The Great Famine in China, 1958–1962

The Great Famine in China, 1958–1962

A Documentary History

Edited by
Zhou Xun

Yale

UNIVERSITY PRESS

New Haven & London

Yale University Press books may be purchased in quantity for educational, business, or
promotional use. For information, please e-mail sales.press@yale.edu (U.S. office) or
sales@yaleup.co.uk (U.K. office).

Designed by James J. Johnson.
Set in Sabon type by Westchester Book Group, Danbury, Connecticut.

Library of Congress Cataloging-in-Publication Data

The great famine in China, 1958–1962 : a documentary history / edited by Zhou Xun.
    p. cm.
    Includes bibliographical references and index.
    ISBN 978-0-300-17518-9 (cloth : alk. paper)   1. Famines—China—History—20th
century—Sources.   2. China—Population—History—20th century—Sources.   3. Food
supply—China—History—20th century—Sources.   4. China—History—1949–1976—
Sources.   I. Zhou, Xun, 1968–
    HC430.F3G74 2012
    363.80951'09045—dc23

                                                                         2011045260

A catalogue record for this book is available from the British Library.

This paper meets the requirements of ANSI/NISO Z39.48-1992 (Permanence of Paper).

Contents

Acknowledgments

THIS book is part of a bigger project undertaken in collaboration with my colleague Frank Dikötter at the Faculty of Arts, University of Hong Kong. Between 2008 and 2010 we were in receipt of research grant HKU743308H from the Research Grants Council, Hong Kong, and research grant RG016-P-07 from the Chiang Ching-kuo Foundation in Taiwan. These grants, which I acknowledge with gratitude, allowed me to carry out essential research for this book. My deepest gratitude goes to Frank Dikötter, for he has given me enormous help and valuable suggestions throughout the course of my research. He has also been generous in sharing his research material—in particular, the archival documents at the Gansu Provincial Archive included in this book. Without his kindness in sharing his time and knowledge, this book would not have been possible.

As I researched the famine in China I benefited greatly from conversations with Gao Wanling at Renmin University of China, Beijing; Cao Shuji at Shanghai Jiaotong University; and Jia Yanmin at Hefei University, Anhui.

I also wish to thank Sander Gilman at Emory University, Atlanta, for his enthusiastic support. He kindly read a draft version of the manuscript, and his useful comments were much appreciated.

My heartfelt thanks go to my friends Robert Williams and Father Edmund Ryden, SJ, as well as Rachel Barrett. They spent many hours carefully reading a draft manuscript and made many invaluable comments for improvement, particularly with the English wording.

Several people read portions of the manuscript, or listened to my ideas, or made insightful suggestions: Gerard Lemos, the former acting chair of the British Council, now a partner at Lemos and Crane Social

Research and a professor in international social policy at Chongqing Business and Technology University; Poppy Sebag-Montefiore, a freelance British journalist and filmmaker who has spent many years in China; Julie Kleeman, chief editor of the *Oxford English-Chinese Chinese-English Dictionary;* and Stephan Feuchtwang at the London School of Economics and Political Science.

I am grateful to the School of Humanities, the History Department, the Centre for the Humanities and Medicine, and the Hong Kong Institute for the Humanities and Social Sciences at the University of Hong Kong for providing me with a hospitable environment and essential support for continuing my research and completing this book.

When I was preparing the manuscript, Abraham Kaleo Parrish, director of the Map Department at Sterling Memorial Library, Yale University, made the map used in this volume. I am very grateful for his kind assistance.

Finally, I wish to thank Yale University Press for its commitment and enthusiasm—in particular, its reference editor, Vadim A. Staklo, and my manuscript editor, Mary Pasti, for their crucial assistance.

Introduction

THE history of the Great Famine in China has long been obscured by official taboos and restricted access to primary sources. Until 1990 very little essential archival material on the subject was available either to historians or to the general public. In November 1990 the Chinese government published a new archival regulation (revised in May 1999) that theoretically made documents more than thirty years old available. In practice, the documents are not always available even today. A great number of documents are still classified as "unsuitable" for public access and are in "closed" files.

Access varies from one archive to another, from province to province, and from county to county. In general, the Central Archive in Beijing remains the least accessible. So far, only a few Chinese Communist Party historians have gained access, by means of letters of approval issued by appropriate ministries and the rubber-stamped passes given by the archive. But even with these at hand, the historian is limited in the type of material he or she is allowed to consult. At provincial and county levels the situation is variable. For instance, the provincial archives for Anhui and Henan, as well as the Yingjing County Archive in Sichuan, are among the most closed collections in the country. In all three places, *every* document after 1949 is regarded as "sensitive" and is therefore "forbidden." In other provincial, municipal, and county archives, even where famine is still seen as an off-limits subject, there are nonetheless a fair number of open documents that can shed crucial light on the years of the Great Famine.

I began work on my project in 2006. Over the next four years I traveled in Sichuan, Hunan, Henan, Anhui, Shandong, Yunnan, Guizhou, Guangdong, and Guangxi provinces and visited many remote places to interview famine survivors and to read as much archival material on the subject as I could. I was able to see many of the "official" accounts in contemporary documents, which rarely, if ever, have been examined before. Through painstaking work in small and large archives throughout China I was able to piece together a fuller story of the Great Famine of 1959–1962 than was previously known.

The Great Famine in China was the worst in human history, claiming tens of millions of lives; countless individuals were deliberately starved or beaten to death. It also led to the destruction of agriculture, industry, and trade and affected every aspect of human life, leaving large parts of the Chinese countryside scarred forever. The conventional view is that the catastrophe was a rural event, yet, as this book shows, the cities, too, were badly hit by the famine.[1]

The famine was a direct consequence of the Great Leap Forward, Mao's attempt to achieve full communism and economic progress instantly. On November 18, 1957, in a speech at the Moscow Meeting of Representatives of Communist and Workers' Parties, in response to Nikita Khrushchev's announcement that the Soviet Union would overtake the United States in economic production, Mao declared that China would overtake Britain in steel output within fifteen years. Meanwhile, a massive water conservation campaign was launched in China; it marked the beginning of the Great Leap Forward. China's peasants were forced to sacrifice their homes, land, and possessions to build socialist collectives.

More than fifty years after the famine, many survivors are still without basic security, health care, or even sufficient food. Despite the current economic boom in the cities, the destructive consequences of the Great Leap Forward are still felt in everyday life in the countryside. The social unrest, the robbery, and the corruption that were widespread at the time of the famine are not only found today, and feared, but are on the increase.

The year 2012 marks the fiftieth anniversary of the end of the Great Famine. For nearly forty years, this horrific episode in modern Chinese history was kept hidden. According to the official explanation, the famine was an unfortunate series of "natural disasters." There is no collective memory of the famine, no public monument, no museum, no remembrance day, no mention of it in any textbook. In recent years, however, there have been a growing number of books and articles on the subject by historians and journalists, inside as well as outside China, who have managed to gain access to various archival collections.

One researcher is Yu Xiguang. During the past twenty years, he has visited over fifty county archives in various parts of China and built up a private collection of material. His anthology *The Great Leap Forward and the Years of Bitterness,* published in Chinese, is based on a handful of letters to Mao written by local cadres during the famine.[2] The book, one of very few primary source books on the subject, is a powerful account of how millions of Chinese suffered under collectivization and of the many different ways people died during the famine. The book was published in Hong Kong in 2005 but remains banned in China and is largely unknown to non-Chinese readers.

Three years later, Yang Jisheng, a former senior journalist working for the official Xinhua News Agency in China, brought out the two-volume *Tombstone* in Chinese.[3] A number of readers have recognized Yang's volumes as "precious," since he was the first to use archival collections from the provinces. Yang is one of a handful of authors who have managed to research and publish work on the famine in Hunan province. He is also one of the first to point out that the top leaders in the Chinese Communist Party already knew about the famine in 1958 and to establish that the famine lasted into 1962.

One of the most solid accounts of government politics of the time is *Utopian Movement* (2008), by the political scientist and Party historian Lin Yunhui, which is based mainly on published sources; it was published by the Chinese University of Hong Kong in its multivolume History of the People's Republic of China series.[4]

Frank Dikötter's highly acclaimed book *Mao's Great Famine* (2010) is the first in the English language to use a wealth of archival evidence from across China to capture how and why decisions that led to the famine were taken at the top and how these decisions affected the lives of ordinary people.[5] The book makes a key contribution to our understanding of how, why, and what happened during the Great Famine in China. It shows that Mao and other key leaders knew very well that the Party was starving people to death. Still, the leaders were willing to carry out Mao's orders and to "let half the people die" (document 5 in the current book). Dikötter's book challenges the conventional wisdom that the state had mistakenly taken too much grain from the countryside because it assumed that the harvest was much larger than it was. It also illustrates the many ways people tried to survive and came to turn on one another. Dikötter demonstrates the sheer violence in the countryside throughout the entire famine period: two to three million people were buried alive, tortured, or beaten to death; many villagers died not because grain was in short supply but because local cadres deliberately and selectively deprived them of food. Dikötter is the first to use a whole range of archives to come up with an estimate of at least forty-five million premature deaths. His book provides the most comprehensive account to date of the extent of destruction in the Chinese countryside from agriculture to industry, trade, housing, and the environment.

An earlier book by the British journalist Jasper Becker, *Hungry Ghosts* (1996), was the first to show the spread of cannibalism during the famine. By quoting Chen Yizi, a senior Party official who claimed a death toll of forty-three to forty-six million, Becker's famine account was one of the first to bring the official statistic of thirty million deaths into question.[6]

Special mention should be made of Gao Wangling's work on peasant resistance during the famine years. Based on a mixture of oral interviews and local archives, Gao's *Acts of Peasant Resistance in China in the People's Communes* (2006) shows that peasants in various parts of China did not always passively obey government orders. Many of them actively resisted collectivization. To survive the famine, they stole and hoarded food; they suppressed production figures; they slacked off at work; they secretly kept private plots of land, and so on. Gao's study opened up a whole new way of looking at the famine.[7] In 2005, Cao Shuji, a historian based in Shanghai, pioneered the use of official local histories published after 1979 by county or city Party Committees to study the famine. He produced the figure of 32.5 million premature deaths in his widely quoted book *The Great Famine*.[8]

A few additional English-language publications on the famine are worth mentioning here. They include Alfred L. Chan's work on the Great Leap Forward in Guangdong province, *Mao's Crusade* (2001), and Ralph A. Taxton's excellent village study, *Catastrophe and Contention in Rural China* (2008).[9] The latter is based on 400 interviews with villagers in Da Fo (a fictional name) in north China. Through their recollections the book sheds new light on what happened to China's rural population at the time of the famine—how they were driven to starvation and what survival strategies they employed to stay alive under Mao's regime. It also shows that memories of the famine continue to affect the lives of these villagers to the present day.

What sets the current book, *The Great Famine in China, 1958– 1962*, apart from all the other accounts is that it is a documentary history. It offers readers, for the first time in English, access to the most vital archival documentation on the history of collectivization and famine in China from 1957 to 1962. Just as the world came to learn the truth of the mass murder of Polish nationals by the Soviet secret police in the 1940s (the Katyn Massacre) after the revelation of the original execution orders signed by Stalin, readers can learn for themselves, by perusing original documents relating to the famine in Mao's China, that what took place is really beyond any doubt. These documents remove further grounds for denial of what happened, or for defense of the Great Leap Forward, or for attempts to vindicate an "innocent" Party leadership. It reinforces, and takes much further, the evidence presented by Yu, Yang, and Dikötter, as well as Gao.

The majority of the documents included in this book are unknown to the larger world. Although a number of them are referred to in Dikötter's *Mao's Great Famine*, they appear here in full for the first time. Document 26, translated in full in the following pages, is partially translated in Dikötter's book. Document 5, which Dikötter discovered, appears here in print for the first time; it establishes—contra the view of many historians—that Mao knew of the catastrophic events in the countryside in March 1959 and still increased procurement quotas. The full text, given here, is vital to our understanding of the Great Famine.

Since 2008 a large number of documents included in this book have been reclassified by the archives as "closed" files. In other words, they have again become inaccessible. That fact makes this book even more valuable, since for some time to come this documentary history may be the only publication available in English that contains the most crucial primary documents concerning the Great Famine and the fate of the Chinese peasantry between 1957 and 1962.

The archival documents used here cover everything from collectivization and survival strategies to ways of dying and mass murder. They include reports and instructions by the Central Committee of the Chinese Communist Party, the Secretariat of the Party, and provincial Party Committees, letters by individuals, official speeches, conference minutes, and Public Security investigations into robberies, thefts, murders, and cannibalism. All are from Party archives located in various provincial, city, and county facilities. Most of these documents were written by the government's investigating agents or by Communist cadres to serve a particular purpose. Quite often the intention was not to show the failure of the Great Leap Forward but to expose corruption at the local level. It was understood that although numerous local officials were responsible for extreme violence, forced starvation, and countless killings in the countryside, Mao's utopian project was completely blameless. It is therefore important for the readers today to maintain a critical distance from these sources. Despite their original intended audience and the Party terminology—terms such as "sabotage" and "counterrevolutionary" were employed to obscure what was really happening in remote villages—these documents are invaluable since they are full of detail, description, and data. Furthermore, they represent an astonishing variety of official viewpoints as well as individual opinions. Together, they allow today's readers to understand the relationship between the state and individual peasants and its context.

All too often, publications on the horror of the Great Famine focus on bland theories about how crop figures were inflated and how the state procured so much that people somehow died of hunger. Yet any history of the famine is never just about shortages or starvation. It consists of a conflicting set of complex and fragmented stories. Rather than forcing the stories into a single narrative that professes to comprehend and explain the sheer scale of the tragedy, the multilayered range of human behavior, the social chaos, and the instigating politics, a documentary history allows readers to gain a better understanding of the complexity of the past, to find out what actually occurred and what choices were made, and to make sense of how it could have happened. The goal of this book is to break through conventional theorizing and to confront readers directly with the moral compromises, the constant violence, the arbitrary and brutal choices that people had to make in their unceasing struggle to survive. It illuminates in sharp relief the world of the Chinese peasants and their desperate attempts to survive the brave new dawn of Communist rule.

Since I have collected more than 1,000 documents in the past four years, I have had to be selective in what is reproduced here. I do not, for example, include any Party conference documents that are well known and have already been published elsewhere. The documents included were chosen to help the reader understand better how and why the catastrophe unfolded, as well as the enormity and sheer horror of what took place. I have arranged them both chronologically and thematically by chapter. In several places, documents seem repetitive, but I have kept them the way they are without too much editing. I believe these repetitions are necessary. They are part of the story, since they establish that the tragedy and devastation did not occur on a single occasion in one particular place but took place over and over again throughout China between 1958 and 1962.

Unlike the horrors of the Gulag and the Holocaust, what happened in China between 1958 and 1962 has rarely been given much attention by the larger world, even though it is one of the worst catastrophes in twentieth-century history. In China itself, the famine is a dark episode, one that is not discussed or officially recognized. By making more than 100 primary archival documents available in English to students, historians, and general readers, this book provides a whole new set of documentary evidence about China under Mao. I hope it starts a much-needed examination of the history of China under Mao by taking advantage of the wealth of information hidden away in archives in China and by addressing the history according to the same high standards used in recent examinations of Soviet history.

To warn zealots and apologists not to exaggerate Stalin's achievements, Dmitry Medvedev, president of the Russian Federation, points out that "even now we can hear voices saying that those numerous deaths were justified by some supreme goals of the state. I am convinced that no development of a country, no success or ambitions can be achieved through human grief and losses."[10] I hope that one day the Chinese Communist Party leadership will find itself able to express publicly the same value for human life.

A Note on the Documents

THE documents included in this book come from Chishui County Archive in Guizhou province, Fuyang City Archive in Anhui province, Gansu Provincial Archive, Guiyang City Archive in Guizhou province, Guizhou Provincial Archive, Gushi County Archive in Henan province, Hunan Provincial Archive, Kaiping City Archive in Guangdong province, Shandong Provincial Archive, Sichuan Provincial Archive, and Yunnan Provincial Archive. Although the majority of these documents cover the period from 1957 to 1962—the time of radical collectivization and the Great Famine—I have also included a few from 1963 and 1964, since they cover events that happened during the famine years. Several documents, in particular those from the Gansu Provincial Party Committee (Gansu 91), have already been mentioned or partially translated in Frank Dikötter's *Mao's Great Famine: The History of China's Most Devastating Catastrophe, 1958–62* (2010), but they appear here for the first time either in full or in a longer form.

The majority of the documents are from the files of various provincial, city, and county Party Committees, except for Guizhou 90, two files from the Guizhou Province Bureau of Agriculture; Hunan 167, a file from the Hunan Province Bureau of Civil Affairs; JC 9, from the Rural Affairs Working Group of the Sichuan Provincial Party Committee; JC 12, from the Sichuan Provincial Party Committee Office of Ethnic Affairs; JC 44, from the Sichuan Province Bureau of Civil Affairs; JC 50, from the Department of Religious Affairs of the Sichuan Provincial People's Committee; JC 133, from the Sichuan Province Bureau of Health and Hygiene; JC 202, from the Sichuan Province

Welfare Committee; and Yunnan 120, from the Yunnan Province Bureau of Grain.

All the original documents are in Chinese. In translating them into English I have sought to be faithful to the original texts. Occasionally I have added footnotes to explain some special terms, events, and names. I have converted Chinese weights and measures into metric units. Names are given in pinyin—the official romanization system used for transcribing Chinese characters—and cited in standard Chinese order, family name first. Since some of the original documents are far too long to be reproduced in full in this book, I have indicated my excisions by means of standard ellipses in parentheses [. . .]. Each document retains its original title.

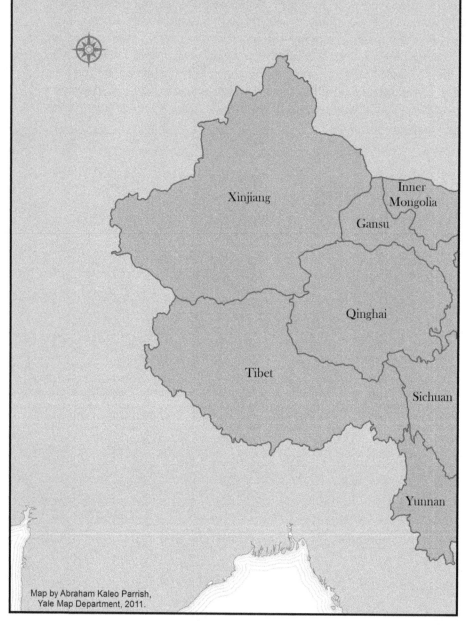

Map of China
in 1959

Xinjiang

Inner
Mongolia

Gansu

Qinghai

Tibet

Sichuan

Yunnan

Map by Abraham Kaleo Parrish,
Yale Map Department, 2011.

Map by Abraham Kaleo Parrish,
Yale Map Department, 2011.

0 75 150   300   450   600   Kilometers

CHAPTER ONE

Famine in the Communes (March–September 1958)

THE Great Leap Forward was Mao's campaign to create a Communist utopia in China: a great, powerful, prosperous, and virtuous socialist state, ultimately a Communist society.[1] It was undertaken in the belief that a socialist system of agriculture would vastly improve land productivity, stimulate rural markets for industrial products, and redirect sufficient numbers of workers and funds toward China's accelerating industrialization. In Mao's view, revolutionary zeal and cooperative effort could overcome all obstacles and transform the Chinese landscape into a productive paradise. In fact, the Great Leap Forward led to the Great Famine of 1958–1962.

Prior to the early 1950s, private land ownership was the basis of agriculture in China, but the growing population contributed to an escalating land-shortage problem, and private land ownership subsequently became directly linked to poverty. In 1943, Mao Zedong, the new supreme head of the Chinese Communist Party, proclaimed that agricultural collectivization was the only way to eliminate rural poverty.[2] After the Party consolidated its power in the early 1950s, it rapidly began enforcing collectivization in the countryside.

Despite the bloodshed that had accompanied the rapid collectivization of 1928–1932 in the Soviet Union, a program initiated by Joseph Stalin, and despite the catastrophic results, including mass famine in Ukraine (1932–1933), Mao wanted a fully socialist agricultural system established throughout China, and he wanted it fast. Once the campaign for agricultural collectivization was launched, it swept across the country like a whirlwind. The pace was astonishing. It proceeded even faster than Mao had anticipated. By 1956 virtually all agricultural households in rural China had been organized into collectives. The 1955–1956 collectivization in the Chinese countryside did not end in bloodshed, but dissatisfaction and unrest spread among the peasant population (document 101).

Faced with these warning signs, Mao showed no hesitation. Although he and the other top leaders were well aware of problems, they simply turned a blind eye. Mao wanted to go further, to begin the Great Leap Forward to move China quickly from socialism to communism and to modernize the economy. On June 8, 1957, he launched the Anti-Rightist Campaign and then the rural Socialist Education Campaign to silence opposing voices within or outside the Party. Anyone who spoke the truth was purged as a rightist.[3]

On March 20, 1958, the policy of total collectivization was formally inaugurated at a Party conference in Chengdu. Mao believed that a socialist system of agriculture, with collective units called people's communes as the centerpiece, would provide the necessary economic and social foundation for the country to industrialize. His goal was to overtake the United Kingdom in steel production within fifteen years. By then, Mao would figure not only as the supreme leader of the Chinese Communist Party but also as the leader of the world Communist movement. In May, Mao hailed the slogan "Going all out, aiming high, and achieving more and faster economic results," and the full force of the Great Leap Forward was unleashed. In August, at the Party's Politburo meeting, people's communes were approved as the new form of organization for rural China: not just agriculture but all aspects of economic, political, and social life would be collectivized. By the end of the year, according to an official estimate, nearly 99 percent of the peasants had joined a commune. Approximately 26,000 communes had been set up, each with an average of 5,000 households.

With the establishment of people's communes in 1958, the Party's goal to control all the land in the countryside, as well as all the wealth, was finally accomplished. The people's communes became the newest and highest form of administrative, economic, and political organization in rural China. Each commune was divided into big brigades (most of which contained several small villages); and the big brigades were in turn divided into production brigades. Households were organized into brigades, the units of accounting and farm production in the large farming collectives. The production or small brigades were lowest in the administrative hierarchy, with big brigades the next level up. The rural leadership structure was built into the Party hierarchy.

The general image of the year 1958, projected then and later, is that the entire country was united in rapturous enthusiasm for the Great

Leap Forward, and that by the end of the year, steel, coal, and industrial output had been massively boosted and the production of grain and cotton had increased considerably. It looked as though Mao's Communist dream was on the verge of becoming a reality in the Chinese countryside. So the fifteen-year goal was brought forward by ten years: it would be accomplished in five years.

As it turned out, the Great Leap Forward was a calamity for rural China. The conventional view is that the failure of the Great Leap Forward did not begin to appear until 1959, that it was only then that famine broke out. The following documents demonstrate, however, that collectivization was disastrous from the outset: famine had broken out in parts of rural China as early as the spring of 1958. (The Great Leap Forward had already started in 1957; it was officially launched in early 1958.) Chronic crop failure compounded the problem. To meet the ever-increasing government procurement quotas, the last grains of wheat and rice were snatched from the peasants.

A report produced by the Jinan Municipal Investigation Team, one of many government agencies whose members routinely went around the countryside to monitor the local situation, shows that between March and September 1958, while radical collectivization was moving ahead at full speed, Gaoguanzhai, a small township in the west of Shandong province, suffered a devastating famine that claimed more than 600 lives. People were forced to sell everything they had, including their children. Around 700 families, as well as some individuals, fled their homes. The parched earth cracked; once lush fields became wasteland. Birds were nowhere to be heard, leaving the countryside in a ghostly silence. In places, the stench of rotting human flesh filled the air (document 1).

The terrible events that took place in Gaoguanzhai were not unique. On April 25, 1958, the General Office of the Central Committee of the Chinese Communist Party in Beijing produced a report citing outbreaks of famine and food riots in sixteen provinces and autonomous regions (document 2). Just five days earlier, in Henan province's Suiping county, the people of Chayashan had celebrated the birth of China's first-ever people's commune, the second in history after the Paris Commune of 1871. Mao loved the constitution of the Chayashan people's commune and held it up with great excitement: "Treasure! A real treasure!" he exclaimed, marching up and down the room.[4] Chayashan became China's hope and its model for prosperity, the bridge to a Communist paradise. In no time, according to Mao, China would become strong and its people prosperous. On the ground, however, as the following documents show, rural China was a picture of hell.

· Document 1 ·

A report by the Jinan Municipal Investigation Team on the outbreak of
famine and deaths in Gaoguanzhai township, Zhangqiu county,
[Shandong province,] January 29, 1959

Huanghe people's commune contains four rural townships, of
which Gaoguanzhai is one. Within Gaoguanzhai there are thirty-
three villages, 5,150 families, and 21,713 people. Before collectivization there were twelve cooperative agricultural units, but they have
since been merged into seven big brigades.

For nearly five months in 1958, from the end of the second month
to the 20th of the seventh month in the Chinese lunar calendar,[5] the
entire population of Gaoguanzhai faced severe food shortages.
Although the county government allocated 455,975 kg of food rations
as emergency relief, this worked out to only 21 kg for each villager, or
0.25 kg per person per day. Furthermore, at the local level these rations were distributed just sporadically. For instance, on June 3, a local
cadre at Lihang production brigade gave just 0.5 kg of wheat to each
villager to last eleven to twenty days. Many villagers were forced to
abandon their homes and became beggars. Some had no other option
but to sell their children. A number of people died of starvation. The
situation was critical.

From spring to early summer, when food first became scarce, people
supplemented their diet with chaff, tree bark, and weeds. Some locals
told us they had eaten at least fifty different types of food substitutes
during this time, including leaves from the scholar tree and castor-oil
plant, grass for feeding pigs, young stems from the tree of heaven,
wheat husks, sorghum flowers, grass seeds, coarse chaff, corn husks,
peanut skins, bean leaves, potato sprouts, elm bark, and watermelon
rind. After everything there was had been eaten, villagers had to go
further afield, sometimes walking for up to 10 kilometers to search for
more. Villagers from Zhangjia hamlet had to cross a small river to
look for food substitutes near the dock, a return journey of about 20
kilometers. During this time, crowds were seen washing newly picked
weeds and leaves from trees around village wells all day long. The
sound of chopping [grass and leaves] never ceased.

Out of desperate hunger, some villagers ate newly planted peanuts
or young beans. To prevent such incidents, cadres at Zhangjia hamlet
confiscated over 100 wicker baskets. Some villagers, such as Wang
Yongbing in the Lihang production brigade, also ate corn seeds while
sowing. Recalling what happened, a local cadre, Du Gang, said, "When

I saw that villagers were eating corn while sowing, I was worried that it might cause a seed shortage. To stop them I mixed the seeds with dog shit." In some cases villagers also ate unripe corn. According to the village cadre Feng Lihe, during one inspection he found that 14,000 corn plants were missing from Zhongmeng hamlet, including most of the husks. That spring, Hongxing production brigade planted 66,700 square meters in corn, while Zhujia hamlet planted 40,020, but by harvest time there was nothing left.

The situation deteriorated further by the summer. Peanut skins were sold at 0.2 yuan[6] per 0.5 kg, stale chaff at 0.3 yuan per 0.5 kg, bean leaves at 0.8 yuan for 5 kg, elm leaves at 0.3 yuan per 0.5 kg, and coarse chaff at about 0.1 yuan per 0.5 kg. People fought to get sweet melons as soon as they appeared and no one dared to bargain over the price. In general, they cost 0.16 yuan per 0.5 kg, but the price doubled if one wanted to select those of better quality. In some cases people gobbled down raw fish the moment they bought them. Worse still, some even ate mud from the nearby bay.

It was also common for people to trade their clothes for food. There were often two lines in front of the town bureau, with people waiting to sell their possessions on the right. This line sometimes stretched almost 50 meters in length, and mainly during this period in 1958, the commune collected 2,752 garments and 7,955 kg of used cotton. On the left were people lining up to buy food from the people's restaurant, although they could wait all day without getting anything to eat.

Owing to a long period of starving and eating food substitutes, malnutrition became prevalent, causing such abnormal symptoms as swollen stomachs, legs, and faces. Some of the food substitutes, such as leaves from the scholar tree and the tree of heaven, were poisonous. After eating a large quantity of these, the entire body would become swollen. In more severe cases, the body could no longer retain excess fluid, which then erupted through the skin, oozing out with a yellowish color.

In Weihualin village, about 80 percent of the population suffered from swollen faces, legs, and stomachs. In Mazhuang, 90 percent of villagers suffered from edema.[7] Their faces became sallow and emaciated, their bodies had no strength, and many people could walk only with a stick. Normally people used barrels to carry water, but during this time the majority of villagers could manage only to hold small jars. Those unable even to manage a jar carried a teapot instead. Men in their prime had to stop and rest four or five times on the 1 kilometer journey from Zhujia hamlet to the town center. Work became inefficient; while weeding the villagers would stop to rest or fall asleep after working for short periods. As a result, over 667 hectares became wasteland.

Most women of childbearing age stopped having periods. Mothers had no milk left to breastfeed, and many babies starved to death as a result. Since mothers were organized to work in big groups, they took their children along to the fields, but they then had to leave them unattended in temporary sheds nearby. As spring turned into summer, many children caught a chill. While a few died of illness, the majority of child deaths were due to starvation. According to our investigation, in Zhongmeng hamlet twenty-eight young and middle-aged women workers had stopped having periods. The birthrate dropped dramatically. According to local statistics, ninety babies were born in Zhongmeng in 1957 but only seventeen in 1958.

These figures also show that 896 people died in 1958, twice as many as in 1957. Our incomplete study reveals that food shortages led to 617 abnormal deaths[8] and 53 children being sold. It also caused two divorces and forced 685 people to leave their homes to beg on the streets. By comparison, only 207 people died of natural causes.

Among the 617 abnormal deaths, 434 were of males and 255 were of females. They comprised 250 children under the age of five, 19 children aged between six and seventeen, 263 adults of eighteen to sixty, and 157 people over sixty. Of those who died, 72 had previously suffered minor illnesses, but it was starvation that caused their deaths. There were also 23 suicides. The whole famine lasted for several months. The first period, between March and May, saw 117 deaths; subsequently, from June to September, 557 people died. Even after [the situation improved in] October there were 15 further deaths. The majority of the 617 deaths were caused by starvation, although the famine also drove a number of people to commit suicide by hanging, jumping into wells, or taking poison. Most families lost at least two family members, some even four.

One example was the family of Bai Daolun from Qianjin production brigade. At the age of thirty-two Bai had been a physically strong man. There were eight people in his family, and they used to make a relatively good living. The food shortages began after the Chinese New Year in 1958.[9] On April 27, Bai's four-year-old daughter died of starvation, and a fortnight later his one-year-old daughter also died. Then on May 30 the famine killed his father, followed by Bai himself, who died on June 29. The day before Bai's death, he worked all day in the fields without anything to eat. In the evening he consumed a bowl of elm leaves before rushing to a meeting. On the way home, he collapsed on the road and was carried home. He died that same night.

Even on their deathbeds, many people still howled for something to eat. Forty-six-year-old Li Mengnian from Zhujia hamlet came from a family of five. His mother used to spend all day looking for food to eat. She counted the days until the promised wheat distribution: "I will die with no regrets if only I could manage to drink half a bowl of wheat porridge." On May 11 the family finally received their wheat ration, but she died the following day. At the time, Li Mengnian was bed-bound, for his legs were completely swollen. Two people held him up and helped him to get to his mother's funeral. After kneeling to kowtow to his dead mother, Li failed to stand up again. He was carried home and eventually died on June 7. The night before his death, he was so hungry that he cried out, "If only I could have two sweet melons to eat, my life would be saved." It was already dark outside. His oldest daughter went out and managed to borrow 0.5 yuan, but she could not find any sweet melons. In the end she boiled some water for him to drink. When dawn came, she went to the town center and bought some lotus-root flour, but Li passed away just as she finished cooking it. By the time Li died, his wife was also crippled by edema from eating food substitutes.

In one case in the Lihang production brigade, Li Shushan's grandfather's body swelled up after eating elm leaves and he died. Soon afterward, Li's grandmother expired. At the time Li was himself confined to his bed, so exhausted by hunger that he could not move. About three or four people carried him to the funeral ceremony, but he lived only until the following day.

Li Haiquan from Zhujia hamlet collapsed while planting potatoes in the fields. Afterward, he tried to make it back home, but died before reaching his family courtyard. Mai Xiansheng went to plant potatoes without having eaten and eventually lay down in the field because hunger had robbed him of his stamina. He was carried home and died that same night. In Mazhu hamlet Mrs. Song's legs were swollen from eating food substitutes, but she still dragged herself along, hoping to find some more weeds to consume. Eventually she collapsed on the hill. She was still breathing as she was carried home. Her family fed her two bowls of vegetable soup but did not manage to save her life.

Quite a number of people dropped dead simply because they had not eaten for so long. For example, Song Shuzhen from Mazhu hamlet, locally known as Old Warrior, used to be a strong worker. He stopped eating altogether after consuming wheat chaff, which gave him serious pain and constipation. He went to the people's restaurant hoping to get some proper food to eat, but could not get into the queue. In the end, he went to the local bar and drank about 200 ml of grain spirits. Soon after he finished the spirits he collapsed on his seat. At the time he was still breathing and was carried home, but he did not last long and died shortly afterward. Zhang Qingzhu from the same village planned to steal some corn to relieve his extreme hunger, but seeing someone else in the field, he hesitated. Right there he collapsed and could not get up. He died soon after being carried home. Elderly people without means of support could not even find food substitutes, and many of them were driven to eat mud from the nearby bay. Mrs. Zhang from Zhangjia hamlet was one such person, and she also died during the famine.

The famine drove twenty-three people to commit suicide by hanging, jumping into a well, or taking poison. Forty-four-year-old Song Shusen from Zhujia hamlet was previously a good worker. From spring to summer as the food shortage worsened he obtained less and less to eat. His body swelled up and he could walk only with a stick. His brother gave him 0.5 yuan to buy some sweet melons to eat, but feeling completely desperate, he hanged himself. In another case in Wang hamlet, Wang Daosan's mother tried to poison herself with some pesticide. After taking the poison, she told her daughter-in-law to take care of her son. Her last words were "You both work outside, but I have nothing to cook with at home. I have no reason to live any longer." In Dujia hamlet, Du Huaibing's family also had no food left. His wife decided to pay a visit to her parental home in Lou hamlet, hoping her family would put her up for a few days. However, they refused to let her stay. Instead, they baked her some bread and then sent her back. After she returned to her own home, she felt so hopeless that she hanged herself as the only way out.

In a particularly shocking incident, one mother even tried to poison her child while taking her own life. The mother was Zhang Linying's twenty-nine-year-old wife from Zhangjia hamlet. The family had run out of food at the end of February, and there were six mouths waiting to be fed. Every day, besides going down the hill to attend to the fields, Zhang's wife had to go and look for food substitutes to feed the entire family. In the spring their one-week-old child died, and things had not improved by the early summer. On the afternoon of June 15, Mrs. Zhang sent her husband, her mother-in-law, and her ten-year-old child away. She then mixed two packets of rat poison with the last bit of flour and baked one loaf of bread. She ate most of it and gave a little bit to her child, who was only six. When they were discovered, Zhang's wife had already died, but fortunately the child was saved. On another occasion, a woman from Linji went to beg in Dan hamlet, taking her six-year-old child with her. They begged all morning but did not get anything to eat. They sat down by the well and rested for a while; she then turned around and pushed her child into the well. The child's body was not discovered until that afternoon.

There were countless cases of extreme hardship ruining family life, causing marriages to break down and children to be separated from their parents. For example, Yan Xizhi from Xin hamlet had a family of eight. Out of six of his children, he sold three of them. The oldest daughter was ten. When Yan went to beg in Licheng, he took her along and sold her to a man named Liu from Chaijia hamlet. Afterward he sold his five-year-old boy to someone else in Taoyuan village for 15 yuan. Again in June he went out to beg for food with his ten-month-old son still in his arms. On the way he sold the boy to a cadre in Shahe cooperative.

A number of people also sold their children through a go-between without knowing the name or location of the surrogate family. In February, Wu Jingxi from Zhujia hamlet gave away his four-year-old son, and shortly afterward he also sold his nine-year-old boy for 5 yuan through a butcher named Zhang from Mazhu hamlet. Wu had no knowledge of who the surrogate family would be. With the 5 yuan he managed to eat one bowl of rice and bought 2.5 kg of peanuts. His wife still cries when thinking of her children. Tears have turned her eyes red, and her sight has deteriorated. In another case at Lihang hamlet, Wang Weitong's wife took her two children with her to beg for food in Jinan. In the northern suburb of Beiyuan, she sold the boy to Sun Taoshan for 1.5 yuan and four rounds of cornbread. The transaction was even sealed with a written deed.

Many were not so lucky as to find a family for their children and simply abandoned them. For example, Teng Zian's wife from Fujia hamlet took her child to beg in June with the intention of giving the child away. Failing to find a family to adopt the eight-month-old baby, she left the child at Laosenkou village. Fortunately, the village head found a family for the child. Xu Jiaoxiang of Lihang production was from the poor peasant class and had a family of seven. After eating food substitutes for a long period, his legs had become swollen like many others' and his body weak. He fainted while planting potatoes on the hill and died soon after being taken home. When he died, his wife was away begging with their children. After Xu's death, she was forced to give away two of their children, leaving one with their neighbor when she remarried.

In Dan hamlet, forty-eight-year-old Sun Yingrong had been married to his wife for seventeen years. They had five children together, and the couple had enjoyed a very good relationship. Earlier on in the spring, when the hardship had become almost unbearable, his wife asked for a divorce. Sun kneeled down before her begging her to stay for the sake of their children. But his wife insisted on getting a divorce because she saw it as her only chance to escape the misery. In the end, not having much choice, they gave away one child, while the wife took another with her and remarried a merchant in Jinan. Before leaving, she left her wardrobe to her mother-in-law and her last pennies to her former husband and her mother-in-law to show that she was obliged by the reality of her situation to marry someone else. Her former husband and mother-in-law still weep about what happened, wanting the local government to help reunite their family. The wife is also said to have regretted the divorce very much.

Another 685 people were forced to leave their homes to beg for food elsewhere. Most of them left in early summer when the situation was most critical. They headed to Licheng as well as Jinan city proper. Thirty-eight-year-old Feng Lichai and his family from Xin hamlet were among them. When summer came, they had no food left, and the entire family of four left for Jinan in order to beg. Some people even went to Jinan Correction Center, pleading to be taken in. A few died of hunger on their journey, including seventy-two-year-old Teng Huzong from Fujia hamlet. By early summer he had no food left, and in August he began to beg and headed for Licheng. He died after reaching Wangsheren hamlet. His body has not been taken back home. Feng Weili also died outside Laosengkou village while on the way to Licheng to beg. His body was discovered only when it began to stink. [...]

· Document 2 ·

A summary report from the General Office of the Central Committee of the Chinese Communist Party regarding food shortages and riots in sixteen provinces and autonomous regions, as well as measures proposed by local Party Committees to resolve the problem, [Beijing,] April 25, 1958

Between April 17 and 19, we received telephone reports from a number of provinces, including Anhui, Hebei, Shandong, Guangxi, Guangdong, Gansu, Shanxi, Sichuan, Jiangsu, Jilin, Liaoning, Hunan, Fujian, Henan, Inner Mongolia, and Yunnan. These reports show there have been food shortages and riots to some degree in each of these provinces or autonomous regions.

Anhui
[A total of] 1.3 million people are without food supplies. In Wuhu, Su county, and Wuwei the situation is particularly critical, involving

some 400,000 people. In these areas famine has forced more than 3,000 people to leave their homes.

Hebei

According to information from Cang county, Baoding, Shijiazhuang, and Handan regions, over 474,000 families took part in a number of food riots recently. The situation is especially serious in Cang county and Baoding, with at least nineteen or twenty families stirring up trouble. In Tianjin prefecture 18 percent of collective farms, out of a total 4,399, have been involved in riots. In many of these villages people have almost no food left. In the market, dried vegetables are now sold at 0.3 yuan per 0.5 kg, and 44,227 people from these areas have left their homes to beg elsewhere. From March 10 to April 9, some 13,700 people have taken refuge in the city of Tianjin, with up to 2,000 arriving in a single day. During this period, Baoding and Shijiazhuang also took in 1,400 refugees.

It is quite common for entire families to become beggars. Normally they go out to beg in the daytime and sleep on the street at night. Discontent is widespread in these regions. In Cang county, Baoding, and Handan there were twenty-eight cases of people selling children, and twenty-nine children were sold. In Yanshan county and Ningji county, famine has driven twelve people to attempt suicide, and nine died as a result. In Tianjin one vagrant beggar was found frozen to death, and another beggar committed suicide. Both of them were originally from another area. At Shen county station, over 600 people from Xian county and Jing county raided the station, robbed around 200 passengers, and ate all their food.

Shandong

Since the end of March, over 670,000 people have had their food supplies completely cut off, and over 150,000 people have been forced to flee and become beggars. Some fifty food riots took place in Mengyin county, which was badly hit by the famine. Meanwhile, at Nanma township and Lijia township in Yishui county over thirty families have demanded to withdraw from the collective due to the poor quality of life.

Guangxi

According to information from 29 counties and 9,065 townships, over 1.2 million people, about 16.2 percent of the total population of Guangxi, are currently living under the poverty line, with very little food or money. In another thirteen counties, the information we received shows that over 57,000 people are without food supplies, and there have been incidents of death from starvation.

Guangdong

According to information from fifty-five counties, the famine in the spring caused 963,231 people to go without food, and seven people have died of starvation. There are also sixty-nine people suffering from edema. In these areas, 547 families have lost their homes and been forced to move elsewhere. Twenty-seven people from among them ran away, ten families sold their children, and sixty-six people became beggars. Huiyang and Zhanjiang have been badly hit by the famine. In Huiyang, 95,444 families are without food, which amounts to about 40 percent of the total number of people without food in the entire province.

Gansu

Degrees of food shortage have occurred in twenty-one counties throughout the province. In Hui county the situation is rather alarming. Severe famine has become prevalent, and people have been eating tree bark and grass roots to satisfy their hunger. In some areas people have consumed all of the geese, dogs, and cats. From last December until now, 2,031 people have suffered from edema, and 795 have died as a result. Eight townships have the highest death rates, and in one commune about 15 percent of those who became ill are now dead, including four entire families. In a number of places it is no longer possible to carry out any productive labor owing to severe malnutrition.

Shanxi

Food-related riots occurred in twenty-seven counties, and signs of unrest can be also seen in another nine counties. According to the information from some of these counties, 950 people have been directly involved in these riots. Meanwhile, 493 people have fled the famine, 339 people have become vagrant beggars, and two people have committed suicide. The crisis in Shanyin county is most critical: around 664 collectives have no food left and urgently need a fortnight's provisions in advance. Seventy-one people from these communes have become vagrant beggars, and 131 people have fled the famine. [. . .]

Inner Mongolia

At least 800,000 people are facing food shortages and are in need of five months' provisions. We predict that after the spring planting season there will be an outbreak of famine in the region.

Sichuan

Famine is prevalent in some twenty counties, but the situation is particularly critical in Luzhou and Jiangjin regions. In Yongchuan county about fifty-one townships lack sufficient food supplies and 50 to 80 percent of people from ten townships have been affected by the food shortages. According to an investigation by the provincial Party Committee, 5 percent of the population of the Sichuan plain do not have sufficient food supplies, with the rate increasing to 7–9 percent in the hills. In the mountain regions, the situation is even worse at around 15–20 percent. In general, the food shortages could last up to thirty-five days. In some areas of Yanbian county, people have stopped working owing to lack of food. They are demanding that the county government resolve the current crisis. In Jingyan county, a retired soldier committed suicide because he could not buy food anywhere. Fifteen hundred have fled from Wushan county to Hubei province. Many have become vagrants.

Jiangsu

In Yancheng region 27,000 families are facing a shortage of food, and 80,099 families have nothing to eat. Seventy people from Huai'an county went to the county government to protest about the food shortage, while in Suzhou about twenty-nine families have formed an alliance and refuse to work. They have also caused a number of riots. Since March, disasters have continued to hit Xuzhou region. According to statistics from thirty-three townships in Pi county, Feng county, Donghai county, and Ganyu county, over 12,000 families are short of food and money, and 1,040 families have gone out to beg. Although a number of victims have been forced to become vagrants, others have no other means but to pull down their houses or to sell their houses and furniture. There are also incidents of people selling children or committing suicide, especially in Yangzhou region, where the famine is extremely severe. In this region over 7,400 agricultural production brigades—around 20 percent of the total—are facing a serious food crisis. In each of these brigades, around five or ten families do not have enough food to eat, and in some cases the number can be as high as 60 percent. For instance, in Baoying county about 30,000 families have insufficient food, some 3,500 families have fled the famine, and 520 families have become beggars. In the same area, 6,000 families have also been affected by a series of natural disasters.

Jilin

There have been twenty-three cases of food-related riots throughout the province, involving six counties and 871 people. One of the biggest incidents took place in Yushu county, with about 500 participants. In Dongfeng county there have been eleven cases of riots, involving 45 people.

Liaoning

In the disaster-struck regions, the failure of local relief work has led to famine. For instance, in five townships in He county, 817 families lack sufficient food, and residents have already consumed 2,616 kg of chaff and 7,625 kg of soybean residue. In Changtu county's Taiping township more than 100 families have requested to move away. In Guanlibao township in Shenyang prefecture there has been one case of suicide and one of selling children.

Hunan

Nearly 10 percent of peasants from the entire province have been facing a shortage of food for over a month. In the lake region about 2,000 people have gone into exile in Hubei, and more than 900 peasants took refuge in the provincial capital, Changsha. However, after the Great Debate Campaign[10]—an attempt to tackle the grain procurement problem earlier this year—no food riots have occurred, even though peasants do not have enough to eat. A number of families have less than 0.5 kg of rice per day and they manage to eat only three watery porridge meals each day. Still, they rarely express any complaints.

Fujian

In certain counties there have been some problems with grain procurement, including in at least 20 percent of the townships in Minhou county, leading to a shortage of 3,220,000 kg of grain. In Taiyu township over seventy peasants have no food left. In Qifeng township about ninety peasants gathered outside the district government [office] demanding an increase in the amount of food provided. In Changle county's Daxi township eight production brigades jointly sent twelve signed letters to the provincial, prefectural, county, and district governments, asking them to transfer food from elsewhere and to provide them with food subsidies. In some townships, over 300 families are lacking one month's provisions. In almost every town there are at least three to five families in need of food subsidies.

Henan

In certain counties, a number of people from a few collectives have jointly stirred up riots. According to the information from Fugou county, Jiyuan county, Qinyang county, and Nanle county, 715 families have been involved in food riots, but only 106 families among them are facing a serious food crisis.

Yunnan

In a small number of poorer collectives, particularly in Wenshan and Zhaotong regions, there have been quite a few food-related riots. In Wenshan, such riots occurred in 133 townships; that is 18 percent of the total number of townships in the region. In Zhaotong, similar riots occurred in forty-three townships, or 4.1 percent. Famine is prevalent across 5 to 10 percent of the total geographic area; in some regions, up to 20 percent, and even 40 percent in a few places. Food-related riots have seriously affected productivity. In Yanshi county's Hongbu collective, for instance, only 50 percent of peasants go to work. About twenty to thirty people even announced a strike, and they have gone to the local government to stir up trouble. In Jilin county's Changhan township, peasants from one production brigade also carried out a one-day strike. In some areas there have been cases of absconding. In Luliang county, for instance, about 45 percent of townships have seen families move away. In three of these counties, 386 families fled elsewhere, a total of 1,345 people. After persuasion, 182 families comprising 642 people have already moved back. In Dongchuan mining region, the food shortages also caused a peasant from Wanghui town to commit suicide.

The causes of these food-related riots are various. First of all, local cadres failed to discover the real food situation in crisis areas and thus underestimated the extent of the problem. Some cadres were afraid of making mistakes or being accused of "right-deviationism"; they therefore refused to believe complaints about shortages and failed to adopt any measures to solve the crisis. Second, the provision plans for some areas have fallen short, and after riots occurred, the local cadres failed to pay close attention to the resale of grain. As a result, people already facing food shortages did not receive provisions in time, causing the riots to spread. Hui county in Gansu, for instance, has the highest incidence of food riots. Here over 10 million kg of grain, enough to feed the entire population for two months, were kept by the county and not distributed to the areas in need. In Sichuan's Kai county, farmers facing food shortages have still not received their ration books.

Furthermore, over winter and spring the workload has intensified because of the Great Leap Forward, resulting in increased food consumption in some areas. The need to put energy into the Great Leap Forward also caused a slowdown in the production of agricultural by-products. Meanwhile, close planting and replanting required more seeds than before. For example, in certain areas in Fujian and Jiangsu, every 667 square meters of land used to be sown with 4 to 7 kg of seeds. With the introduction of close planting, however, the amount of seeds needed for every 667 square meters of land increased to 5 to 12.5 kg, resulting in less grain available as food. Also, the estimated yield for some areas was much higher than the actual amount produced at the last fall harvest, and arrowroot and corncobs were counted as grain to make up the missing surplus. Another problem was that in some potato-growing areas the potatoes were poorly stored, with the result that large quantities went rotten. In Jiangsu province, for instance, at Haibing county's Daguan collective, 235,000 kg of potatoes out of 375,000 became inedible. All these factors have undoubtedly propelled the outbreak of famine throughout the country. [...]

CHAPTER TWO

Terror, Repression, and Violence
(1958–1961)

RADICAL collectivization in China was as bloody and violent as it had been in the Soviet Union twenty years earlier. Millions of Chinese peasants were forced to live communally. In pursuit of utopia, private possessions were collectivized: villagers lost their homes, their land, their personal belongings down to pots and pans, tools, bricks, wood, needles, diapers, and quilts to keep warm, and their livelihoods—and many lives were sacrificed (documents 3–4, 30). Yet unlike in the Soviet Union, where collectivization turned into a civil war between state and peasantry, in China Mao pitted everyone against everyone else. He called this "mass struggle." It began with land reform in the early 1950s, when the "liberated" peasants were encouraged to "struggle" against the "feudal" and "exploitive" landlords. In 1955–1956, during the initial phase of collectivization, poor peasants were told to "struggle" against middle and rich peasants. After radical collectivization was launched in March 1958, terror and repression were extended beyond the "enemy circle" and used directly against the Chinese peasantry.[1]

Peasants in the people's communes struggled among themselves, and some family members fought with each other. Mao conceived of the people's communes as environments without legal safeguards, as organizations operating strictly on military lines. "We have got to be relentless," he said. "This will mean being precise and accurate; it can't be seen as being vicious" (document 5). In some parts of the country, violence and repression could be practiced with impunity. "Struggle" also provided opportunities for personal revenge and other selfish pursuits. Local cadres used their positions of power to extract benefits for themselves and to punish those they disliked or with whom they

disagreed. The outbreak of famine on the eve of radical collectivization took thousands of lives; but as radical collectivization continued,
many others—an estimated two–three million—were buried alive, tortured or beaten to death, or deliberately starved.[2] Some of these people
happened to have been born into the "wrong class," and others had
simply clashed with the local cadres. The methods of torture were
brutal; on occasion, family members were even forced to torture one
another (document 3).

As famine took hold in China in the spring of 1959, grain production failed. The procurement systems for the acquisition of grain and
other agricultural products broke down in large sections of the country. But crop failure and famine conflicted with Mao's vision of abundance, and he refused to accept reality. To him, the success of the Great
Leap Forward was much more vital than the lives of ordinary peasants.
Mao put pressures on local cadres, forcing them into competition with
one another.[3] On February 22, in a letter to provincial leaders, he indicated his belief that the food shortages had not been caused by crop
failure but rather by a conspiracy: peasants, he believed, were hiding
grain. He maintained that the real cause was corruption at the local
level, so he gave orders for the launch of the Anti-Hiding Campaign to
"educate the peasants."[4] A month later at a Communist Party meeting
in Shanghai (March 25 to April 1), Mao again told top Party leaders to
"be relentless" toward the peasants and to procure "a third" of the
total crop produced. In order not to retard the Great Leap Forward,
Mao was quite willing to sacrifice half of China's population (document 5).

Local cadres had to make up for false production figures showing
praiseworthy success. This led to the ever-increasing procurement
quotas based on the false figures. Guangdong province, under provincial Party secretary Tao Zhu, was the first to undergo the Anti-Hiding
Campaign, which was launched at the end of 1958. Guangdong has a
long revolutionary tradition. The Chinese Communist Party was extremely active there from its earliest days, and in 1927, China's first
rural Soviet base was established in Haifeng and Lufeng counties in
eastern Guangdong. One legacy of Guangdong's revolutionary culture was a propensity for political violence. With the people's communes, the region's military tradition was restored by Mao's order;
oppressive control was revived and reached an unprecedented level
(documents 6–7).

The Anti-Hiding Campaign soon turned into a nationwide crusade
against peasants. Local cadres forced starving peasants to hand over
their very last kernels of grain and to work day and night in scorching

summer and freezing winter. Anyone who did not follow orders was severely punished. Many were tortured or starved to death.

To ensure the success of the Great Leap, Mao constantly put pressure on provincial leaders. Under pressure, provincial leaders turned on those at the level immediately below them. As the popular Chinese saying goes, "The big fish eats the small fish, the small fish eats the little shrimp, and the little shrimp eats nothing but sand." Violence permeated the bureaucratic structure, becoming more extreme at each lower level, from the county to the communes to the production brigades. Terror had always been a feature of Mao's regime, but when the Great Leap was pushed further forward after the Lushan plenum of the Chinese Communist Party in late July and early August 1959,[5] the violence intensified. At the local level, Party meetings became the platform for the promotion of terror and the place of decision for its execution. Mass campaigns engineered by the Party turned into a "beating frenzy" that spread across the country at terrifying speed.

In Hunan, the native region of a number of Communist leaders, including Mao Zedong and Liu Shaoqi, terror and violent cruelty became endemic, spreading from the county level down to the production brigades (document 8).

West of Hunan, in Sichuan, the proverbial land of abundance, provincial Party boss Li Jingquan—a man Mao once called more ruthless than the earlier warlords—was eager to please Chairman Mao Zedong. While he continued to receive praise from top leaders like Mao and Deng Xiaoping for Sichuan's generous provision of grain to the rest of country, millions of Sichuanese died of starvation or were tortured to death during the rigorous Anti-Hiding Campaign. Although a serious food shortage afflicted the Sichuan countryside early in the spring of 1959, Li Jingquan launched a Balance the Books Campaign in March to achieve the unrealistically high procurement quotas. This campaign was part of the nationwide Anti-Hiding Campaign, and it was accompanied by the Rectification Campaign. At the local level, rectification did not clean up corruption among the cadres, but it often enabled the looting of peasants' homes and the theft of the very last reserves of food they had. If no grain could be found, peasants risked torture or total food deprivation.

The situation was particularly severe in eastern Sichuan. High up in the hills, in houses clinging to the banks of the Yangtze River, peasants faced harsher conditions than in the western plains of the province. Though not far from prosperous Chongqing, Shizhu county had an average death rate between 20 and 50 percent from mid-1959 to mid-1961. In some areas of the county the death rates were as high as

60 percent. While the majority of those who died did so as the result of starvation, many were also beaten to death. In the Xianfeng big brigade of the county's model Huaban commune, more than 70 percent of the local population were battered during the Anti-Hiding Campaign. Some areas not only had special "people-beating squads" but local cadres even encouraged children to attack other children (document 9).

In nearby Fuling county the situation was no better. The death rate in Baozi commune in 1959 and the first half of 1960 was as high as 29 percent. This county was once considered Fuling's granary. With its lush green terraced fields, the area had produced such an abundance of food that over 2.5 million kg of grain were sent to the state granary in 1958. The main road used to be full of people every day, carrying grain and pigs to the local market. It was always bustling. At the time of collectivization in 1958, Baozi commune had 15,455 people. But by January 1961 the population had dropped by 46 percent. More than 667 hectares of farmland were covered in weeds. The grain output plummeted by 87 percent, and the local population relied entirely on government food provisions. In addition, 70 percent of the workforce was diverted from agricultural work to build communal projects such as collective canteens and piggeries. The Anti-Hiding and Rectification Campaigns accompanied the crop failure; people in the commune's Qinglong big brigade were beaten to death during the former campaign (document 10).

Humiliation inflicted as much pain as torture. In traditional China, public humiliation was used as a form of punishment. Under the Maoist regime humiliation was an essential tool for carrying out political violence, and it was widely practiced in people's communes. In December 1958, for example, eight citizens from Wugang county in southern Hunan sent a letter to Chairman Mao to report a case of humiliation in which more than 300 female peasant workers from the Red Flag people's commune were forced to work topless in freezing weather (document 11).

All but one of the following documents are from Sichuan, Guangdong, and Hunan—major agricultural provinces in China. They show the extent of violence, repression, terror, and brutality in the countryside from the launch of the people's communes in 1958 to the height of the famine in 1961. Document 5 is the exception. Discovered by Frank Dikötter in the Gansu Provincial Archive, it is a transcript of Mao's responses and interjections at a March 25, 1959, conference. It deserves close attention. As Dikötter has pointed out, this document shows, for the first time, that Mao knew very well what was happening in the countryside at large and nonetheless ordered that procurements be *increased,* not decreased.[6]

What makes the Great Famine in Mao's China different from famines in late imperial China and the brief Republic is the extraordinary level of violence that was meted out. Under Mao, violence was a very effective means of control. The aim was to "kill one in order to deter one hundred," or, as a Chinese proverb says: "Kill the chicken to scare the monkey." Violence became the foundation of the Great Leap Forward and contributed to the escalating problem of scarcity that eventually led to millions of deaths by starvation.

· Document 3 ·

A report on how to mobilize the masses and rely on the poor peasants to reveal the problems in the commune, as well as suggestions for future work, by the Wanxian Region Party Committee, [Sichuan province,] 1961

[In Wanxian region, local cadres] unlawfully set up private courts, jails, and labor camps. The methods of torture included hanging people up, beating them, forcing them to kneel on burning charcoal, piercing their mouths, clipping off their fingers, stitching their lips, pushing needles into the nipples, force-feeding them feces, stuffing dried beans down their throats, and so on. They also punished ordinary peasants by making them wear tall hats and marching them in front of the local populace. Some people also had their faces tattooed. Some parents were made to beat up their children, and children, to beat up their parents. The cadres tried every possible means to break down the peasants emotionally as well as physically. Many committed suicide as a result. Others were beaten to death, and quite a few were even buried alive. To destroy the evidence, they burned all the dead bodies. In addition to beatings, food deprivation, looting of houses, and heavy fines, openly robbing peasants is also widespread. Many peasants have lost not only their possessions but also members of their families: parents have lost their children, and wives have been forced to leave their husbands.

In Fengle commune, the former Party secretary, Zhan Xianchun, together with his deputies, Yang Xinghua and Wang Kaiyuan, ran the commune like dictators. They waged an extremely cruel war on ordinary peasants. Zhan even held special meetings to announce his plan to raid peasants' homes and to use torture. [. . .] When deaths became commonplace, he publicly declared: "A few deaths are nothing. If one dies, we can just pull out the dead body; if a couple die, we will carry the bodies out. There are too many people in our country, the more people who die, the more food for us to eat." He told other cadres and peasants: "A few dead is nothing. The amount of food is limited. It's the result of our socialist system." He continued: "Our socialist system determined that death is inevitable. In the Soviet Union, in order to build the socialist system, about 30 percent of the population died."

In this commune, from the winter of 1959 to the spring of 1960, about 2,357 people died, which is 14.5 percent of the total population. Of those who died, 40 were beaten to death, and 32 were forced to commit suicide. More than 300 were deliberately starved to death. Some of them were not given anything to eat for more than half a month. [...] According to our preliminary investigation in Dongyang commune, 438 people from that commune were physically tortured, 297 were forced to flee elsewhere, 113 people died as a result of a physical beating, plus 57 people were severely injured, and some were permanently disabled. [...] In Nanmen commune the number of deaths has exceeded 4,303, which is 19 percent of the total population. According to our preliminary investigation, 82 were beaten to death, while 510 were deliberately starved to death. In addition, more than 200 people were forced to flee from their homes, and 13 people went mad. In this commune at least 868 have been beaten, and 562 households have been looted. [...]

· Document 4 ·

A report by Comrade Yang Wanxuan on the Rectification Campaign
and production work in Fuling region, [Sichuan province,]
January 7–August 7, 1961

[...] Gaoan commune in Dianjiang county introduced the slogan "To destroy all thatched houses within one night, to establish collective housing within two days, and to enter Communism within one hundred days." In one night more than 200 peasants' houses were burned down. Pingshan administrative district's Yongping commune even organized a special squad, consisting of eleven people, that was responsible for burning down houses. Altogether they burned down more than 1,150 houses. In Pingxi administrative district, more than 310 houses were also burned down. In Pingshan district's Baijia market, more than 200 families were forced to relocate. In Sanhui market and Yanjia market, all the families were moved elsewhere. [...]

· Document 5 ·

Chairman Mao's words at the Shanghai Conference, March 25, 1959

TOP SECRET

The following document is to be handed out only to comrades attending the meeting and must be returned after the meeting.

[Comments] during Comrade Li Xiannian's[7] report on the current trade and financial situation, as well as further suggestions.

[Li]: [. . .] The amount of agricultural products procured over the past few months has been rather disappointing.

[Mao]: It's more than just disappointing. In some aspects it's terrible. In some areas the problem is very serious.

[Li]: [. . .] Throughout the country, the grain procurement quotas have not been uniformly accomplished.

[Mao]: Let's publish the results showing who have fulfilled their quotas and who have not. We have got to be relentless. This will mean being precise and accurate; it can't be seen as being vicious. [. . .]

[Li]: [. . .] Many parts of the country have failed to allocate and transfer [agricultural products] effectively.

[Mao]: Announce their names and shame them.

[Li]: [. . .] Many major oil production areas have failed to achieve their procurement quotas.

[Mao]: Which are these areas? How come their names are not listed here? Afraid of losing votes?

[Li]: [. . .] It's essential to collect at least 15 billion kg of oil.

[Mao]: Before the end of this conference, let's make a pact with each province and decide how much oil they must hand in within the next three months.

[Li]: [. . .] Shandong, Hebei, and other regions have set a rule not to slaughter any pigs in the next three months, and residents living in cities must eat less pork so that more effort can be put into increasing productivity [in the countryside].

[Mao]: Excellent. Why doesn't the whole country follow their example? [. . .]

[Li]: [. . .] It is crucial for all Party members to put their efforts into achieving the [procurement] targets.

[Mao]: By this we mean provincial, regional, and county Party Committees. As long as the amount of grain being procured does not go above a third [of grain produced], peasants will not rebel.

[Li]: [. . .] Although the harvest was good throughout the country, only Heilongjiang, Jilin, Henan, Hebei, Sichuan, Hunan, Shanghai, and Beijing have managed to seize the opportunity and succeed in grain collection. Each of these provinces "struck while the iron was hot" and paid close attention to [grain] procurement.

[Mao]: Why did the rest of the country fail? Every province must adopt Henan's method: "He who strikes first prevails; he who strikes late fails." This is a real lesson.

[Li]: [. . .] Our policy always puts the stress on procuring grain in good time. Let the prosperous regions support the less prosperous ones; each region should first eat what it has and leave the state granary as the last resort.

[Mao]: Let's keep it that way for the next ten years. Even if we manage to solve the grain problem in ten years' time, we should not disclose the news.

[Li]: [. . .] As for grain consumption, we should continue to be cautious, constantly "looking ahead and behind," and economize at every stage to avoid going short. We should also continue the state monopoly over collecting and selling grain, taking one step at a time to slowly but steadily build up our grain reserves.

[Mao]: Excellent.

[Li]: [. . .] With regard to procuring local produce and waste—

[Mao interrupts]: There is no waste in the world. One man's rubbish is another man's food. [. . .]

[Li]: [. . .] Priority should be given to the domestic market and the export market should come second.

[Mao]: We should talk about this slogan. There are times when domestic trading should be subjugated to export needs. The export market is extremely important, and we mustn't neglect it. We shouldn't become too comfortable. We should eat and consume less. We should live frugally to guarantee the export market. We need to stress this. Some people don't eat meat. Old Xu is a human being and he doesn't eat meat, yet he has managed to live to eighty-three. Horses and cows don't eat meat, but they are capable of plowing the fields. We should keep up with the spirit of Old Xu.[8] [. . .]

In the course of Comrade Bo Yibo's[9] report on the implementation of the industrial development plan over the first quarter and arrangements for the second quarter, when [Bo] was talking about the arrangements for the second quarter.

[Mao]: It would be great if we could complete what's on the list. Is this Marxism? If 90 percent [of targets listed] are accomplished, then it's Marxism. [. . .]

When [Bo] suggested there were two ways to arrange production and construction over the second quarter:

[Mao]: [. . .] In the next three months we need to put our efforts into developing our industry. We must be forceful, relentless, and precise. Our leadership in charge of industry should act like the First Emperor of Qin.[10]

To distribute resources evenly will only ruin the Great Leap Forward. When there is not enough to eat, people starve to death. It is better to let half the people die so that the other half can eat their fill.

· Document 6 ·

A report on the criminal case of the counterrevolutionary Wu Xing
and his followers in Encheng commune, to the Guangdong Provincial
Party Committee, December 29, 1960

Wu Xing and some of his associates set up five illegal labor camps in 1958 using the commune and a need for deep plowing as an excuse. Under their evil influence, individual production brigades set up a further eighteen [illegal] labor centers. [. . .] Any cadres who were ill or happened to disagree with what Wu Xing and his group were doing were regarded as "right deviationists" and "lacking enthusiasm." Any peasants who failed to turn up for work or showed discontent were labeled "stumbling blocks." As a result, they were punished with hard labor.

It has been revealed to us that 605 cadres and ordinary people have been detained and sent to labor camps. [. . .] For example, Zhen Zifan, the Party secretary of Pingtang big brigade, could not go to work owing to severe tuberculosis, which caused him to spit blood. After learning this, the commune's Party secretary Wu Qin not only refused to let Zhen have any treatment but even accused Zhen of "doing a bad job" and ordered him to be sent to the labor camp. For over ten months, from September of last year to July, Zhen was forced to do hard labor. [. . .]

In the first lunar month of this year, Wu Qin was staying at Jingjiang big brigade. At that time, peasants were collecting soil from the pond to make fertilizer. It was already 9 p.m., and as the weather was cold, many requested a stop to the work. Wu Qin reported this to Wu Xing. [. . .] Wu Xing then ordered the head of the militia to go to Jinjiang brigade, along with the cadre in charge of security for that brigade and another 120 militiamen. They surrounded the three villages and used guards patrolling both ends of each street to force more than 800 peasants, men and women, old and young, to run to the public meeting place. They denounced several individuals and used guns to scare people. [...]

Worse still, in 1958 Wu Xing suspected an elderly lady named Wu Ducai, from Dachongling big brigade, of stealing corn, and she was punished with hard labor. Wu Ducai became frightened and attempted to commit suicide by jumping into a river, but she was saved by some people nearby. Wu Xing, however, did not apologize to her. Instead, he called this woman a "shameless deadweight" and tied her up with a rope in public. Once more Wu Ducai was driven to commit suicide, and this time she hanged herself. [...]

As well as the problem of illegal labor camps, looting of private houses has become a poisonous wind sweeping across the commune. So far 86.2 percent of villages and 83.1 percent of individual peasants' houses have been looted. One serious outbreak of looting took place during the period when peasants and villages were collectivized. Peasants' land, houses, oxen, agricultural tools, pigs, poultry, grain, and seeds were all collectivized; this was known as the "eight collectivizations." At the end of 1958, during the Anti-Hiding Campaign, another two severe bouts of looting took place, accompanied by over 200 more minor incidents.

The most severe looting took place at the end of 1958, when Wu Xing, using the Anti-Hiding Campaign as an excuse, led another six cadres from the same commune, ten cadres from other big brigades, and forty-five militiamen to Hejing big brigade. They established their headquarters and targeted a number of houses as a priority for looting. Under Wu Xing's command, the looters surrounded four villages within the brigade and arrested the local cadres. Some cadres were detained for more than five days. The looters also imposed curfews forbidding people to go out. If anyone broke this curfew, the militia would shoot him or her with impunity. The looting was carried on for eleven days, and the looters spared neither the interiors nor grounds of people's houses, or even the woods on the hill. They not only excavated people's land and dug under their walls but even dug beneath their beds. They also rummaged through boxes and cupboards. In the end they confiscated 230 kg of rice, 424 kg of fennel, 4 kg of rice flour, 10 kg of seeds, 83 kg of grain, 85.5 kg of sorghum and wheat, 144 kg of beans, and 268.5 kg of rice cakes, as well as ten plows and some beef fat, salt, sugar, and poultry. The poultry, fat, and sugar were taken to Shadi big brigade and were feasted on by those who took part in the looting. [...]

It has been revealed to us that 471 peasants have been deprived of food. [...] In 1959 a poor peasant named Lu Maonü, from Huancheng big brigade, stole some rice while she was working in the collective canteen. When she was found out, the local cadres searched her home and confiscated 9 kg of grain rations [intended] for her entire family. They also punished her with two days of hard labor. For five days, they even refused to serve any food to her father[-in-law] and mother-in-law. Lu, while desperately hungry herself, felt worse watching her husband and family being punished. She told her husband, "I must accept responsibility for my own sin," and committed suicide. After hearing about Lu's death, the Party secretary, He Yaoting, did not make any effort to help solve the problem. Instead, he said, "Once it's dead, it's over." He went on: "Ten dead bodies makes five pairs; using them to make fertilizer will guarantee a high yield." [. . .]

While ordinary people are finding it difficult to survive, Wu Xing and his followers are having feast after feast. This year, during a conference at Liufang big brigade, they ate proper rice at every meal. This was at a time when the peasants in the brigade had been out of food supplies for thirteen days. They were displeased watching Wu Xing and others eating rice. They complained, "We do the work but have no food to eat, whereas you, who simply stroll around all day, get 250 grams of rice." Wu Xing replied: "I did not eat 250 grams of rice strolling around. I ate it sitting down." Later he told this to cadres in the commune as a joke.

The most unbearable aspect is that in the spring of this year, around eleven big brigades went without any food supplies for more than ten days. However, in the commune granary more than 224,000 kg of grain, 20,000 kg of yam, and 5,000 kg of wheat and beans were left to go rotten. Even then, [the cadres] did not give any food to the villagers. A significant number of villagers died as a result. For instance, in Jinhu big brigade forty-three people died, about 4.5 percent of the total population. Nine babies were born at this time, but because of lack of food, the families had to kill them. [. . .]

· Document 7 ·

A report on several recent cases [of commune cadres] violating the law, written by the Guangdong Procuratorial Party Committee and authorized for dispatch by the Guangdong Provincial Party Committee, June 1959

[. . .] Currently a number of communes have unlawfully set up their own detention centers and "private prisons." Judging from what has been seen and heard by the [Guangdong] Provincial Investigation Team, these include at least Guangli commune in Gaoyao county,

Heping commune in Chaoyang county, Dazhen commune in Wengyuan county, Shengtang commune in Kaiping county, Huangliu commune in Ledong county, and Jialai commune in Chengmai county. According to the reports we have, these are not isolated cases: "private prisons" run by the commune are widespread in many regions. In most cases these private prisons are used to deal with "the people" rather than "the enemy." Intended as an instrument of government control, they have now become a means for cadres to violate the law and to force their own orders on the people.

Between April 13 and May 7 this year, within twenty-five days, thirty-two people were arrested in Huangliu commune. Apart from two criminal offenders, one former soldier, and one former guerrilla fighter for the [Japanese] puppet government, these were all ordinary people. Zhen Lianqin, the Party secretary of Shengtang commune, also set up two labor camps. Of the people sent to these two camps, except for three people classified as belonging to the Five Types,[11] more than seventy were there for being "unruly" and "disobedient" grass-roots cadres and activists.

There are no proper procedures for making arrests. Anybody is able to make an arrest and have other people sent to labor camps. All of the cadres have the power to go to rural areas, arrest people, and bring them into the communes. People have been detained for hours or days, even months, without their cases being properly dealt with. Some have also been deprived of food and sleep. At Dazhen commune in Wengyuan county, because of a housing shortage, the urinal is used as the detention center. Following the example of cadres at the commune level, cadres and a few villagers from production brigades have also started to openly arrest and detain people. In Huangliu commune, for example, there have already been fifteen arrests in three big brigades. In the spring, when Tan Mujing, a peasant from Kaiping, got lost on his way to visit his relatives in Taishan county, he was detained for two weeks by the local Public Security Bureau. Huang Qihan, the deputy head of Hushan big brigade in Pingsha commune, Zhongshan county, decided to use slave labor and arrested nine peasants. After the first campaign to suppress counterrevolutionaries,[12] it was decided that no district or town should set up its own prison. However, since the establishment of the people's communes, private prisons have been springing up. Worse still, some cadres in charge of political administration pay no attention to the seriousness of the situation; they even praise [the private prisons] as "having helped to defeat the enemies in good time and played a powerful supporting role to the core work." [...]

Unlawful physical torture was particularly prevalent before April. Although the situation has improved slightly, the damage is irreparable. According to incomplete figures from Wenchang, Hua, Kaiping, Leibei, and Zengcheng counties, thirty-four people died from their injuries or committed suicide as a result of unlawful searches and physical assaults. In Liangyang county, the deputy Party secretary of Pinggang commune ordered a public denunciation meeting to be held once a month at Fuchang big brigade. Denunciation meant physical violence. One peasant was so badly beaten that his intestines emerged.

At an April 18 meeting at which the villager Ning Wenjun was denounced, Liu Zhenyu, the deputy head of Xiaojiang commune in Hepu county, tortured Ning with the "frying beans" method,[13] as well as cuffed and beat him until [he] started to spit blood and eventually lost consciousness. Ning died three days later. The peasant woman Chen Yukui was from Renhe commune in Hua county. She complained that her local cadre refused her request to have time off because of pain in her legs. Beginning on March 1, the head of her production brigade, Li Qiucai, attacked her for two nights in a row, driving Chen to commit suicide by drowning herself with her six-month-old child on her back. For some cadres arresting people has become an addiction.

In Huaiji county, Yang Wenhua, the Party secretary of Zhongzhou commune, struck eleven people, wounding three of them. In one day, he hit the leader of a small unit, Mo Chonglou, three times. People compared him to a ferocious tiger and called him the "tiger man." In Haikou county's Longtang commune, the female committee member Wang Meilan struck ten peasants, including a sixty-seven-year-old and some pregnant women. Some cadres do not differentiate people from the enemy. Zumiao Hardware Factory in Foshan county hired some released prisoners as well as persons still under public surveillance to beat up discontented workers. Cadres at Dasi Law Court in Qin county hired a number of bad elements to interrogate and assault a man suspected of pig theft.

In areas where unlawful attacks are particularly severe, people are simply terrified. In Diaofeng commune in Leibei county, Chen Shaoying and forty other teenagers were placed under house arrest for a whole night for playing cards over the Chinese New Year holiday. After they confessed their faults to the public, local cadres did not let them off but paraded them through the village and handed out criminal sentences. This led two youths to commit suicide by throwing themselves into a river. When Lin Rongfang from Baoluo commune in Wenchang county asked for leave from her work on a water reservoir construction site because she suffered painful menstruation, Gan Qin, the cadre from the commune, not only refused her request but threatened to arrest and denounce her. Lin had to carry on working despite her menstrual pains and later died at the construction site. This incident has generated extremely negative feelings among the people.

Torture was used to extract forced confessions. [. . .] For example, in one recent case the head and the deputy head of the Public Security Bureau, as well as the section head of the Political Security Department, employed the so-called wheel-war tactic[14] during interrogation, taking turns to flog each suspect. Under their influence, more than ten other cadres also slapped culprits' faces during interrogation.

In March a bag of money went missing at Huadong commune's brick factory in Hua county. After he "had closely watched everyone's expression and weighed up their words," the security section head Chen Zhao suspected that the peasant Chen Renjia was the thief. Chen Zhao, along with the commune's political and legal section head and other committee members, tortured Chen Renjia in order to extort a confession. They tied him up and used such techniques as hanging him up and beating him, forcing him to kneel down, force-feeding him by pushing grain chaff into his mouth, applying electric shocks, setting his mouth on fire with kerosene, and using sleep deprivation. They also brought Chen's wife to watch him being tortured, and she burst out crying at the scene. After returning home, she committed suicide by jumping into a well holding their seven-year-old child in her arms.

In Shantou, a peasant in Xiapeng commune named Cai Yayou twice reported that he had happened to lose 5 yuan. However, the head of security, Wang Song, decided that Cai was making false reports and forced him to confess. This eventually drove Cai to commit suicide by jumping into a river with his two children tied to his body. [. . .]

In Qin county's Dasi commune, Chen Fujing, the cadre in charge of political and legal work, even threatened people with "fake executions" in order to track down hidden firearms. In some areas grass-roots cadres also pushed gun barrels into people's ears, or forced people to stand naked in the rain or under the scorching sun.

Some details of these cases are horrifying, and many involved personal abuse or humiliation. [. . .] For example, the deputy Party secretary of Longmen commune, named Lin Juqing, smeared the faces of sixteen "lazy" workers with paint in five colors and forced them to wear dunces' hats and carry white flags.[15] He then paraded them around the construction site and forced them to shout "I am a lazy bastard; whoever wants to be a lazy bastard, look at me."

In Puning county's Jiangkou commune, head shaving was used as a punishment, and one time, six people had their hair completely shaved off. In Wengyuan county's Dazhen commune, the cadre in charge of security paraded down the street with drums and gongs a woman who had been caught stealing. On her body was hung a cardboard sign reading "I am a thief."

All sorts of personal humiliation were widely promoted in many regions. In Dan county's Nada commune, two women stole things to survive. Local cadres together with several militiamen tied them to a tree and stripped off their clothes. They then focused torchlight directly on their genitals. One of the cadres also painted two big turtles on their backs and forced the two women to wear them for three days.[16] In the end both women committed suicide. [. . .]

· Document 8 ·

A preliminary report to the Hunan Provincial Party Committee regarding the case of cadres violating discipline and the law in Liling county, by Comrades Lou Qinan, Zhao Chuqi, Zhang Tongzuo, and Yang Shuqing during their investigatory trip to the countryside, June 2, 1960

[. . .] [Cadres] from the top down violating the law is a very serious situation.

Since October last year, during seven county-level conferences, including the county Party congress, the conference of county-level administrative departments, the conference of third-level cadres in the county, and [other] conferences concerning grain, there have been a number of incidents of physical assaults, involving 127 victims. Some 71 people were forced to kneel down and were subjected to beatings. A few were badly injured as a result.

For instance, in the second half of October last year, during the county's third-level cadres' conference, cadres from individual communes were scrutinized. Guo Jiyao, the deputy head for Taohua commune, was beaten unconscious, and two doctors had to be called in to try to bring him back to life. [. . .] Cadres from fourteen communes attended this conference, and physical violence occurred within thirteen communes. [. . .]

Since several county-level conferences have set the example, physical violence has become prevalent in communes and in big and small production brigades, becoming worse at each level down.

It is normally more violent at the commune level than it is at the county level. According to statistics from eleven communes, 235 people were denounced at a Party conference inaugurating the Rectification Campaign, and 120 people were beaten up—this was 51 percent of the total number of people denounced. Three people died as a result, seventeen were seriously wounded, and thirty-five suffered minor injuries. More than twenty types of torture were employed, most of them extremely dangerous. They included hanging people up like pigs waiting to be slaughtered, using burning incense [to cause damage to parts of the body], whipping the feet, smearing saltwater [over open wounds], pouring ice water [on people], burying [people] alive, and so on.

Some areas even advocated extremely cruel "beating slogans" to describe the methods of torture used, such as "big group operation"—a group of activists jump up onto a platform to attack victims; "beat up a fierce tiger trying to leap over a gully"—victims are lined up in two rows, kneeling on a platform, while a militiaman flogs them with a bamboo whip, turning rapidly as he flogs them; "tie up firewood"—the victim is tied up with rope and then beaten; "beat twenty-four gods"—twelve victims kneel down on a platform while twelve more kneel down below the platform; "double cook"—repeated beatings; "white up and black down"—the victim is brought up to the platform naked and then beaten until his or her body turns black and blue; "lie on the ground"—knock the victim down hard till his body rolls around on the floor, and so on. In some communes, "beating frenzy" is like an evil wind sweeping through society from the top down. Worse still, some commune cadres believe there should be a beating campaign and that it must be "carried out properly and thoroughly." They also praise those who take part in the beatings as "enthusiastic activists" who "stand and fight firmly."

· Document 9 ·

A report by the Shizhu county branch of the Rectification Campaign Working Team, [Sichuan province,] January 1961

To the Provincial Party Committee and the Fuling Region Party Committee,

We arrived in Shizhu county on January 17, and on the 20th we went down to Dahe commune. [...] From the information we have gathered so far, the problems described in letters of complaint sent by ordinary people were fairly accurate. Below is our report of the situation there.

1. Problems with [cadres] violating the law

Cadres in this county regularly violate the law. They torture people by hanging them up, beating them, looting their houses, and depriving them of food. They have even beaten and starved people to death. They have become completely lawless, and it is no longer possible to tolerate this.

[The trend] began with cadres at the county level, many of whom tortured and beat up other cadres during denunciation meetings. In the autumn of 1959, during the Anti–Right Deviation Campaign, more than forty cadres were assembled together to study [Party policies] and to confess their sins. The county Party secretary Diao Hongyuan chaired the meeting. During this meeting a number of cadres were tortured. They had their ears and hair pulled and were smacked across the face. Through torture, cadres were forced to confess their "right deviationist thoughts." Altogether, about thirty cadres were physically assaulted at the meeting. According to the Party secretary of Dahe commune, Liu Xuefa, the headmaster of Shizhu Middle School, Huang Kung, could no longer bear the physical punishment and jumped out of a window in the provincial government guesthouse. He did not manage to kill himself, however, but broke the bones in his feet.

During that winter, the Three Anti-Hiding Campaign—against concealing grain, against concealing income, and against withholding labor—was launched in the countryside. The county Party secretary Kang Maogui was in charge of the campaign at Huafeng commune. During an Anti–Right Deviation Campaign meeting, he condemned those cadres who did not stand up to denounce others for "lacking a firm stand against right deviationist thoughts." The meeting continued for three days, and many people were physically attacked and denounced. Party secretaries, brigade leaders, and accountants from Shangyou, Yuejin, and Yongqin big brigades were so badly beaten that their faces became swollen and their mouths twisted. Xiao Haiyun, the Party secretary of Yuejin big brigade, had his eardrums punctured. After they returned to their local areas, grass-roots cadres also held denunciation meetings and physically tortured villagers. [. . .]

At the grass-roots level, incidents of cadres beating and hanging up peasants have become prevalent, and the problem is very serious. Any commune Party secretary, or brigade leader, or even administrator can beat people up, deprive them of food, and loot their homes. Many villagers have been beaten or starved to death. No one is spared, from elderly people to young workers and even five- or six-year-old children. Cadres not only physically assaulted people themselves but encourage villagers to beat up villagers, and children to beat up children. In some areas, there are even special "people-beating squads." These squads regularly torture people with corporal punishment as well as hair- and ear-pulling. Some even used burning kerosene or hot iron to hurt people; they have also driven bamboo sticks into people's bodies and fingers. Their methods of torture are too savage and horrendous to relate.

Chen Zhilin, the former deputy Party secretary of Dahe commune, has physically tortured 311 people in Number 5 big brigade, eight of whom were beaten to death. At Huafeng commune's Xianfeng big brigade, Wang Dexing, the cadre in charge of propaganda work for the whole county, joined up with the deputy head of the brigade, Wei Zhenxing, the leader of the small production brigade, Ma Peijin, and another three people to form an "attacking tiger squad." If they saw smoke coming from a house, they would go there to make a search. If they found that the family were secretly cooking food, they would smash their pots and pans and beat them up. In this brigade at least 70 percent of peasants have been physically assaulted, and two peasants were beaten to death. Six people were made too sick to walk, and they were left with no families to look after them. Wang Dexing, however, insisted on their going to the collective canteen to eat, and no other villagers were allowed to bring back any food for them. As a result, these six people died of starvation. To this day, peasants still grind their teeth with hatred whenever Wang Dexing's name is mentioned.

Tao Sisheng is the head of Number 1 production brigade, which belongs to Lichang commune's Number 8 big brigade. He is also the head of an attacking tiger squad. The squad has hung up and flogged fifty people, and three people have been beaten to death. They also looted sixty-eight houses and deprived 145 peasants of their food. They have not only physically assaulted peasants from their own brigade; peasants from other brigades who disobeyed orders were also sent to them to be punished.

Dong Zhifu, the Party secretary of Lijia commune, has beaten five people to death, and he even claimed that "any cadre who does not take part in beating is a rightist." Once, a poor peasant, Yan Nongkui, picked up a pack of buckwheat flour off the ground, but Dong insisted that Yan had stolen it. He hung Yan up and tortured him with a heavy beating. Yan died the next day. The villager Liu Sandou could not go to work owing to sickness, but Dong accused him of pretending. He called a meeting to denounce Liu by pulling Liu's ears and hair. As a result of being hung up and severely physically assaulted, Liu died the day after. Dong's treatment of the poor peasant Yan Qifa was even more brutal. After discovering that Yan had secretly slaughtered a farm ox, Dong poured kerosene over Yan's head and set him on fire with rush straws. Yan's head was badly burnt, and he died the night after his release. Among Dong's many savage tortures, one is impaling fingers, which he calls "tearing up fingers to bring out blood." First he ties up the two big thumbs of the person being punished, and then he drives bamboo sticks into both thumbs through the fingernails. [. . .]

Liu Xingpei, the Party secretary of Nanmu big brigade in Qiaotou commune, not only looted all the peasants' pots and pans but smashed every single one. When twelve-year-old Tan Benjing fought to get more food to eat, Liu hung him up and punished him with a physical beating. Tan was also forced to eat feces. The boy died the day after. Liu also regularly assembled villagers who were labeled "blemishes," often about thirty or forty of them, and used "making improvements by following good examples" as an excuse to force them to go down to the river in the snow to search for stones. Owing to his savage treatment, a number of peasants froze to death, while others starved to death. A few were also disabled by heavy beatings. Worse still, he did not permit anyone to mourn for the dead or to bury the bodies. Also, Liu's entire family eat their three meals at the local nursery, where his wife is the head teacher. They steal food from the children's grain rations and regularly deprive children of their food. There used to be over seventy children at the nursery, but now only twenty are left.

Examples of local cadres' brutality towards peasants are countless [. . .]. Even today, there are still incidents of villagers being physically tortured to death. On January 14 this year, the villager Ma Qunzhi from Huafeng commune stole some vegetables from Guihua big brigade in Tianquan commune. She was caught by the manager of the local collective canteen, Ma Jiangzhi, and the [storeroom] keeper, Tang Yonglin, who beat her to death and threw her body into a pond. Ordinary villagers always wept and choked with sobs when telling us of the brutality they suffered. [. . .]

2. Deaths

Our investigation shows that at the commune level, the lowest death rate is 20 percent and the highest goes above 50 percent. Some entire families have perished. There used to be 688 people in Qiaotou commune's Nanmu big brigade, but there are now only 388 people left. Besides those who were forced to move away, 51 percent of the population has died. Dahe commune used to have more than 7,000 people, but only 4,000 are left now. The Number 3 big brigade of this commune had 1,400 people when the commune was first formed; now only 470 people are left. The death rate in this brigade is above 60 percent, and the majority of those who died were poor peasants. Huafeng commune's Dalin collective canteen had twenty-five families and 128 people; among them at least twenty families had family members killed [by the famine], and altogether about sixty-six people died. [. . .] When the former Qiaotou commune's Qiaotou big brigade was dissolved by the brigade's Party secretary, Chen Xinghua, more than 400 people were forced to move to Nanmu big brigade, and many people died as a result. We are still investigating this case.

The day after we arrived in Dahe commune, an elderly lady named Tian Yuying from the commune's old people's home complained to us in tears about how elderly people were badly treated in this home: they were refused any medical treatment when they were ill, and many were deprived of food. There were about twenty people there when Tian was first admitted into this home, but since then, at least half of the people have died, and only nine people are left now. [. . .]

· Document 10 ·

A report on how ordinary peasants from Qinglong big brigade in Baozi commune were encouraged to expose [corruption] and seize power, by the Fuling branch of the Investigation Team of the Sichuan Provincial Party Committee, January 1961

[. . .] The current population of [Baozi] is 8,017 in total, composed of 3,123 families. Since 1959, 6,158 people have either died or moved away. In 1959 and during the first half of 1960, 4,408 people died, or 29 percent of the total population of the commune. [. . .] The population decline has weakened the workforce, and this in turn has led to a shortage of pigs and to a very limited amount of fertilizer. It has seriously damaged agricultural production and seriously affected people's lives. At the moment, 30 percent of the land has been allowed to go to waste, and 40 percent of the spring crops are of very poor quality. Since October 1960, the local food supply has been completely reliant on government provisions. How did the situation get so bad? Natural disaster may be one reason, but the most fundamental cause for such a disaster is human. [. . .]

Qinglong big brigade is one of the "backward" brigades in the commune. Its problem lies with its leadership, which was in the hands of Lü Fangqin and Zhou Shunliang. [. . .]

[Lü Fangqin] joined the Party in 1954, and in 1958 he became the Party secretary of this brigade. [...] According to our incomplete statistics, Lü Fangqin has been personally involved in torturing at least twenty villagers, and we know for sure that seven people died at his hands. Lü regularly concealed grain and dealt on the black market. In August 1958 he illegally sold 1,500 kg of grain. In April and May 1959 he again stole more than 1,500 kg of grain and 250 kg of wheat. Yet he used the Anti-Hiding Campaign as an excuse to loot peasants' houses and to rob them of any personal property they had. Furthermore, Lü also regularly deprived peasants of their food supplies so that he himself could feast. Peasants hated him to the marrow of their bones, and they called him a "money-grabbing big dog."

Zhou Shunliang was a member of the commune's Party Committee and the deputy head of the commune. [...] In April 1959 he became the deputy Party secretary of the Pingqiao brigade, and he regularly used beating, hanging people up, and other forms of savage torture to harm ordinary peasants. Once he tied up a poor peasant named Yang Jiankang and one other person with an iron chain and then pulled the chain back and forth continuously until the two were badly injured and died. Another peasant, Xu Zhizhong, once mentioned behind Zhou's back the fact that Zhou had eaten a large amount of pork from dead pigs. When Zhou found this out, he accused Xu of stealing and physically tortured him to death. According to accounts given by a number of villagers and our incomplete statistics, at least six people were beaten to death by Zhou. Together with Wang Lunchang, the Party secretary of Pingqiao big brigade, and a few other people, Zhou also stole and sold communal timber. Worse still, Zhou and the others looted peasants' private property and confiscated things for their own use. Zhou often boasted to others, "Other Party secretaries have no personal money to spend, but I am the Party secretary with everything I want."

In November 1959, Zhou was appointed by the commune to be the resident cadre at the Qinglong big brigade. He and Lü Fangqin took complete control of the leadership. They regularly deprived peasants of food supplies so they could have feasts themselves. [...] In December 1959, during the Anti-Hiding Campaign, Lü and Zhou ordered their henchmen to bully a number of ordinary peasants into attending a meeting for Anti-Hiding activists. They carried on all night long and took turns at beating people up. One poor peasant, Gao Yongsheng, was beaten to death at the meeting. Another two people were badly injured during the meeting and died afterward. One person was handicapped by the heavy beating and could no longer carry on working.

The most evil thing was that Lü Fangqin used the opportunity for personal revenge and flogged the deputy Party secretary, Xu Daifu, to death. Xu had twice reported Lü for stealing communal grain, and Lü therefore hated Xu's guts. During the meeting, with the support of Zhou Shunliang, Lü savagely tortured Xu by giving him a heavy beating and hanging him up. They also hung a stone mill around Xu's neck and tormented him by every possible means. [This treatment] afterward caused Xu's terrible mental disorder and eventual death.

In September 1960 the current Party secretary [Zhang] took up his position at the Qinglong big brigade, but Zhou tried to control him in every possible way. Whenever Zhang tried to speak during meetings, Zhou scolded him for being "long-winded" and interrupted his sentences. In this way, Zhou tried to weaken Zhang's leadership. Recently, when the current Party secretary tried to report an incident in which Zhou Shunliang continued to beat up people during the county's congress of fifth-level cadres, Zhou verbally abused the current Party secretary by saying, "How dare you try to mess me up?" He then went on to threaten the current Party secretary.

At the start of the Rectification Campaign, Zhou Shunliang was the commander of Qinglong big brigade. Lü Fangqin and Zhou pretended to care about the Youth League leaders and their work, with the real intention of getting them on their side. They went on to threaten the Youth League leaders by saying: "Number 4 brigade has spies who are very vicious; they may well kill you."

When this investigation team tried to hold a meeting for the activists, Zhou used agricultural work as an excuse to try to stop the meeting. After the investigation team learned some of the things Zhou and Lü had done, Zhou and Lü turned to us and said: "You should see our achievements as well as our shortfalls," and "Lü Fangqin did make a few errors, but he has corrected them since." [...] Furthermore, Zhou continued to encourage his close associates by saying: "The Party trusts you. Good or bad, alive or dead, it all depends on you now." With his encouragement these people continued to cause massive destruction without restraint. They slaughtered pigs and other farm animals; they also stole seeds and ruined crops. Furthermore, they stirred up many troubles in the collective canteen. [...] Their actions have seriously undermined the Rectification Campaign.

· Document 11 ·

A report regarding the incident in which female workers from Numbers 3, 4, 5, and 7 regiments of the Red Flag people's commune were encouraged to work topless during their supportive work in steel production, and regarding as well the negative feelings it caused among the general public, by the Wugang County Supervision Committee, [Hunan province,] December 18, 1958

On November 23 our county launched the mass steel campaign. The Red Flag commune sent 4,200 steelworkers to boost production at the commune's steel factory. Among them, 1,713 were from Numbers 3, 4, 5, and 7 regiments,[17] including 443 male and 1,270 female workers. On the 25th, 316 female workers from these regiments worked without wearing any tops. Below is a report of the incident.

It began with the Number 5 regiment. On that day, workers from the regiment showed little enthusiasm while working. After discussing the situation, the deputy heads Xiong Benli and Zhang Mucheng decided to set an example to encourage other workers to put all their effort into the work. They were the first to take off their tops.

Workers from other regiments also began to take off their tops to follow their example. Different regiments and male and female workers started to challenge each other to remove their tops, and the spirit of competition was fierce. At this time, a small-unit leader called Zhang Songlin and a peasant worker called Zhou Jinsheng told [female workers], "You women only talk about challenging us men, but we work without our tops on. Why don't you?" A forty-five-year-old female worker named Zhong Lao'er asked the regiment deputy leader Zhang Mucheng, "Should we take off our tops?" [Zhang] replied, "Why not, if you feel the drive to work hard." So Zhong Lao'er and two other female workers, named Deng Dingxiu and Deng Guixiu, also removed their tops. Ouyang Wen, who is normally in charge of irrigation work, was acting as a visiting cadre [at the steel factory]. He used a loudspeaker to encourage more and more female workers to work without their tops on.

The commune's Youth League secretary, Li Zhaofeng, had just arrived at the work site. After seeing the enthusiasm in Number 5 regiment, he regarded female workers working topless as a new phenomenon, a break away from tradition and feudalistic superstition. So he decided to hold an onsite meeting. [. . .] A slogan was sent out: "To celebrate the onsite meeting, more female workers must take off their tops." By the time the meeting started, about twenty female workers had taken off their tops.

Cadres, including small-unit leaders from Numbers 3, 4, 5, and 7 regiments, were called to the meeting. As soon as they arrived, Li told all female leaders to stand in the front row, and then he said, "Have you seen their enthusiasm? They are women; you too are women." Li then asked Number 5 regiment's Youth League deputy secretary Ding Renan and the women's director, Ding Yinjiao, to stand without tops and give a presentation of how they started to work topless, how the number of topless female workers had increased from two to thirty, and so on and so forth. They told everyone at the meeting: "In order to support steel production, we women should try to become equal with men. We must break away from feudal traditions; we mustn't be afraid of looking silly. Only by taking off our tops can we show our enthusiasm as women."

Li Zhaofeng followed this by praising the enthusiasm in Number 5 regiment. He complimented the female workers in Number 5 regiment on their soaring enthusiasm and their remarkable ability to break away from thousands of years of feudal tradition. He also said, "Cadres, ordinary people, and women in Number 5 regiment are the same as everyone else: how come they can take off their tops and be full of enthusiasm? Some of them are still unmarried young girls: how come they are not afraid of feudal traditions or looking silly? Some of you are leaders of small units: why don't you set a good example by taking your tops off? [Workers] in Number 5 regiment have taken off their shoes, their socks, and their tops so that they can work harder: how come you are still wearing your shoes, your hats, and your padded jackets? Judge from today's situation. On behalf of the Party Committee of Red Flag people's commune I present a red flag to the Number 5 regiment for their soaring enthusiasm. Those women who took off their tops to work will each receive material rewards." After the talk, he gave an order to Numbers 3, 4, and 7 regiments requesting them to make real changes and to be full of enthusiasm within ten minutes. He commanded all small-unit leaders to set an example by taking their tops off until all other women also began to go topless. He also said that the more women worked topless, the more enthusiasm there would be. [. . .]

As Li had ordered regiments to make a real change within minutes, cadres from each regiment took immediate action after returning to their own work sites. Liu Fuchen, the commander of Number 6 battalion in Number 4 regiment, told his team that anyone who refused to take off his or her top would be showing a lack of enthusiasm, and anyone lacking enthusiasm would be given a white flag. Yang Junwen, a cadre from the regiment investigation team, called out with a loudspeaker, "Isn't it ugly to refuse to take off your tops? Isn't it wrong to refuse to take off your tops?" In Number 7 regiment, Zhen Guangzhi also used a loudspeaker. He called out: "Comrades, let's respond to the call of the Party. Let's take off our tops and work hard."

The trend of working topless spread quickly and led to 316 women taking off their tops at work. In Number 3 regiment, women felt rather embarrassed after taking off their tops, so they crowded inside a water ditch and did not dare to come out. In Number 4 regiment some women also felt embarrassed after they took off their tops, so they used an apron, an underskirt, or a face cloth to cover up their breasts. In the letter [sent to Chairman Mao] it also says that after Zhou Chunjiao put on an underskirt to cover up her breasts, the commander of Number 1 battalion pulled it off. The female worker Mao Xiuzhen and others also told us: "We felt really silly taking off our tops, but we were afraid we'd get a white flag if we didn't take them off, so in the end we had to." [. . .]

[Li Zhaofeng] later told cadre Jiang Dongfa, "The situation is great. For women to take off their tops and to work topless is a mighty, earth-shaking event." He then walked to the Red Star regiment and Number 2 middle-school work sites and asked them to send representatives to visit [Numbers 3, 4, 5, and 7 regiments] in order to promote the experience. Halfway there, some female students from Number 2 middle school felt embarrassed to see women working without tops on and wanted to return, but Li stopped and criticized them.

From 2:30 p.m. to 6 p.m., [female workers] had worked topless for over three hours. After the work finished at 6 p.m., Li Zhaofeng called all battalion commanders to a meeting to sum up the day's achievements. Li said, "Today's number one achievement is that we managed to collect 90,000 kg of iron ore; and, second, female workers have broken with thousands of years of feudal tradition. The young, unmarried girls worked topless with their tits pointing up, whereas the married women worked with their tits hanging down." While speaking, he also began to laugh, looking rather comical. He then went on to say: "We must carry on like this, or become even better. We should try to become number one [in steel production] in the county, or even number one in the province." Li also regarded his mistaken behavior as a worthwhile innovation and felt it should be promoted. That same evening, when he was making his report to the [commune's] steel production headquarters, he even imitated the women by using his hands, saying: "With tits about the size of apples, those young, unmarried girls worked without wearing any tops."

After the incident, a number of people were very disturbed by what had happened. Female workers such as Du Laojiu and Zhou Laochun from Number 3 regiment said, "Since the day we came out of our mothers' wombs, we had never felt so humiliated. [What happened] was more humiliating than being caught having an affair." [. . .]

According to our investigations, more than thirty women became ill and vomited as a result of working topless. [. . .] A female worker named Zhou from Number 5 battalion in Number 4 regiment caught a cold after working without wearing any top. This, together with the extremely heavy workload, caused her to begin spitting blood the day after and then to collapse. For two days she could not carry out any work.

CHAPTER THREE

Seasons of Death (1959–1962)

AS month followed month, the famine worsened, exacerbated by intense violence in the communes, endless political campaigns, and, after the Lushan plenum in August 1959, a redoubled effort to propel the Great Leap forward. By the winter of that year, chronic scarcity was felt almost everywhere in China. Very few places were spared from devastation. Whole families perished; villages were wiped out; large swaths of countryside fell silent.

Nineteen fifty-nine was the Year of the Pig in the Chinese calendar. According to tradition, it should have been a happy year for China's agricultural population. To bear children in the Year of the Pig is normally considered to be fortunate, for the pig is associated with fertility and virility. But 1959 and the following three years turned out to be barren years of great misfortune. Amenorrhea, the cessation of menstrual periods, and uterine prolapse, the weakening of the muscles that hold the uterus in its normal place, became widespread among rural women. Take Sichuan, for example: in 1961, between January and April, an estimated 1.4 million women were reported to have these and similar gynecological problems (document 12). The majority of cases were the result of starvation and malnutrition added to exhaustion (document 13). In many villages no children were born between 1959 and 1961. Sichuan was transformed from the "land of abundance" into a "valley of death." Between 1958 and 1962, according to local government statistics, nearly eleven million people died. In some areas, the death rates were as high as 50 to 60 percent (document 14). In the nearby province of Guizhou, in Meitan county's Suiyang commune, more than 12,000 people died within a few months in late 1959 and early 1960, or 22 percent of the total population. More than 1,500 families lost their last member (document 15).

Of the tens of millions who died in the course of the famine, about 20 percent were children. Sichuan, one of the worst-hit regions, had the highest number of orphans: between 1958 and 1962 more than two million children lost their parents. Because government relief agencies failed to deliver adequate food and medical supplies, many of these children ate unwholesome things, if they ate anything at all, and died of food poisoning as a result (documents 16–17). Others were regularly abused by orphanage staff or host families (documents 16–18).

To ease desperate hunger and stay alive, villagers consumed anything they could find. In Sichuan, as in other parts of the country, many turned to the ancient practice of earth eating. Geophagy may be universal, but in China it has unique historical, cultural, and religious meanings. Since the practice is thought to have originated in Daoist tradition, as part of the diet to achieve immortality, the type of earth consumed is commonly known as "immortal earth" (*guanyin tu*). Ordinary people ate earth to stay alive, much less to achieve immortality. In eastern Sichuan, a provincial government investigation team sent to Qu county discovered that earth eating had become prevalent and had caused a number of health problems, including severe constipation. Qu county used to produce some of the best-quality pork and tangerines in the province. But the "Wind of Communism" had swept the region almost bare.[1] For many months in 1961 local farmers had to eat earth to fill their empty stomachs (document 19).

Death as the consequence of eating poisonous food substitutes was common throughout the country. In November 1960, after failing to deliver famine relief, the central government in Beijing launched a nationwide movement to collect and manufacture food substitutes or alternative foods. The result was another disaster. Within a month, outbreaks of food poisoning had spread across the whole of China, to the alarm of the central government. On December 25, the State Council in Beijing made an emergency announcement to local governments (document 20).

Fresh outbreaks of food poisoning never ceased occurring. As the famine progressed, illnesses such as edema became endemic. In Hunan province, Mao's native land, an estimated 35,816 people died of edema in just forty days in 1961, their bodies and limbs swollen with fluids (document 21). In Sichuan, 450,000 people were reported to have edema in 1960 and the first part of 1961. After suffering a long period of starvation, the grief and pain caused by losing family members and homes, and the extreme violence that accompanied collectivization, many people were affected by various forms of mental illness. According to one estimate, at least one in every thousand people in the whole country suffered from a mental illness; one group of women suffered from "mass hysteria" (document 22).

The situation was not better in cities. As part of the Great Leap Forward, the movement toward urban people's communes began in many cities in the summer of 1958. The movement was also a means for the Communist Party to mobilize the urban population. Although the urban communes were built more slowly and tentatively than the rural communes, the effect they had on city residents was profound and often devastating. Family life was destroyed. Eighty percent of women were forced into low-paid, full-time employment, and family members had no option but to eat in collective canteens, often in different canteens. Communes were supposed to provide social welfare facilities such as schools, nurseries, and day-care centers, but many children were left at home uncared for, as were disabled people. In 1961, after the famine hit cities, severe malnutrition and rickets became widespread among urban children (document 23).

Overwhelmed by the number of famine victims across the country, the already exhausted health-care system finally collapsed, contributing to further deaths. In Sichuan, health officials from the Bureau of Health went out to investigate the prevention and treatment of edema. They witnessed neither treatment nor prevention, only scenes of horror. Hospital staff seeking to survive the famine themselves had lost every sense of professional responsibility. Corruption and abuse became commonplace. Instead of being institutions for saving lives and treating death with respect, hospitals and mortuaries collapsed into chaos (documents 24–25).

· Document 12 ·

Request [from the Sichuan Province Welfare Committee] for additional medical relief funds for the year 1961 to treat edema and gynecological problems, June 1961

To the Ministry of Finance, Ministry of Civil Affairs, and Ministry of Health and Hygiene of the People's Republic of China:

Between January and April, more than 1.4 million women in Sichuan province have been found to be suffering from gynecological problems each month, including amenorrhea and uterine prolapse. That is about 4 percent of the total female population in the province. [...]

According to our priority investigation as well as reports from various local areas, we reckon in the next eight months more than 3 million women will be in need of treatment. [. . .]

· Document 13 ·

Problems relating to the Rectification Campaign, agricultural production, distribution, and living arrangements in Fushun county, by the Yibin branch and Fushun sub-branch of the Rectification Campaign Working Group of the Sichuan Provincial Party Committee, January–November 1961

In Fushun's Hongzhu administrative district, the former commune deputy head He Changhua forced pregnant women to work in the fields, causing twenty-four cases of miscarriage.

· Document 14 ·

Report by Comrade Yang Wanxuan on the situation in Shizhu county, [Sichuan province,] and the current work arrangements, January 27, 1961

To the Provincial Party Committee:

After spending one week in Shizhu county, I confirm that the problem here is very severe and shocking. The number of deaths is enormous. According to the police investigation, the total population in 1958 was more than 346,000. In 1959 and 1960 the death rate reached 63,792. [. . .] According to several further investigations, in some communes the number of deaths has reached 40 percent. For instance, in Shuitian commune, the death rate is 40.5 percent, while in Qiaotou commune the death rate is 39 percent. The lowest death rate is around 10 percent. [. . .] In a number of the most problematic administrative districts, the average death rate is between 50 and 60 percent. In Dahe commune, for instance, the death rate in the Number 3 administrative district is as high as 66.4 percent, and in Qiaotou commune's Wafang administrative district, the death rate is 58.2 percent. The most severe case is Xianfeng administrative district in Donghua commune. The Banzhulin collective canteen used to have nine families, a total of thirty-seven people, but now only three families, comprising seven people, are still alive.

I have heard very shocking things. For instance, because the number of deaths had grown very high in Shuitian commune, the commune simply dug a big hole and threw more than forty dead bodies into it.

The corpses were left there unattended. Two kilometers from the county town in Dengjian commune, over sixty dead bodies were buried by the river embankment. More than twenty were left exposed, attracting a few scavenging dogs that tried to pull the bodies away. No one seemed to care. There have also been at least five incidents of people eating dead human flesh, and we heard that in Dahe commune there were even incidents of living people being devoured by others. In Qiaotou commune's Nanmu administrative district nursery there used to be more than seventy children, but now there are only twenty left. The dead children were carried out in bamboo baskets, one basket after another.

· Document 15 ·

Report on how to clean up the Party and the cadres, as well as how to improve the backward brigade, by the Central Supervision Commission, [Guizhou province,] January–December 1960

In Guizhou province's Meitan county, in the Suiyang commune, the Party secretary, Rong Jing, is a bad element. Together with other criminals in the commune, they have absolute control over the commune. Last winter and spring this year, when the famine broke out, they refused to take care of the livelihood of ordinary peasants. Instead, they regularly tortured peasants, either by physical beating or by hanging. They also set up prisons illegally. During the three-month Anti-Hiding Campaign, they unlawfully arrested many peasants. Within a few months, the number of deaths in the commune had reached more than 12,000, about 22 percent of the total population. More than 1,500 families had no family members left. To forge their "success," last December, with the support of county Party secretary Wang Qingcheng, they removed more than 10,000 kg of grain from the state granary and put it in a cave, pretending [that securing] the grain was their Anti-Hiding achievement. The county even held a celebratory meeting in the commune. Before the meeting, Rong Jing ordered the militia to drive all edema suffers up the mountain. About forty people with severe cases could not walk. Rong Jing locked them up in a tobacco-curing chamber and deprived them of food and drink for several days. All of them died as a result.

· Document 16 ·

Report on relief work by the Famine Relief Department of the Sichuan Province
Bureau of Civil Affairs, February 2–December 1961

Wang Jiarong at Neijiang county's Gaoliang district orphanage
failed to feed the orphans regular meals, leaving the children starving.
A number of orphans have been regularly seen rummaging around
local market restaurants for leftovers. Some also went to look for wild
grass, dead fish, shrimp, and toads to eat. Within three days in April
1961, three children died of food poisoning as a result, and eight others became severely ill. In Dianjiang county's Hongqi commune orphanage, the staff regularly abused children with physical punishment.
There are at least fourteen physical punishments being used, and more
than eighty-two children have been subjected to hanging and tying up;
that is nearly 50 percent of the total number of orphans. Some fourteen children became severely ill and have died because of abuse.

· Document 17 ·

Report and feedback on the settlement and education of orphans, by
the Party Committee of the Sichuan Province Bureau of Civil Affairs,
March 5–May 24, 1962

In the districts of Tongsi and Daisi, in the suburbs of Fushun town,
illnesses among orphans are common. Most of these orphans have lice
[...] and lack clothes and quilts to keep warm. Stealing is prevalent
among them. A number of children even went to the toilet to fish out
dead rats to eat.

· Document 18 ·

A report to the Sichuan Provincial Party Committee regarding the condition of
orphans in Ya'an, Bishan, and other areas, by a joint investigation team from
the Provincial Internal Affairs Bureau, the Provincial Bureau of Civil Affairs, the
Women's Association, and the Jiangjin Regional Office, May 24–November 20,
1962

In Sichuan's Ya'an region, there are more than 6,600 orphans at the
moment. More than 800 of them have been adopted into the collective
care centers, and over 1,600 have been adopted into the state-owned
care centers. There are, however, more than 4,100 orphans still on their

own and scattered around in different places. There are many problems regarding the living conditions of these orphans.

[. . .] In some poor brigades, most of the orphans are left on their own without any care. They wander about all day long, and a number of them have resorted to thieving. Some have suffered physical abuse and become injured or disabled. In Tianquan county's Yongxing commune, an orphan named Wang Shigao from Number 4 production brigade in Number 2 big brigade was forced to sell the family home, furniture, and clothes after the death of his parents so that he could buy some food and vegetables to live on. At the moment he is temporarily living in a villager's home. He has no padded jacket nor any quilt to cover himself up. In Yingjing county, some families regularly abuse adopted orphans, depriving them of food, as well as beating and scolding them. Some families, after eating up the orphans' grain ration, have pushed the orphans outside and left them to wander about.

[. . .] A number of care centers are badly managed, and the staff is extremely irresponsible. Some centers also suffer from overcrowding, poor hygiene, and poor living standards. Many orphans have become ill, and the number of deaths is very high. From January to September this year, Yingjing county care center adopted over 900 orphans, and more than 100 have already died, about 10.8 percent of the total number adopted. In August an average of one orphan died per day. One class has about forty-five orphans: about 70 percent have become ill, and 50 percent have died. Maggots and lice have also been found growing in the hair of a number of orphans.

In addition, a number of orphans in care centers are urgently in need of clothing, covers, and other necessities. In Tianquan county's Yongxing commune care center, there are eighty-seven orphans without any clothes to wear or any bedcovers or mattress straw. Some orphans were found squatting on the floor or hiding inside a stove in an attempt to keep warm. More than 30 percent of the orphans have become ill as a result.

· Document 19 ·

Report regarding villagers in parts of Qu county, [Sichuan province,]
who are digging for "immortal earth" to eat owing to hardship and lack
of famine relief, August 31, 1961

Towards the end of June, more than fifteen out of the twenty families living near Sancha River in Daxia commune's Wenxing big brigade went to Pujia Mountain to dig for "immortal earth" to fill their hungry stomachs. By July more and more people had joined in. [. . .] When we went to Pujia Mountain, Taigongshi, Hedizi, and Longfeng to investigate the matter, we found that around 10,000 people have dug up more than 400 cubic meters of earth, almost 250,000 kg in weight. On Pujia Mountain alone, some 7,500 people have dug up 200 cubic meters of earth, around 190,000 kg in weight. Because of the large crowds and limited space, people had to line up under the scorching sun. Some villagers had to travel from far away, so they arrived the night before and slept in the old temple on top of the mountain. [. . .] Around forty or fifty people have been regularly sleeping there overnight, but on one occasion more than 100 people stayed overnight. Some villagers in Xinhe commune's Number 3 brigade even assigned one old farmer to the task, and he came back with more than 40 kg of earth to share with everyone. One old lady not only burned incense and paper money during the dig but also kowtowed to the earth [gods]. A number of people were so desperately hungry that they even gulped down the earth during the dig. In order to dig faster and to have more, some people ignored their own safety. The earth collapsed and four people, including children, died as a result. A number of little children fainted after climbing up the mountain in such hot weather on empty stomachs. [. . .] Some people have been eating earth for thirty-eight days. One villager, Xiong Jishu, and his family have already consumed more than 50 kg of earth. Many people complained about stomach pains and constipation after eating earth. In some areas the old health problems of many people recurred, causing a number of deaths. A report from the regional Party Committee says: "In Chenbei commune's Hongqi big brigade, sixty-nine families, amounting to 240 people, suffered stomach pains and constipation after eating earth; three people among them suffered from liver problems, nineteen people suffered from edema, and two people suffered from other infectious diseases. Worse still, six people died as a result."

According to our preliminary investigation, among three production brigades in this commune, more than thirteen people have died as a result of eating earth. This is a very serious matter.

· Document 20 ·

The State Council's emergency announcement to prevent incidents of food poisoning while the movement to collect and manufacture food substitutes continues, [Beijing,] December 25, 1960

According to local reports, recently there have been outbreaks of food poisoning caused by eating food substitutes. On December 16 the Bureau of Grain in Fujian province made a telephone report to the Central Bureau of Grain. The report shows that since the end of November, 6,591 people from forty-three counties in that province have suffered from food poisoning, and 294 people died as a result. [A total of] 2,071 people have been reported as suffering from food poisoning after eating cassava, and 286 were killed as a result. A telephone report by the Bureau of Grain in Shaanxi, dated December 15, stated that in Luonan county's Xinjian commune's Xinmin district, fifty-eight people suffered from food poisoning after eating flour made of wild hemp flowers. The symptoms include total paralysis as well as nervous disorders. [...] The State Council appeals to various levels of local government to pay attention to the following: The movement to collect and manufacture food substitutes must continue, and there should not be any slowing down. Meanwhile, there should be more technical instructions on the ground to avoid any further incidents of food poisoning.

· Document 21 ·

A report by the Hunan Province Bureau of Civil Affairs regarding disease prevention work, 1961

Within forty days after January 1, according to an estimate, 35,816 people throughout the province died of edema, at an average of 895 deaths per day. Within twenty-eight days after March 8, again, 10,650 people died of edema, at an average of 409 deaths per day.

· Document 22 ·

[Sichuan Province] Bureau of Health and Hygiene's special summary report on treating edema, January 1960–October 1961

According to reports from Leshan, Mianyang, Da county, Ya'an, Luzhou, Yibin, Chongqing, and Chengdu, between January 16 and

January 20, 1960, 35,373 people were found to be suffering from edema, and 574 people died as a result. The rate is on the rise; there is no sign of a slowdown. At the moment 450,000 people are found to be suffering from edema in the province. [...] In the first half of March, the number of edema sufferers had reached 107,160; of them, 41,410 were new cases, and 65,750 were recurrent cases. Renshou, Leshan, Xiushan, Nanjiang, Tongliang, Jiangbei, Jiangjin, Yongchuan, Santai, and Beishan were among the worst-hit counties, with Renshou being the worst hit of all. The number of edema sufferers there is 22,900, which is the highest number among the above counties. [...] Between April 11 and April 17, 1960, 171,270 people were found to be suffering from edema, and 3,220 people died of edema within the week after April 16. [...]

Around July 9, a strange mental illness broke out in Xiushan, Youyang, Fengdu, Nanchuan, Fuling, Changshou, and nearby counties. More than 360 people were affected by it. The patients are all young women or women in their prime. Each day patients would break into mass hysteria two to three times and each time the symptoms would last one to two hours. After each incident, the patient would become normal again. The symptoms include headache, rapid heartbeat, lack of strength in all four limbs, hysterical laughter and crying, and muddled speech. Some also ran around and attacked people physically.

· Document 23 ·

Report on rickets and malnutrition currently [afflicting] children, as well as on necessary measures to treat the problem, by the Chongqing City People's Committee, Sichuan province, January 30–September 7, 1962

To the Provincial People's Committee:

Malnutrition and rickets have become prevalent among children in the city. According to an incomplete estimate in January this year, more than 167,000 children have been suffering from these two problems, and more than 100,000 children are reported to be very feeble physically. At the moment there are more than 9,500 children in seven factory nurseries, including those of Chongqing steel factory, Number 2 steel factory, Chang'an factory, and Number 601 factory; among them, 898 children—that is, 9.4 percent—have been reported to be suffering from poor health. In the city center, the Zhonghua Road branch of the Jiaochangkou urban people's commune gave 1,466 children a health checkup, and the result showed that 596 children—

that is, 40.65 percent—were suffering from malnutrition. Of those, 15.6 percent are in a critical state. There are also 313 children, about 21.35 percent, diagnosed with rickets. Both symptoms are found among children of all ages, but malnutrition is particularly widespread among children under the age of two. About 65 percent of children in this age-group have been diagnosed with the problem. Rickets is more widespread among children under the age of four, and about 72 percent of children in this age-group have been diagnosed with the condition. Most of these children have very little chance of surviving. Last year, in all seven districts, an estimated 11,306 children under the age of seven died. Of these, 9,633 were under the age of three, which is about 85 percent. The chance of children surviving with these two conditions is very slim. Even if they do survive, they are most likely to end up disabled for life.

The causes of malnutrition and rickets among children can vary; there are, however, several main factors contributing to the problem.

1. Birth defects and undernourishment. Owing to the famine, food supplies in the city have become scarce. Many pregnant women have suffered ill health, which in turn has affected the health of their babies. The problem seems more severe in the city than in the countryside.[2] According to reports from several hospitals, a large number of women's hemochrome [red blood count] was below 50 percent, and many suffered from low blood pressure and other health problems. These problems affected the development of the fetuses, and most newborn babies weighed only about 2–2.5 kilograms. At the same time, because the mothers suffered poor health during their pregnancy and are malnourished during the postnatal period, most of them have very little milk. According to an investigation among seven municipal factories, about 90 percent of mothers stopped producing milk within three months of giving birth. Without either their mother's milk or an adequate supply of cow's milk or good-quality milk substitutes, many babies had to survive on rice porridge. As a result, they have become undernourished and are physically very weak.

2. Lack of care and feeding. Since the Great Leap Forward, many women have been encouraged to go into full-time employment, leaving a number of children at home with no one to care for them. In some families, since the mothers went out to work, older children were left to take care of younger ones. Some children were simply left to crawl on their own and to find food to eat from the floor. Because of poor hygiene, many children were infected with hookworm and suffered regular diarrhea. Because of their busy work schedules, some mothers have no time to cook for their children, so they take the children to eat in

the canteen. The food in the canteen is generally rough and coarse, and the quantity and temperature vary from meal to meal. Many children have developed a poor digestive system. As a result, they are suffering from malnutrition and rickets.

3. Appalling living environment. Because of the population density, many residents in the city live in very crowded accommodations. Many houses lack sunshine and are very damp. In the cold and dark winter, children barely get a chance to be exposed to any sunlight. Even during the other seasons, when there is plenty of sun outside, the mothers lock up their children indoors because they have to go to work. A number of children have suffered from rickets owing to lack of sunlight. According to our investigation, 37.6 percent of children have developed rickets as the result of an insufficient exposure to sunlight.

4. Parasitic diseases are another cause of malnutrition among children. After examining the stools of 163 children suffering from malnutrition, 107 of them, about 65 percent, were found to have been infected with roundworm.

From the above, we can determine that malnutrition and rickets among children are a serious health problem in the city.

· Document 24 ·

Reports on edema prevention and treatment by the Department for Disease Control, Sichuan Province Bureau of Health and Hygiene, 1961

In Guangyuan county's Jinyu commue, the Party Committee has little awareness of the local edema problem. On January 17, 1961, they reported only 359 edema sufferers, but according to our investigation, there are 626 cases, and 21 died between December 8 and January 18. A number of patients are in a very critical state; they have to share beds, and there is a shortage of food for them to eat. Furthermore, the patients' ward is not secure against wind or cold.

The standard of hygiene in the canteen is also very poor, causing many to suffer stomach problems. [. . .] Hospital staff lack a sense of responsibility, and as a result, there have been some serious incidents of death. [On one occasion,] after a patient lost consciousness, he was locked up in a coffin for twenty-eight hours. The hospital staff realized that he was still alive only after he woke up and started to scream. [On another occasion] the head of the local health center went to sleep while on duty and failed to notice that one patient had died during that time. From the beginning of January to the 18th, some thirteen patients have died in the commune hospital. [. . .]

In Pengshui county 110 people died between January 1 and the 15th [. . .] and every day about three to five people died in the hospital on the outskirts of the county town. [. . .]

In Qingjiang township's Hongxing district, in Jintang county, the medical personnel rarely undertake any health inspections. Even when they do, they only go to the canteen to talk to the canteen staff and to find out from them whether there have been any edema sufferers. In some areas, because the local cadres were worried about failing to achieve the procurement quota, they refused to let minor sufferers of edema go to the hospital for treatment. Some sufferers themselves also refused to go to the hospital for treatment for fear that their homes might be robbed. Also, the hospital requires patients to bring their own bedding. Since many families have only one quilt to share among the family members, this leaves other family members with nothing to cover themselves. In Qingjiang commune, patients have to sleep in a cowshed, which is covered in dirt. In Jintang county's Zhao district [edema] center, the patients' ward has a terrible, cold draft from the window. The weather has turned very cold, but there is no fire in the room.

In Hechuan county's Yongxing commune, between January 17 and February 15, 1961, there were six incidents of fire. Of these, five took place in the commune hospital, and three patients were burned to death. The other fire took place in this commune's Shihe district edema center, causing the unnecessary deaths of the patients Zhang Zhu'en and Zeng Shuying. The accident happened at noon on January 17. Because of the cold weather and inadequate facilities in the hospital, plus the lack of responsibility among the hospital attendants, many patients suffered terrible cold and hunger. When patient Zhu Haiquan lit a fire in his bed to keep warm, the hospital staff was queuing up in the canteen for deep-fried sweet potatoes. When other patients discovered the fire and called for help, no member of the staff responded. The patient Zhang Zhu'en was badly burned and died as a result. On February 2, the patient Zeng Shuying was shivering badly from a severe cold. She called out for help, but no staff member answered. Listening to her terrible moaning, the patient in the next bed told her to light a fire in the bamboo warmer and sit on the chamber pot to keep warm. Unfortunately Zeng's clothes caught on fire, and the fire caused bad burns all over her body. Emergency treatment did not save Zeng's life; she died as a result. [. . .] Also, there is neither attendant nor lighting at night. Patients have to get up to go to the toilet by themselves in the dark. On one occasion a patient knocked down the chamber pot and wet himself. After he slept in cold and wet clothes his condition worsened, and he nearly died as a result of the incident. [...]

The Party secretary of Tonggu commune in Youyang county refused to attend many edema prevention and treatment meetings. The region has held eleven meetings so far, but he only attended four. He also slept through all four meetings. After each meeting, he also failed to follow or pass down any instructions.

In Dingshi district's Tianguan commune, Youyang county, a doctor added croton oil to edema medicine. After taking it, 150 people suffered diarrhea, causing their edema to become more severe. Even worse is that this commune has buried several patients while they were still alive.

In Jiangbei county's Tongjing district, there are some serious problems concerning local health work. Not only is the standard of medical care very poor, but the problem of corruption is also serious. Some hospital personnel use their position and every possible means to create problems for patients. Some of their actions are not only immoral but also extremely harmful. For instance, in Tongjing commune's Zhongping hospital, a doctor, Zhang Youtang; a chemist, Li Sufang; Zhang's aunt and son; a nursing staff member, Zhou Dezhi, and his apprentice, Yang Zuozhen; and the hospital director, Lu Weiwen, have ganged up to steal patients' food and other provisions. Worse still, they have also taken medicines and tonics provided for edema patients for their own use. [...] They even used hospital bandages to wipe their shoes or to make shoe pads. Zhang Youtang and Li Sufang also tried to cheat people of their money. [...] They sometimes charge patients as high as 10 or 20 yuan for one course of medicine. [...] While patients have nothing to eat, Zhang's home is filled with tonics and health supplements. He even used cod liver oil to fry vegetables and glucose to make sticky-rice pudding or pancakes. [...] Zhang also tried every means to prevent patients from being admitted into the hospital, and in this hospital there have been a number of deaths as a result of treatment being withheld. According to one local health official's report, in Minzhu district, where Zhang is responsible for the local health work, thirteen entire families out of sixteen families died. Zhang gave inpatients a routine checkup just every four or five days and medicine just once or twice a month. The patient Liu Haiqing has been in the hospital for more than seventy days, but he has received only one course of medicine. After a number of patients had reached a very critical condition, Zhang still refused to treat them or give them any medicine or food. Two of them were deliberately left to die. The patient Ye Jinfang had to ask several times before being admitted into the hospital. But during her ten days there, only once was she given some purslane juice to drink. At each meal she was given only a small amount of rice soup mixed with sweet potato stalks. As a result, her condition became worse and worse. [...] When she became severely ill, she was not given any emergency treatment, and eventually she died. After her death, Zhang told Zhou Dezhi to forge a ten-day prescription in Ye's name. He said: "This person was of no use while she was alive; now that she is dead, she can at last help me."

Not only has the Long'an district hospital doctor Liu Heren neglected treating edema patients, but he has also used every possible means to refuse to admit them to the hospital. A twenty-eight-year-old patient, Tian Jianyun, was taken to the hospital suffering from edema. After ten days his condition became worse, but Liu Heren insisted on his family taking him home. Tian cried and cried, begging to be allowed to stay in the hospital, but Liu still insisted on his departure. Tian died the same night after he was forced out of the hospital. Another patient, Liu Daixin, was also chased out of the hospital when he was already very weak. On his way home he fell down. He died after reaching the collective canteen in his village. According to an investigation, about eleven severe edema suffers died after being forced out of this hospital. Being extremely sinister and ruthless, however, the hospital staff made sure that no patient actually died on the hospital premises. By this means they managed to be made the recipient of various honors, including being named "model hospital" and "model doctor." [...]

The central hospital doctor He Shiwei is not only rude toward patients; he also totally neglects his duties and refuses to give out prescriptions or to treat emergency cases. His negligence has caused a number of deaths. For instance, the nineteen-year-old patient Li Chaolun died within ten hours after being admitted to the hospital because he was deprived of all medicine and treatment. Doctor Tang Bihai from the same hospital gave an eleven-year-old boy an overdose of *yangdihuang* tablets,[3] which led to the boy's death. After the incident, he asked a nurse, Lu Weizhen, to keep quiet. Since October, eighteen patients have died in this hospital, but at least ten cases were not reported. The hospital staff have also deprived patients of their food and stolen the government's special provisions for patients, including food, oil, salt, sugar, and medicine. [...] Being desperately hungry, some patients went out to pick sweet potato shoots; when the staff found this out, they exclaimed: "Let's take out those patients who have stolen food and denounce them." They also tried to deprive patients of their food openly by making rules such as "No food outside mealtimes" and "No rations if one returns home." Once, after a home visit, the patient Huang Suzhen was a little late for her meal. When she took up her bowl, one member of the hospital staff took it away from her and forbade her to eat. Huang was so desperately hungry that she burst into tears and cried. [. . .] He Shiwei and others used patients' oil to fry salt for their own consumption.[4] They also stole patients' vegetables for late-night feasts. After they stole patients' meat, oil, and sugar rations, they tried to justify their actions by saying "Uterine prolapse is caused by eating too much" and "Edema patients must avoid eating oil." [. . .]

The medical care and standards of hygiene in the central hospital are also very poor. Patients cannot wash their faces, and they must share one tub if they want to wash their feet. The chamber pot in the upstairs ward sometimes became so full that the urine overflowed and wet patients on the floor below. Also, after some patients had been dead for some time, their bodies had still not been removed, so living patients have had to share the same room with dead ones. [. . .] Since March 1960, this hospital has admitted 263 edema patients, and 68 have died. Since October 1960, 112 patients have been admitted, and 18 have died.

· Document 25 ·

Instructions regarding the prevention and treatment of edema and other diseases, by the General Office of the Sichuan Provincial Party Committee, the Chongqing and Fuling Region Party Committees, and various local Party Committees, January 10–December 20, 1961

In Guan county's Happy commune, there have been several incidents in which a living person was locked up in the mortuary. For instance, the mechanical worker Yan Xishan had been suffering from epilepsy. Instead of treating him, he was tied up and locked in the mortuary. Also, after several patients died, the commune failed to inform their families in time. Meanwhile, rats got into [the mortuary] and ate the eyes and noses of six corpses.

CHAPTER FOUR

Cannibalism (Late 1959–Early 1961)

S URVIVORS are not necessarily heroes, and surviving is rarely an experience worth glorifying. It is more often full of misery, pain, and remembered horrors. During the Great Famine, survival meant enduring extremely cruel and degrading conditions. To survive, people had to resort to every possible means, from eating earth and poisons to stealing and killing and even to eating human flesh. While cannibalism is normally understood to be a savage and taboo practice, for those surrounded by unremitting violence, horror, and death, eating human flesh may not seem so extraordinary. In the beginning, the government tried to dismiss stories of cannibalism as idle rumors, but by the end of 1959, as the famine worsened and the violence in the countryside became frenzied, it was no longer possible to deny that people in many parts of the country had resorted to eating human flesh in order to survive. As the land turned barren, not much else was left to eat.

The spread of cannibalism varied from region to region. In Linxia autonomous region in Gansu province, for instance, more than fifty instances of cannibalism were uncovered in one city between late 1959 and the following summer. Situated on the upper reaches of the Yellow River and bordering the Tibetan plateau and the Gobi desert in northwest China, Linxia was a major historical crossroads between China and central Asia. The region had always been culturally diverse; the current population comprises twenty-two ethnic groups. Although the Hui, or Chinese Muslims, form the predominant group and Islam is the major religion, Buddhism, Tibetan Lamaism, and Catholicism have also taken root there. The local diet is heavily meat-based, with beef, lamb, chicken, duck, and rabbit being favorites.

These are eaten with different types of wheat bread and strong black tea.

Following the Communist takeover of Linxia in the early 1950s, constant clashes occurred between the Hui population and the Chinese authorities. Many Muslims were assaulted by the Chinese police, and on one occasion, eight Muslim prisoners froze to death in the office of the Linxia Region Political Department. The abandonment of their bodies in a nearby wasteland caused a huge public outcry. In November 1951 a riot broke out, and an army of 8,000 Muslim rebels attacked the city of Linxia. Around 400,000 residents fled, and more than 1,000 died or suffered serious injury.[1] Three years later, the region was chosen as the principal site for two of China's biggest hydropower dams, and in 1957 it was designated one of China's first two Hui autonomous regions. In the course of resettlement, local villagers were persuaded to join farming collectives. The Communist government showed little concern for how or even whether the resettled villagers could cope with the breakup of their community and their lost livelihoods.[2] In 1958 these collectives were forcibly merged into people's communes, and all private properties were confiscated. The construction of the Yanguoxia and Liujiaxia dams commenced in 1958, but villagers were given no prior warning. Suddenly one day they were driven from their homes. They watched as their houses were demolished and their villages, farmland, trees, ancestral tombs, mosques, and temples were obliterated by engineered flooding. The few villagers who tried to resist were badly beaten by the militia.

A devastating famine broke out in the Linxia region at this time, killing half a million people between 1959 and 1960. Everything living or growing was consumed; indeed, people even ate lime plaster torn from the walls of buildings in attempts to dull their hunger. After every goose, dog, and cat had been killed and consumed, and trees had been stripped bare of their bark and leaves, all that was left to eat were the bodies of the famine's victims. Given the choice between dying or eating human flesh, a number of people chose the latter. Often the acts of cannibalism were carried out on the corpses of the dead, but murder also took place to provide a source of sustenance (document 26).

Cases of cannibalism were also reported elsewhere in Gansu province. Take Zhangye, for example, situated on the ancient Silk Road in the far west of the province. This oasis town is blessed with fertile land, numerous streams, and plenty of sunshine. Historically, it was an important frontier station for Chinese merchants and adventurers traveling farther west into central Asia and beyond. Marco Polo called it a "great and noble" city, where many religions and ethnic groups lived side by side.[3] But in 1961, Zhangye became a marketplace for human flesh; this trade was carried on at the central train station (document 27).

Further inland, near Shaanxi province, Xili county is one of Gansu's most important agricultural regions. With plenty of rainfall and pleasant weather all year round, Xili has dense green forests and vast grasslands. Xili horses are highly sought after in China. At the time of the Great Leap Forward, Xili was at the forefront of radical collectivization. In August 1958 it took a mere eleven days for the twenty-three townships in Xili to complete the process of collectivization, and by August 22, most of the population—85 percent—had joined collective canteens, where they could eat for free. The free food did not last for long, however: between 1959 and 1960 the famine killed 10 percent of the local population.

Xihe commune in Xili's mountain region had always been relatively poor. During the Great Leap, the commune was involved in fifteen different construction projects, including three irrigation canals, two dams, one dike, and two steel factories. These projects completely exhausted the already very limited resources that Xihe possessed. The devastating famine persisted for more than two years, leading many people to flee from their homes. Those who could not escape died. A few survived by resorting to killing and eating other people (document 27).

In southwest China the situation was equally bleak. Officials at a people's commune in eastern Sichuan not only robbed villagers of their very last reserves but punished villagers caught consuming food substitutes. People found cooking wild fruit or grass were beaten up and had their pots and pans smashed to pieces. In Qiaotou district in Shizhu county—where the death rate reached nearly 26 percent between 1959 and early 1961—7,334 people out of 28,352 died. The provincial Party Committee's investigation team discovered eighteen cases of dead bodies being consumed. In nearby Huafeng and Dahe communes, several cases of cannibalism were reported (documents 28–29).

The following four documents are official reports on cannibalism in Gansu and Sichuan provinces. These reports were compiled by government agents sent to investigate the problems or by the local police. The status of individuals, where it is cited in the reports, refers to official categories arising from the land reforms in the late 1940s and early 1950s. By redistributing land previously owned by individual families and landowning trusts the Party aimed to take control of the land and to destroy private ownership, enforcing its administrative and political power in the process. Related goals were to destroy existing kinship groups, to recruit new village leaders—cadres—to serve the Party, and to reorganize rural society. The Party classified all village families into classes—landlords, rich peasants, middle peasants, poor peasants, and hired peasants and other workers—based on the economic position of the family and the amount of land they owned at the time. After the land reform of 1950, a number of poor peasants managed to improve their living standard and wealth; in 1954 they were reclassified as "new middle peasants," and the former middle peasants became known as "old middle peasants." The class labels were passed from one generation to the next until the 1980s. Under the new village social structure, the village cadres became the ruling class in the countryside; the landlords and rich peasants were moved to the bottom of the hierarchy. The famine affected all these classes, and in the struggle to survive, status in some cases determined who was in a position to literally eat someone else.

· Document 26 ·

A study of cases of cannibalism in Linxia municipality, by the Ningxia branch of the Government Solicitude Group, [Gansu province,] March 3, 1961

Date: January 24, 1960. Location: Tiejia village in Maji commune. Culprit's name: Tie Erge. Number of victims: 2. Manner of crime: Exhumed victims' corpses and consumed the flesh. Reason: To survive.

Date: February 25, 1960. Location: Yaohejia village in Hongtai commune. Culprit's name: Yang Zhongsheng. Culprit's status: Poor peasant. Victim's name: Yang Sanshun. Relation to the culprit: Younger brother. Number of victims: 1. Manner of crime: Killed the victim and consumed the body. Reason: To survive.

Date: February 1960. Location: Zhangzigou backside village in Hanji commune. Culprit's name: Yi Wucheng. Culprit's status: Poor peasant. Number of victims: 4. Manner of crime: Exhumed the victims' corpses and consumed the flesh. Reason: To survive.

Date: July 2, 1960. Location: Kangjia village in Hanmasigou. Culprit's name: Zhao Bannai. Victim's relation to the culprit: Daughter. Number of victims: 1. Manner of crime: Exhumed the victim's corpse and consumed the flesh. Reason: To survive.

Date: March 13, 1960. Location: Zhaojia big production brigade in Hongtai commune. Culprit's name: Zhao Xiangxiang. Number of victims: 1. Manner of crime: Killed a child and consumed the body. Reason: To survive. Result: Arrested.

Date: March 1960. Location: Dahe: Dazhuang village in Liuji big production brigade. Culprit's name: Zhang. Number of victims: 1. Manner of crime: Exhumed the victim's corpse and consumed the flesh. Reason: To survive.

Date: March 1960. Location: Shiyuan small production brigade in Dahe. Culprit's name: Shi Wanshan. Number of victims: 1. Manner of crime: Exhumed the victim's corpse and consumed the flesh. Reason: To survive.

Date: March 1960. Location: Dazhuan small production brigade in Dahe. Culprit's name: Fan Changpincheng. Victim's relation to the culprit: Father. Number of victims: 1. Manner of crime: Exhumed the victim's corpse and consumed the flesh. Reason: To survive.

Date: March 1960. Location: Dazhuang village in Liuji big production brigade, Dahe. Culprit's name: Wang Guojiangcheng. Number of victims: 1. Manner of crime: Exhumed the victim's corpse and consumed the flesh. Reason: To survive.

Date: March 1960. Location: Kaixin village in Dahe. Culprit's name: Fan Zhemaji. Number of victims: 1. Manner of crime: Exhumed the victim's corpse and consumed the flesh. Reason: To survive.

Date: November 1959. Location: Zhaizi village in Linjiaping production brigade, Chuimatan commune. Culprit's name: Kang Shoupeng. Culprit's status: Poor peasant. Number of victims: 1. Manner of crime: Exhumed the victim's corpse and consumed the flesh. Reason: To survive. Result: Arrested.

Date: November 1959. Location: Zhaizi village in Linjiaping production brigade, Chuimatan commune. Culprit's name: Zhu Wushiliu. Culprit's status: Poor peasant. Name of victim: Wang Yucheng. Victim's relation to the culprit: From the same village. Number of victims: 1. Manner of crime: Exhumed the victim's corpse and consumed the flesh. Reason: To survive. Result: Arrested.

Date: April 1960. Location: Zhaizi village in Linjiaping production brigade, Chuimatan commune. Culprit's name: Li Zhengyuehua. Culprit's status: Poor peasant. Names of victims: Ma Hashan and Ma Labirong. Victims' origin: From elsewhere. Number of victims: 2. Manner of crime: Killed the victims and consumed the bodies. Reason: To survive. Result: Arrested.

Date: January 2, 1960. Location: Luojiaping in Caojiaopo, Hanzhai commune. Culprit's name: Ma Wende. Culprit's status: Rich peasant. Number of culprits involved: 1. Victim's name: Ma Younu. Victim's relation to the culprit: From the same village. Number of victims: 1. Manner of crime: Killed the victim and consumed the body. Reason: To survive. Result: Arrested.

Date: January 12, 1960. Location: Qiaojiaping in Hanzhai commune. Culprit's name: Ma Ba'nai. Culprit's status: Poor peasant. Number of culprits involved: 1. Victim's name: Ma Gamai. Relation to the culprit: Daughter. Number of victims: 1. Manner of crime: After the victim died of illness, the culprit cooked up her body and consumed the flesh. Reason: To survive. Result: Died.

Date: March 1960. Location: Liuji in Dahejia commune. Culprit's name: Fan Cunxiwa. Culprit's status: Poor peasant. Number of culprits involved: 1. Victim's relation to the culprit: Husband. Number of victims: 1. Manner of crime: Consumed the victim's corpse. Reason: To survive.

Date: March 2, 1960. Location: Zhenhua production brigade in Nanlong commune. Culprit's name: Qiu Sande. Number of culprits involved: 1. Number of victims: 1. Manner of crime: Consumed the victim's corpse. Reason: To survive.

Date: March 1960. Location: Xiaogoumen in Nanlong commune. Culprits' names: Zhu Shuangxi. Number of culprits involved: 2. Victims' relation to the culprits: Husband and oldest son.[4] Number of victims: 2. Manner of crime: Consumed the victims' corpses. Reason: To survive.

Date: 1960. Location: Gaojiagou in Yiji commune. Culprit's name: Ma Paishan. Number of culprits involved: 1. Number of victims: 1. Manner of crime: Consumed the victim's corpse. Reason: To survive.

Date: 1960. Location: Longhuwan in Yiji commune. Culprit's name: Shang Debao. Number of culprits involved: 1. Number of victims: 1. Manner of crime: Consumed the victim's corpse. Reason: To survive.

Date: 1960. Location: Xihe commune. Culprit's name: NA. Victim's origin: Vagrant. Number of victims: 1. Manner of crime: Killed the victim and consumed the body. Reason: To survive.

Date: February 17, 1960. Location: Nansheng big production brigade in Hongtai commune. Culprit's name: Yang Shengzhong. Victim's relation to the culprit: Son. Number of victims: 1. Manner of crime: Cooked the victim's corpse and consumed the flesh. Reason: To survive.

Date: December 26, 1959. Location: Taiyangwatan in Maiji. Culprits' names: Yang Zhanlin, Yang Zhanming, and Yang Zhanquan. Culprits' status: Poor peasants. Number of culprits involved: 3. Name of victim: Wang Gahu. Victim's relation to the culprits: From the same brigade. Number of victims: 1. Manner of crime: Cooked the victim's corpse and consumed the flesh. Reason: To survive.

Date: January 6, 1959. Location: Taiyangwatan in Maiji. Culprits' names: Yang Zhanlin, Yang Zhanming, and Yang Zhanquan. Culprits' status: Poor peasants. Number of culprits involved: 3. Name of victim: Wang Kanzhu. Victim's relation to the culprits: From the same production brigade. Number of victims: 1. Manner of crime: Exhumed the victim's corpse and consumed the flesh. Reason: To survive.

Date: January 16, 1960. Location: Taiyangwatan in Maiji. Culprits' names: Yang Zhanlin's entire family. Culprits' status: Poor peasants. Number of culprits involved: 12. Victim's name: Luo Galu. Number of victims: 1. Manner of crime: Exhumed the victim's corpse and consumed the flesh. Reason: To survive.

Date: January 9, 1960. Location: Zhangsama village in Maiji commune, Yashi. Culprit's name: Kang Gamai. Culprit's status: Poor peasant. Number of culprits involved: 1. Victim's name: Maha Maiji. Relation to the culprit: From the same production brigade. Number of victims: 1. Manner of crime: Hacked the victim to death with an axe and consumed the body. Reason: To survive.

Date: January 17, 1960. Location: Maiji commune. Culprits' names: Jiao Wenzhong and family. Culprits' status: Poor peasants. Number of culprits involved: 2. Victim's relation to the culprits: From the same village. Number of victims: 1. Manner of crime: Cooked and consumed an aborted fetus. Reason: To survive.

Date: January 27, 1960. Location: Tuanjie production brigade in Xinzhuang commune. Culprit's name: Shui Wangying. Culprit's status: Poor peasant. Number of culprits involved: 1. Victim's name: Bao Yousu. Relation to the culprit: From the same village. Number of victims: 1. Manner of crime: After the victim died of illness, [the culprit] cooked up the victim's body and consumed one leg. Reason: To survive.

Date: January 21, 1960. Location: Daping village in Sanshilipu. Culprit's name: From the Ma clan. Culprit's status: Poor peasant. Number of culprits involved: 1. Victim's name: Ma Ersha. Relation to the culprit: From the same village. Number of victims: 1. Manner of crime: Exhumed the victim's body and consumed the flesh. Reason: To survive.

Date: January 28, 1960. Location: Dachuan village in Sanshilipu. Culprit's name: Ma Junxiang. Culprit's status: Poor peasant. Number of culprits involved: 1. Victim's name: Zhang Youcai's daughter. Relation to the culprit: From the same village. Number of victims: 1. Manner of crime: Exhumed the victim's body and consumed the flesh. Reason: To survive.

Date: January 28, 1960. Location: Dachuan village in Sanshilipu. Culprit's name: Ma Junxiang. Culprit's status: Poor peasant. Culprit's name: Zhang Mage. Status: Landlord. Culprit's name: Unknown. Number of culprits involved: 3. Victim's name: Zhang Youcai. Relation to the culprit: From the same village. Number of victims: 1. Manner of crime: Cooked up the victim's body and consumed the flesh. Reason: To survive.

Date: January 28, 1960. Location: Xinying village in Maiji commune. Culprit's name: Ma Waiyoubu. Culprit's status: Poor peasant. Number of culprits involved: 1. Victim's name: Sun Zhaxi. Relation to the culprit: Wife. Number of victims: 1. Manner of crime: Exhumed the victim's body and consumed the flesh. Reason: To survive.

Date: February 1, 1960. Location: Puba village in Yanzhi commune. Culprit's name: Wang Liangxia. Culprit's status: Poor peasant. Number of culprits involved: 1. Victim's relation to the culprit: Sister. Manner of crime: Cooked up the victim's corpse and consumed the flesh. Reason: To survive.

Date: January 1960. Culprit's name: Ma Hakelin. Culprit's status: Poor peasant. Number of culprits involved: 1. Victims' names: Ma Fajimai, Ma Yang, Ma Deli, Ma Bu, etc. Number of victims: 5. Manner of crime: Exhumed the victims' bodies and consumed the flesh. Reason: To survive.

Date: February 7, 1960. Location: Liujiashan in Youai production brigade. Culprit's name: Ma Seerbu. Culprit's status: Poor peasant. Number of culprits involved: 1. Number of victims: 8. Manner of crime: Exhumed the victims' bodies and consumed the flesh. Reason: To survive.

Date: February 7, 1960. Location: Liujiashan in Youai production brigade. Culprits' names: Ma Ma'nai and family. Culprits' status: Poor peasants. Number of culprits involved: 4. Number of victims: 13. Manner of crime: Exhumed the victims' bodies and consumed the flesh. Reason: To survive.

Date: April 1, 1960. Culprit's name: Ma Ganu. Culprit's status: Poor peasant. Number of culprits involved: 1. Number of victims: 1. Manner of crime: Exhumed the victim's body and consumed the flesh. Reason: To survive.

Date: January 28, 1960. Location: Daping in Sanshilipu. Culprit's name: Ma Mage. Culprit's status: Poor peasant. Number of culprits involved: 1. Victim's relation to the culprit: Culprit's own child. Manner of crime: After the victim died of illness, the culprit consumed his body. Reason: To survive.

Date: March 27, 1960. Location: Xiyan village in Caotan town, Xinmu. Culprits' names: Yang Wenyi, Yan Shuyin, etc. Number of culprits involved: 8. Number of victims: 1. Manner of crime: Picked up a child's corpse and consumed the flesh. Reason: To survive.

Date: May 1960. Location: Dashu commune in Dongxiang county. Number of culprits involved: 1. Number of victims: 1. Manner of crime: Exhumed the victim's body and consumed the flesh. Reason: To survive.

Date: March 1960. Location: Baihe commune in Dongxiang county. Number of culprits involved: 1. Number of victims: 1. Manner of crime: Exhumed the victim's body and consumed the flesh. Reason: To survive.

· Document 27 ·

Reports on two cases of cannibalism, [Gansu province,] April 15, 1961

To Comrade Bingxiang, Office of the [Gansu] Provincial Party Secretary, the Northwest Bureau of the Central Committee, and the Ministry of Public Security:

According to telephone reports from the local police in Xili county and Zhangye city, there have recently been two cases of cannibalism in both areas. The details are below.

1. On March 31, some people from Xihe commune's Mengjia brigade in Xili county reported that a local peasant, Meng Zhengjie, was cooking meat. The commune Party secretary suspected that Meng had stolen and killed a sheep from the commune, so he went to Meng's home to search. At Meng's house, however, he not only found some meat in a jar but also discovered a hank of female hair alongside a floral-patterned cloth hairband and head-scarf. After careful investigation, it was confirmed that these items belonged to thirteen-year-old Meng Naonao from the same brigade, who had disappeared on March 20. After the Party secretary had a talk with Meng, Meng admitted that he had first choked Meng Naonao to death and then cooked and eaten the flesh. In January and February, Meng Zhengjie had twice dug up corpses of dead children, intending to take them home to cook and then eat. On both occasions he was stopped by local cadres. Regarding the case reported above, the local police have already sent a team to the brigade for further investigation.

2. On April 4 at Zhangye's railway station, a local peasant named Zhao Yuyin bought 1.5 kg meat and a pair of leather shoes. On his way back, he opened his purchases and discovered that the meat was in fact flesh from a human head, with a nose and ears. He reported it to the local police. The Zhangye Public Security Bureau is currently investigating the incident.

· Document 28 ·

On humans eating corpses and killing children for consumption: a report by
Comrade Wang Deming from the Shizhu branch of the Investigation Team
of the [Sichuan] Provincial Party Committee, January 27, 1961

To the Provincial Party Committee and the Fuling Region Party Committee:

After investigation, we have found that reports of humans eating corpses, as well as killing and consuming children, are all true:

In February 1960, the peasant Ma Luzhi from Shizhu county's Huafeng commune was beaten to death by Ma Peiling, a cadre from Yongjin brigade and others after being caught trying to steal grain. [After his death, Ma Luzhi's] sister-in-law Ma Lanzhi cut off the flesh from his leg and cooked and consumed it. [. . .] Ma's mother, Ran Yulu, had also eaten the flesh of four corpses. In the winter of 1959 several production brigades were reorganized into big units. The grass stored in peasants' homes [to feed animals] was taken away to make fertilizer. It was during this time that the remains of human bones were discovered hidden underneath a pile of grass [at Ran's home].

On another occasion, Li Shiyou from Xinhua production brigade went to the commune to attend a meeting, taking his dog with him. On the way he bumped into Ran Yulu. Suddenly the dog jumped onto Ran's back. It turned out that Ran was carrying a dead human body, which had already been chopped into two pieces. After Li left, Ran took the corpse home and consumed it. Other villagers told us that Ruan had eaten seven corpses, but Ran only admitted to four, including the bodies of Tan Jiuzhen, Ma Peifang, Tan Yushu, and a boy named Ma Peisheng. All of them had died of illnesses.

In Dahe commune's Number 2 big brigade, Zeng Bifa's wife cooked and consumed the flesh taken from the body of Zeng's nephew after he had died. Another villager, Liu Chengyu, also attempted to consume his dead nephew's body, but was stopped by some cadres from the commune. He was discovered by the cadres after he had already cut the body into pieces ready for cooking. The peasant woman Liu Chengzhen from Xinhua production brigade had three children: one aged eight, one aged five, and the other aged three. In the winter of 1959, the three-year-old child went missing. Soon afterward, Liu Chengzhen became ill with edema and was taken to a hospital. In February 1960 she asked for leave to go home. At home she strangled her five-year-old son to death with a towel. She then cooked up his body and consumed it in four separate meals. Such shocking and disturbing incidents are by no means unique. Recently we also heard of people being buried alive in Dahe big brigade. We are still investigating the matter.

· Document 29 ·

The problem of humans eating human flesh, by the Shizhu branch of the Investigation Team of the [Sichuan] Provincial Party Committee, February 9, 1961

In Qiaotou district, the problem of people eating human flesh is most severe in Wawu brigade. Xiang Xuezhen and two other villagers from Number 1 production brigade were involved in the consumption of human flesh. According to them, some sixteen corpses, including the bodies of Ma Fahui, Ma Faxiang, and Chen Shilan, have been consumed since last winter—see List 1.

It began around December 20. An old lady named Luo Wenxiu was the first to start consuming human flesh. After an entire family of seven had died, Luo dug up the body of the three-year-old girl, Ma Fahui. She sliced up the girl's flesh and spiced it with chili peppers before steaming and eating it. In the same brigade, Xiang Chaobi—who has already been arrested and subsequently died—consumed the corpse of the eighteen-year-old Yuan Jialin. After consuming the body of her five-year-old son, Yuan Ertou, Chen Shilan also died, and her corpse was eaten by others. Feng Houzhen was another who consumed the corpse of her own son, the seven-year-old Yuan Mao.

In this big brigade, eighteen people were found to have consumed corpses—see List 2. The corpses were highly toxic, and after eating them, thirteen people showed symptoms of edema and their skin turned yellow. They all died eventually. The reason that the other five people did not die was because they tasted only small pieces of flesh. Cases of cannibalism were also found in other communes. For instance, in Maliuying big brigade, the day after Liu Qingshu, Xiang Guofang's fifty-eight-year-old mother, had died and been buried, someone chopped off her thighs and arms and consumed them.

List 1: Names of Victims
Ma Fahui, female, 3 years old
Ma Faxiang, female, 10 years old
Xiang Xuerun, female, 8 years old
Yuan Jialin, male, 18 years old
Chen Shilan, female, 20 years old
Sun Baocheng, male, 3 years old

Sun Baolu, male, 1 year old (Sun Baocheng's younger brother)

Chen Sanshu, male, 30 years old

Ma Zemin, male, 30 years old (Ma's heart was scooped out and eaten)

Qin Xingqiang, male, 10 years old

Qin Mao, male, 5 years old (Qin Xingqiang's younger brother)

Yuan Mao, male, 7 years old

Yuan Ermao, male, 5 years old (Yuan Mao's younger brother; their corpses were consumed by their mother, Feng Houzhen)

Yuan Ertou, male, 5 years old (Yuan's corpse was consumed by his mother, Chen Shilan)

Anonymous, male, 10 years old (died on the wild grass plain without any family)

Anonymous, male, 8 years old (died on the wild grass plain without any family)

List 2: Names of Those Who Consumed Corpses

Name: Chen Jialan. Sex: Female. Age: 20-plus. Class: Old upper-middle peasant. Current condition: Dead. Previous number of people in the family: 2. Remaining family members: 0.

Name: Feng Houzhen. Sex: Female. Age: 30-plus. Class: Old upper-middle peasant. Current condition: Dead. Previous number of people in the family: 5. Remaining family members: 0.

Name: Wu Jiazhi. Sex: Female. Age: 40-plus. Class: Old upper-middle peasant. Current condition: Dead. Previous number of people in the family: 5. Remaining family members: 1.

Name: Yuan Jiacai. Sex: Male. Age: 7. Class: Old upper-middle peasant. Current condition: Dead. Previous number of people in the family: 6. Remaining family members: 0.

Name: Yuan Jiawu. Sex: Female. Age: 12. Class: New upper-middle peasant. Current condition: Dead. Previous number of people in the family: 6. Remaining family members: 1.

Name: Chen Shilan. Sex: Female. Age: 20. Class: Poor peasant. Current condition: Dead. Previous number of people in the family: 4. Remaining family members: 0.

Name: Luo Wenxiu. Sex: Female. Age: 70. Class: Poor peasant. Current condition: Dead. Previous number of people in the family: 2. Remaining family members: 0.

Name: Sun Guozhen. Sex: Female. Age: 40. Class: New upper-middle peasant. Current condition: Dead. Extra information: Sun is Luo Wenxiu's daughter.

Name: Luo Honghan. Sex: Male. Age: 12. Class: Old upper-middle peasant. Current condition: Dead. Previous number of people in the family: 6. Remaining family members: 0.

Name: Ma Faxiang. Sex: Male. Age: 12. Class: Poor peasant. Current condition: Dead. Previous number of people in the family: 7. Remaining family members: 0. Extra information: Older brother of Ma Faxiang (below). His corpse was consumed by others.

Name: Ma Faxiang. Sex: Female. Age: 10. Class: Poor peasant. Current condition: Dead. Previous number of people in the family: 7. Remaining family members: 0. Extra information: Younger sister of Ma Faxiang (above). Her corpse was consumed by others.

Name: Wang Fazhen. Sex: Female. Age: 48. Class: Landlord. Current condition: Dead. Previous number of people in the family: 2. Remaining family members: 1.

Name: Xiang Chaobi. Sex: Male. Age: 30-plus. Class: Old upper-middle peasant. Current condition: Dead. Previous number of people in the family: 6. Remaining family members: 4. Extra information: He was arrested and subsequently died.

Name: Chen Shimei. Sex: Female. Age: 30-plus. Class: Old upper-middle peasant. Current condition: Alive. Extra information: Wife of Xiang Chaobi.

Name: Xiang Shengmei. Sex: Female. Age: 54-plus. Class: Poor peasant. Current condition: Alive. Previous number of people in the family: 2. Remaining family members: 2. Extra information: Ate only one small piece of human flesh.

Name: Shi Xianpei. Sex: Female. Age: 20. Class: Poor peasant. Current condition: Alive. Previous number of people in the family: 2. Remaining family members: 1. Extra information: Ate only one small piece of human flesh.

Name: Ma Peilan. Sex: Female. Age: 20-plus. Class: Old upper-middle peasant. Current condition: Dead. Previous number of people in the family: 4. Remaining family members: 3. Extra information: Ate only a small piece of human flesh.

Name: Xiang Shizhen. Sex: Female. Age: 16. Class: Landlord. Previous number of people in the family: 2. Remaining family members: 1. Extra information: Ate only a small piece of human flesh.

CHAPTER FIVE

Devastation in the Countryside
(1958–1961)

T
HE radical collectivization that began in 1958 robbed the rural populace of all private possessions. The Wind of Communism blew away many differences in status, leaving imposed egalitarianism in its wake. Furniture and household items became communal property (document 30); pots and pans were smelted for steelmaking; building material, including bricks and timber from private houses, was removed to build collective canteens, nurseries, communal halls, pigsties, and dams. Even coffins were collectivized (document 31). Many homes were demolished to clear the ground for various construction projects or to be used as fuel for the collective canteens and backyard furnaces, or, if made of earth, were flattened to make fertilizer. Many people in the countryside were left with nowhere to live (documents 32–33). In parts of Hunan human corpses were removed from their graves and simmered into fertilizer (document 34).

The destruction went beyond private housing, household items, and coffins. Throughout the country much of the fertile agricultural land was turned into construction sites for Great Leap projects, including backyard steel furnaces, coal factories, and collective pigsties (document 35), as well as "Ten Grand Buildings." The showpiece for the achievements of the Great Leap Forward, Ten Grand Buildings were erected in Beijing in the autumn of 1958. They were the People's Hall, the Beijing Railway Station, the Workers' Stadium, the National Agricultural Exhibition Hall, the Diaoyutai State Guesthouse, the Overseas Chinese Hotel, the Cultural Palace of Nationalities, the Hotel of Nationalities, the China Revolutionary History Museum, and the People's Revolutionary Military Museum. The capital set the example, and the rest of the country had to catch up. Provincial capitals, counties, and even villages began building their own Ten Grand Buildings. In the race to achieve the Great Leap Forward, no place dared to be left behind. The waste was enormous, the consequences devastating. Liu Shaoqi—China's president and number two in the Party after Mao—was shattered by the damage he saw in Huaminglou, his hometown in Hunan province. Under Liu's orders, his chief bodyguard, Yang Shuqing, and an investigation team produced a report showing the destruction wrought by the Great Leap Forward to agriculture and indeed to every other aspect of local life (document 36; also document 113).

Just south of Huaminglou, in Chairman Mao's home village, Dongmaotang in Shaoshan township, the situation was just as bad. When Liu Shaoqi was setting off for Huaminglou, Mao's nephew, Mao Huachu, was visiting Dongmaotang. There Mao Huachu learned from local people that radical collectivization was extremely destructive and, in any case, failed to accomplish its goals. At the end of his trip, he produced a report on the situation in Dongmaotang based on his conversations with villagers. Mao Huachu's report was sent to his uncle Chairman Mao by Mao's secretary, Hu Qiaomu, on April 10, 1961 (document 37).

Without homes to live in, without tools to work with, and without food to eat, China's peasants lacked the resources to engage in communal labor and had little incentive to do so. Because the entire rural population was mobilized to transform China into an industrial powerhouse, no one in the countryside was available to plant rice or to cultivate half-grown crops, which were left to wither in the fields. Agricultural land became wasteland, and unattended livestock died (documents 38–40). The "Wind of Exaggeration" further damaged agricultural production.[1] To match the inflated government procurement figures, local cadres and peasants had little choice but to lie (document 41). During a twenty-five-day official tour of the Central China Plain, Hu Yaobang,[2] head of the Communist Youth League, was staggered by the destruction in the countryside. On October 1, 1961, after traveling more than 1,800 kilometers to visit thirty counties, Hu wrote a long report to the Central Committee of the Chinese Communist Party (documents 42, 46).

To transform China into the dreamed-of industrial superpower required a lot of steel. Many of the mountainous regions in China were deforested as trees were cut down to feed backyard furnaces. In some areas the idea was to convert the treeless land into rice fields or to make way for irrigation canals. These efforts turned out to be counterproductive. Deforestation led to soil erosion and sandstorms. It turned paddy fields into "sandy beaches" and farmland into bogs. The destruction was particularly bad in China's northwest, where about one-third of the forestland disappeared. Elsewhere, in Hunan province's Anhua county, for instance, unrestrained deforestation after 1958 brought drought, seriously damaging local agriculture (documents 43–44).

To generate power, gigantic dams were built throughout the country, as a result of which millions of people were uprooted from their homes. While most of these half-baked projects turned out to be an enormous waste of time and resources, the ecological consequences of these schemes continue to affect the environment today. In the agricultural heartland of Henan, one of China's most populous provinces, more than 1.3 million peasants were drafted into water-conservation or fertilizer-making projects under the radical provincial Party head Wu Zhipu. By the autumn of 1958, it was reported that the entire Henan countryside had been fully irrigated. But this apparent achievement turned out to be a complete disaster for the province. Excessive irrigation made large swaths of land alkaline and no longer fertile. On top of that, the waterlogged soil not only destroyed crops but damaged houses to the extent that many eventually collapsed. In December 1961, in a letter to Premier Zhou Enlai, the distressed newly appointed provincial Party secretary, Liu Jianxun, noted that "in a few years, the vast plain along the Yellow River will turn into a total wasteland" (document 45).

Similar calamities afflicted nearby regions, including Shandong, Anhui, and Jiangsu provinces. Like Henan, all were densely populated agricultural areas. New irrigation not only created alkaline, waterlogged soil but also prevented water from draining downstream. This caused the worst floods in Shandong's history in 1960 and 1961, leaving many villages "like small islands in an ocean" (document 46).

· Document 30 ·

Comrade Hu Jizong's speech at the December 22 meeting, from the transcripts of the [Hunan] Provincial Party Committee plenum, December 20–24, 1958

In some areas [. . .] even private furniture, clothes, quilts, and mosquito nets were "collectivized" and became the property of the people's commune. [. . .] In Liuyang county's Hongqi commune, a family of five had only three quilts. The commune insisted that the family contribute one to the commune, making it very embarrassing for the family. This family consists of one old couple and one young couple, as well as one unmarried daughter. It was already quite difficult for them to share their possessions.

· Document 3 1 ·

An investigative report on the compensation situation in Qu county, by the Daxian branch of the Investigation Team of the Sichuan Provincial Party Committee, June 8, 1961

According to our investigation, in Yongxing commune's Yongxing big brigade, peasants were told to "contribute" their private property, including pots and pans, jars, and coffins during the iron- and steel-work campaign. Although the cadres used the term "contribution," in most cases the peasants were forced to give up their possessions. This type of "contribution" occurred three times. The first time was on a voluntary basis. The cadres encouraged individual peasants to give their pots and pans to the collective. The second time was compulsory, and the peasants were given little choice. The third time was by force, and if anyone refused, his private possessions were smashed into pieces and taken away. Almost all of the private coffins were taken away by force. For instance, the peasant Chen Zirong refused to "contribute" his family coffin. When he was confronted by sixteen cadre and militia members, he held the coffin in his arms and cried. But he could not compete with sixteen strong people, and they took the coffin apart piece by piece. Every piece of wood was taken away in the end. [. . .] When village cadres went to the peasant Peng Xuexin's home to remove the family coffin, Peng's mother resisted by lying inside the coffin. She wailed to the cadres: "If you want to take away my coffin, bury me first." There were many peasants watching at the time. They tried to persuade the cadres not to take Peng's coffin away. They pleaded: "She is of such an advanced age, please spare her this time." [. . .] After the incident the old lady became very ill, and she died a few days later.

· Document 3 2 ·

A report to the Bureau of Internal Affairs and the Political and Legal Committee [in Beijing] regarding the current crisis in nine regions and counties, by the Sichuan Province Bureau of Civil Affairs, January 9–November 1962

Since 1958 the destruction of rural housing in Daxian region has been very serious. Today there are more than 50,000 families with nowhere to live. Some people have slept in sedan chairs[3] underneath the eaves of the houses of other families, and some people have slept in caves. There are many cases of a father- and daughter-in-law or a brother- and sister-in-law sharing one room. It is also common for people to share their space with animals.

There are two mains reasons for the reduction in rural housing.

1. Many private houses were occupied or demolished in the campaign to mass-produce iron and steel, during the construction of collective canteens, during industrialization in the countryside, while building collective pigsties, and in the course of road construction work. In particular, in some hilly regions, which used to have shortages of fuel, each local population, after collectivization, was moved to live collectively around the collective canteen. The houses were demolished and used as fuel for the canteen or for the backyard furnaces. Some old houses built of aged earth were flattened to be used as fertilizer. According to our investigation in Da county's Waibei commune, in Number 1 big brigade's Number 2 production brigade, about 70 percent of the total number of houses destroyed were demolished as a result of the construction of collective canteens and rural factories. Lianhua big brigade in Dazhu county's Wenxing commune demolished 45.4 percent of the private houses during the iron- and steelwork campaign. In Linshui county, in order to build a hydropower station, Changtan commune's Number 4 brigade demolished 50 percent of the private houses. Some individual peasants have received compensation, but the amount is very low. Without any building materials available, it is almost impossible to construct another house with the money paid out.

2. Because of the Wind of Communism,[4] many peasants are no longer enthusiastic about building private houses.

· Document 33 ·

An investigative report about problems resulting from compulsory relocation due to construction of the Yangmei reservoir [in Gaoyao county, Guangdong province], 1960

Construction of the Yangmei reservoir began in the winter of 1958, and it was completed in the spring of 1959. [. . .] In February 1959, 725 families, including 2,300 people from seven villages, were forced to relocate. [. . .] After relocation, villagers' housing, livelihood, and health care were left unresolved, so a number of people died. According to our incomplete estimate, at least 279 people have died, which is 13.4

percent of the total number of people being relocated. Forty-seven entire families have died out.

The worst-affected village is Baiyingen village: 203 people were forced to move out of their homes in this village, and 48 people, about 16 percent, have died as a result. Among those who died, one committed suicide, four died in the process of relocation, three died of sudden illnesses, nine died of edema, and seventeen died of emaciation and exhaustion. [. . .]

Sixty-five-year-old Chen Yugeng, a poor peasant, has four sons. Because they were not allocated any housing after relocation, the family were forced to go their separate ways to live in four different villages. [. . .] Initially Chen wanted to join one of his sons in Dingjiang village, but the cadre there refused to take him in because he was too old and frail to work. Since he could not get any food there, he went to look for his other son in Guangtang, where he received the same treatment. In the end, he was forced to go to Yinjiang village. On July 1, 1960, he committed suicide. Huang Zhangqing used to live with his brother and sister-in-law. After they moved to Dingjiang village, the cadre there refused to take Huang in because of his old age. He was sent back to Yinjiang, where he died alone on July 13. His body was discovered a few days later, but only when it began to smell foul. [. . .]

Some peasants put up a poster of complaint outside the commune's headquarters, which reads:

> Yangmei reservoir used to be our home; after we were moved to Guangtang, life became a complete mess. We have no houses to live in, and when someone dies, there is no one to bury the body. [. . . We] report to the commune, but the cadres turned a blind eye to our problems. They live in luxurious places, and they don't care whether we live or die. After they feasted and indulged enough, they pulled down our houses. [. . .] Many people have become homeless, and families have been forced to live apart. [. . .] Please help us to build some new houses, so we can have homes to return to.

· Document 34 ·

Hou Shixiang's letter to the Political Department of Shaanxi [Province] Military Region, March 1959

On December 5, 1958, Hou Shixiang from Shaanxi Military Region's Supporting Unit wrote a letter to Director Zhang in the Political Department. In the letter, Hou wrote:

In October, I went for a home visit to Guandu big brigade in Xinhe people's commune, Li county, Hunan province. I was quite disturbed by the situation there, and I feel I should write to the Party and let the Party know what's going on.

[...] I arrived home on October 18. On the morning of the 20th, I saw that the graves in front of our house had been flattened and the coffins left uncovered. So I asked what had happened to those graves. Someone told me that they had been flattened the previous night. A few days later I saw smoke near the house of the brigade Party secretary, Song Jinliang. A large number of human corpses had been put into four big pots. They were simmered into fertilizer. On another occasion while I was strolling along in the countryside, I saw stoves being set up in a graveyard. I ran into a peasant who was transporting grain, so I asked him what those stoves were doing there. He told me they were there to make fertilizer. I asked again: Why is it being done in an open field? He explained that because the smell is too foul, it is not suitable for indoors. After making some inquiries, I learned that this was the second time the same thing had happened. Both my mother's and my aunt's graves were destroyed the first time. [...] I went to the county afterward and spoke to Liu, director of the People's Committee. He was very angry about what had happened. He said to me: "They have started doing this again. Aren't they afraid they might die of it?" Apparently, the liquid fertilizer made of human corpses is poisonous; a number of people were poisoned after touching it. He also told me that a similar thing had also happened in his home village. [...]

[...] From what I understood, this is not Party policy. [...] To build a resting place for the dead has been a Chinese custom for thousands of years. To destroy such a tradition has a terrible effect, [...] I am very concerned that it might damage the Party.

· Document 35 ·

Report from the regional conference of third-level cadres, [Guizhou province,]
June 23, 1961

In Zunyi region, in order to build the Chatieshan coal factory in Tongzi county, more than 34 hectares of agricultural land were used, and fifty private houses were occupied. To build collective pigsties in Yangchuan commune, more than twenty family houses in Minzhu production brigade's Houjia enclave were pulled down. People were forced to move in with the pigs and cows.

· Document 36 ·

A survey of Huaminglou commune in Ningxiang county by the Central
Committee of the Chinese Communist Party, the Investigation Team of the
Hunan Provincial Party Committee, and Comrade Yang Shuqing, April 4, 1961

From the winter of 1959 to the spring of 1960, under the leadership of Hu Renqin [Huaminglou commune's Party secretary] and others, the Wind of Communism has become widespread. To build the
so-called Ten Grand Buildings, many houses were randomly pulled
down; labor and money were wasted in large quantities. For instance,
during a telephone conference, the commune decided to build a "Six-
Kilometer-Long Pig City." Each big brigade was given a quota: to
build 100 pigsties. And they were to be completed within one month.
This all took place during the spring planting season. Not only has
the project wasted the equivalent of 54,000 days of work, but it has
also led to the destruction of 1,994 residential homes and occupied
222.4 hectares of paddy fields and dry rice-fields. Construction of the
"Hilltop-Cooling Pavilion" took more than 4,000 agricultural laborers.
In addition, it cost 8,000 yuan to make the dragon and phoenix carv-
ings. There were also plans to build a "Ten Thousand People's Conference Hall" and "The Mountain of Fruits and Flowers," a new residential
quarter, and a new road through the [nearby] mountain. Fortunately the
regional Party Committee stopped these projects halfway, but a huge
amount of resources and labor had already been wasted.

In the past two years, 10,605 private houses in total have been
pulled down, and 15,824 have been unlawfully occupied [by the com-
mune]; that is more than 40 percent of the total number of residential
homes in the area. Huaminglou commune has 59,000 people; dividing
up [the losses shows that] each person has lost the equivalent of more
than half of one room, two-and-a-half pieces of furniture, two-and-
a-half agricultural tools, 14 kg of agricultural products, 180 square
meters of land, eight pieces of timber, and thirty-five working days.
The total value in terms of cash is 2,481,138 yuan. Divided up, the
cost is 43.2 yuan per person.

· Document 37 ·

Report on collectivization in Shaoshan, [Hunan province,] by Mao Huachu,
sent on April 10, 1961

On April 1, I went back to my ancestral home in Dongmaotang,
where I lived some twenty years ago. [...] After hearing about my

visit, many villagers came to see me and wanted to have heart-to-heart talks with me. After dinner on my first day there, I visited Mao Weixin's home. As soon as I was seated, more than ten men and women turned up spontaneously, and we talked almost until midnight. Those who did not attend sent messages asking me to visit their homes. On the following three days, from April 2 to the 4th, I visited different families one by one. [...] We talked about a number of issues they were most concerned about. These included the low standards in the canteen: the place is run down, and there is a lack of cooking facilities. They complained that the local situation has deteriorated in the past few years, and the destruction of woodland is extremely severe. Most of them were not hesitant in sharing their thoughts with me. Auntie Shun'er even asked me: "Huachu, does your uncle[5] have any idea what has been going on in the past two years? You must let him know the situation here."

From what I have seen, there are a number of problems I would like to mention in particular.

1. The problem of the collective canteen. [...] When I mentioned the collective canteen, sixty-two-year-old Mao Yukun complained: "Our canteen is far too big." The deputy brigade leader went on to explain: "Our brigade has twenty-three families; except for Uncle Yukun, who lives on his own in the lower part of the village, and the two widows who cook in their own homes, seventeen families have joined the canteen. There have been many complaints and the standards in the canteen have been very low. Worse still, the canteen has completely run out of cooking fuel." [...] Mao Hanxing told me: "The problem with the collective canteen is that people are individuals with different thoughts. Some are very selfish." His wife, Auntie Gui, went on to say: "The canteen manager, Mao Yuanshou, always tries to play tricks. As you can see, only his children look fat and healthy. He stole the grain from the canteen and sold it for 1 yuan per 0.5 kilogram." Mao Renchu also told me: "The former canteen manager was the same. She stole more than 20 kg of grain. After people complained, she was removed from the position. But Mao Yuanshou was no better. Last year the commune distributed some biscuits. Because no one in the village had any food coupons left, he took all the biscuits home. It's always like that. Whenever there is food, it always goes to him first. Other villagers have no part of it." [...] Hu Jiagang went on: "If things carry on like this, we will have nothing to eat, not even vegetables. Nowadays everything belongs to the collective, and no individual is responsible for anything. [...] The hill over there used to be full of trees, but now there is nothing left. There is not even any wood for fuel."

When I asked how the collective canteen started, Mao Caisheng told me: "The order came from above. Just one word from the cadres and we were collectivized immediately." Mao Pusheng continued: "To build the canteen, our bowls, pots, chopsticks, and pans were all taken away. They were loaded into a bamboo basket and removed. Some were broken on the way." Mao Runkai added: "Even eggs and pickled vegetables were collectivized." Mao Pusheng carried on: "To be honest, we did have two good months, especially when the government inspection team came to check. In those few days we ate really well, but the waste was enormous." Mao Hanxing then said: "People were not willing to join the canteen from the start. Plus the canteen has been badly managed; the quality has become worse and worse." [. . .]

2. When I asked about the situation with pigs, [. . .] Mao Yifeng was the first one to speak: "Although the collective canteen has kept three pigs, none of them look healthy." Mao Yukun also said: "I visited a number of places in Changsha and Zhuzhou. At each place I learned that raising pigs collectively could not work. In some farms, the pigs could barely walk without [being prodded with] a stick." At this point Zhao Shaohua took over the conversation: "Uncle Yukun, forget about the others. Let's take a look at our own problems. Why don't the pigs look good? With such a big canteen, how come the canteen cannot keep even three pigs healthy? Where is the food to feed the pigs?" Tan Shiying followed: "People are very selfish. Collectivization will never work."

3. The problem regarding the management of woodland. Why do the woods in the area look much worse than before? [. . .] Mao Yukun told me: "Nearly 6.8 hectares of cultivated fields were used to build the commune's Sanba pig farm. It was supposed to accommodate 6,000 to 7,000 pigs. To build such a big pig farm, not only were private houses demolished, but a large number of trees were also cut down. They were the very best trees in the area." Mao Pusheng added: "They even dug up the roots of all the chestnut trees. There will be nothing left in the future. We will have no more firewood."

When I asked why no one had tried to stop such reckless acts, a number of them answered at once: "Who had the power to stop them? The order came from the commune. We were all called out to build the Sanba pig farm, and there was no one left. One word from the commune, and all the houses were pulled down. Everyone had to join in, and all the pigs were collectivized. After all that, who had any energy left to care for a few trees?" Mao Pusheng added: "Before collectivization, the responsibility of looking after the woods was assigned to individuals. So if anyone was found logging, they'd be stopped immediately.

But nowadays, all the woods belong to the collective, so no one looks after them." Mao Hanxing also added: "Since collectivization, each brigade has been allocated a corner of the woods. As a result, the brigade over here has started cutting down trees that belong to the brigade over there. If this is not stopped, the problem will become even worse."

· Document 38 ·

A work report by the Jiangjin branch of the Agricultural Production
Investigation Team of the Sichuan Provincial Party Committee,
March 20–November 30, 1960

In Jiangjin county's Xianfeng commune, a pig farmer, Wu Yanyun, resented collectivization. He not only chopped down nine orange trees that belonged to the commune but also refused to wash out dirt and sand from the pigs' food. The pigsties were left in very filthy and damp conditions, and most mornings he also skipped feeding the pigs. As a result, five out of eight pigs died. All nine piglets also died under his care. Four pigs died at the hands of another pig farmer, Wang Jiafu. Afterward, Wang claimed that "even human beings are dying" and asked, "How could pigs not die?" The cadres in the production brigades had no idea how many pigs there were altogether. After ten pigs died at the hands of Yang Yichen, the former Party secretary for Number 3 brigade, Yang did not report the incident to the commune. Instead, he cured more than 30 kg of pork and ate the rest of the meat fresh.

· Document 39 ·

A report on the current situation in the countryside, by the Sichuan Province
Department of Agricultural Work, 1960

In Neijiang county, the number of pigs dropped sharply in November [1960]. Compared to 1959, the number of pigs has decreased by 43.6 percent. Compared to June [1960], the number has decreased by 37.2 percent. Even compared to the month of September, the number has decreased by 13.8 percent. One of the causes is that pig farmers lack a sense of responsibility, since there is no incentive for them. Whether there were more or fewer pigs, whether the pigs were well fed or not, there was no reward system for the farmers. Many pigsties were badly managed. In many places, all the pigs—big or small, male or female—were put into one large pigsty and given the same amount of feed. The pigsty was not only dirty but also very damp. Furthermore, there was not enough food to feed the pigs, and the majority of them suffered terrible starvation. [...]

In Hechuan county's Jiuling commune, [...] pig farmers were not paid according to the number of pigs they raised. When some farmers raised extra ones, they were not rewarded accordingly. A number of farmers took the lead in violating the rules. To get meat to eat, they killed the pigs. Since the winter of 1959, Zeng Qingfa from Number 1 brigade and his brother Zeng Haiyuan—the deputy head of this brigade—have eaten or sold 272 dead pigs, four of which they deliberately killed. In this brigade there has been a huge number of deaths among the pigs. There were 1,310 pigs last winter and early this spring, but now only 468 pigs are still alive. Up to 64.3 percent were lost. [...]

· Document 40 ·

Comrade Luo Qinan's report on grain production in Wenshi commune, Liuyang county, [Hunan province,] November 11, 1960

The situation in Liuyang county is very critical. Since 1958 the grain production here has plummeted. In 1960 the total amount of grain produced was 150,650,000 kg. Compared to the amount of grain being produced in 1959, the amount decreased by 41.9 percent, which is 112,840,000 kg in total. Again, compared to 1958, the amount decreased by 45.2 percent, which is 129,280,000 kg. In the past two years, owing to the famine, 27,066 people have fled from the area, and 67,630 have suffered from edema. [...] More than 3,802 hectares of cultivated fields plus 2,707 hectares of other usable land have become wasteland.

[...] Although the cold spring and the autumn drought might have contributed to the low production figures, having spoken to a number of local peasants, I think the main problem was not the weather; rather, the commune Party Committee did not put the main labor force into agricultural work, particularly not into grain production. [...] The Qingjiang reservoir has taken three years to build. It was abandoned early this summer. At one point, a labor force of more than 1,300 farmers was taken away to build it. Even though the number of workers was reduced later on, still at least 700 to 800 people were sent off to work at the construction site. In March this year, during the busy planting season, in order to win a "red flag" for collecting timber, the commune diverted some 10,000 people to go up to the mountain to fell trees. In the end, only 50 percent of the planting was completed, and 246 hectares of rice have [not been planted,] missing the season as a result. In addition, the commune faked last year's grain production figures; [. . .] by June and July this year, each month each person had only 8 kg of unprocessed grain to eat. Meanwhile, the cadres in the commune kept on violating the rules, causing a large number of people to run away. The number of edema sufferers has also increased to 3,164. Therefore, there is a severe shortage of laborers to undertake agricultural work. At this point, more than 667 hectares of crops have not been given fertilizer, which is 33.2 percent of the total number. As a result, more than 15 percent of cultivated fields and other land has become wasteland. It's not surprising the grain production in this commune has plummeted.

· Document 41 ·

A collection of speeches by the Yangzhou Region Party Committee [of Jiangsu province] on corruption among cadres, as reported at the regional conference of fourth-level cadres, from the documents of the Seventh Central Committee meeting at the Eighth Party Congress, March 1959

A cadre from Zhoudai production brigade in Liangxu commune, Taizhou county, revealed that "since last year, the local cadres have forced peasants to use 60 percent of the agricultural fields to grow sweet potatoes. There was no room for discussion: anyone who failed to plant the designated number of sweet potatoes was given the 'white flag.' To make the fields available for growing sweet potatoes, they even ordered peasants to plow under the already sprouting sorghum crop. In the end, only 50 to 100 kg of sweet potatoes were harvested for each 667 square meters of land." [. . .]

One cadre from Wusan production brigade in Yuetang commune, Yizheng county, said, "The commune and the big brigade do things only by the book. They have very bold thoughts and a bold spirit, but they don't look at the reality. Take planting sweet potatoes, for instance. There was an order from above saying that all the young sweet potato plants must be removed and replanted as soon as they had grown about 16 centimeters tall. The big brigade followed that order rigidly but ignored the weather. They told peasants to replant all the sweet potato plants in one day. Because the sun was burning hot that day, all the sweet potato plants died."

[...] The head of Yanliu production brigade, Tang Qijin, said: "Last year we harvested only 150 kg of grain per hectare, but the cadres wanted to save face and insisted that we report [a harvest of] 250 to 300 kg."

The head of Zhangmu commune's Number 1 brigade in Taizhou county, said: "When we reported to the cadres about agricultural work, we had to tell lies; otherwise, we would get a 'black flag.' Last year I lied several times, and as a result, our brigade received several 'red flags.'"

[...] The head of militia in Jiangduo commune's Xuqing big brigade said: "When the government inspection team came to inspect agricultural work, they looked only for activities, not for quality. As long as they could hear us shouting loud slogans, they were satisfied and thought we were working hard. In reality, we just made loud noises but did little work." [...]

Zhong Guoling from Qiulou big brigade said: "Last year when cadres heard that the government inspection team was coming, they became desperate. They forced us to work at night in order to get ready for inspection. We were told to go here and there, to do this and that, but in the end we never completed any work. To be ready for the inspection team, we were told to replant 9.4 hectares of peanuts. At the time, the peanut plants were still too young. We had to pull all of them up within one night. The next day, we were suddenly told that the inspection team would inspect fall planting work, so we had to leave the peanuts lying in the fields and plant wheat instead. The peanut plants were left in the fields for thirty days. Many eventually died of frost. The damage was enormous." [...]

· Document 42 ·

"My Witness: Traveling through the Countryside [of Hunan Province] in Twenty-Five Days, Covering 1,800 Kilometers," by Hu Yaobang, October 1, 1961

The weather and rainfall have been normal in most of the areas we have visited, but the summer harvest was extremely poor, and the fall crops don't look any better. We have been struck by a phenomenon we observed in many of these areas: despite having the same quality of soil and similar weather, where one of the many neighboring counties, or communes, or even big brigades has performed well, the other has done very badly. Why have some of these places performed so badly? One of the major problems was the Five Winds,[6] which have damaged local vitality. Furthermore, agricultural planning in these areas has missed opportunities over and over again. What opportunities? Before the summer harvest, [...] local cadres could not mobilize ordinary peasants to put their effort into farm production; this has caused severe food shortages, leaving villagers with little energy for work. After the harvest, the government's Sixty Articles[7] were never enforced in these areas. Many villagers became disillusioned and had no desire to work. [...]

In Anhui province at least fifteen counties have been severely damaged by the Five Winds, and Fengyang is one of the worst. The destruction here is simply shocking. Last year more than 236,950 hectares of farmland were turned into wasteland. The county ended up having to buy more than 37.5 million kg of grain from elsewhere. [...]

One other thing worth mentioning is how to protect livestock that is still breathing. In some areas animals are still kept together by the collective. In those areas where people have eaten up the animals' food supplies, the commune uses work points[8] as an incentive to encourage villagers to collect grass to feed the animals. We were told a little child could earn up to fifty work points by collecting grass, whereas a laborer gets only twelve work points for plowing fields. Still, the animals look extremely thin and unhealthy, and the villagers become greatly distressed when talking to us. Many of them reckon that the majority of the animals will not survive this winter. [...]

In most of these areas, one thing local villagers urgently need is clothing. We saw a number of families that have only one bedcover for five or six people. Some women went to work in the fields with nothing to cover the upper part of their bodies. A number of children have no clothes to wear. Unless one sees the situation with one's own eyes, it's impossible to believe how awful it is. It seems to me that [the government] should urgently send more relief to these regions to keep people from freezing to death.

· Document 43 ·

Report on the damage to forests in Fujian and four other provinces and eight suggestions for the region, June 1962

[...] In recent years the grain procurement quota in the forest regions has kept on rising. In these regions, the more severe the damage dealt out to agricultural production, the less the amount of grain produced, yet the higher the government's grain procurement quotas. In many of these areas, the local cadres and farmers were forced to focus on grain production and neglect forest development completely. [...] To pump up the grain [production] figure, they destroyed a huge area of forest and converted it to farmland. In some forest areas, no one paid attention when fires broke out. Instead, they considered forest fires a good way to make fertilizer and to scare away animals, thus ultimately contributing to high yields. In Hunan, the problem is turning into a vicious circle. Unrestrained deforestation to create more agricultural land has not only destroyed trees but also caused soil erosion. This means that after two or three years many newly converted areas of farmland will turn into wasteland again. No one will be able to grow anything. On the other hand, [deforestation] has also triggered droughts and floods in the lower reaches of the Yangtze, causing a decrease in grain production in the region. As a result, the procurement burden on the forest regions has become even heavier. This has led to further deforestation because of the conversion of even more agricultural land. Since more forestland is being destroyed, this in turn inflicts more damage on agriculture and ultimately causes more harm to forest regions and the lower plain regions. Take Anhua in Hunan as an example: Before 1957, the county needed to import about 30 million kg of grain from elsewhere each year. Since 1958, however, it has been given a large grain export quota annually. This year the grain export quota for this county was 15 million kg. In recent years, more than 81,240 hectares of new agricultural fields have been created by conversion, but more than 2,031 hectares of those fields have already become wasteland. More than half of the forest resources have been lost, and the problem of soil erosion is very serious. As a result, the climate in the area is also changing. Local people told us: "Previously in the month of June we needed to wear padded jackets when up in the mountains, but nowadays the scorching sun up on the mountains makes our skin peel off." Many paddy fields in the valley have turned into dry land; some even became sandy beaches. But to maintain the agricultural production level, deforestation is continuing. The cadres from the county tell us that if this continues, not only will Anhua lose its forests completely within ten years, but it will have no agriculture left. [...]

· Document 44 ·

Report on the destruction of forestland in the northwest [of China],
October 31, 1962

To the Office of the Secretary of the Northwest Bureau of the Central
Committee:

Following your instruction, we have compiled the following report
on the destruction of forests in the northwest:

[. . .] In recent years the damage to forests in the northwest has
been very serious. In a vast area of plains and hills at least one-third
of open forest has been chopped down, and one-fifth of closed forestland has also been destroyed. For instance, in western Shaanxi, along
the Shaanxi-Qinghai railway and the Xianyang-Tongchuan railway,
at least 60 percent of trees, which were originally planted to protect
the railways, have been chopped down. In major irrigation regions by
the Jing, Wei, and Luo Rivers, more than 30,000 trees along the canals have also been felled. In Gansu province, along Mount Xiaolong
in Tianshui region and Tange in Wushan county, about one-third of
the forests have been destroyed. Longxi county once had a forest covering 27,757 hectares of land, but 15 percent has been destroyed. On
top of that, about half of the trees in the 18.3 hectares of newly planted
forest have also been cut down. In many areas, deforestation is still
continuing, and in some places it has become even worse. The destruction of the forest has caused soil erosion and sandstorms and reduced
the amount of water resources. It has badly damaged agricultural production. In Ziwuling—the border region between Shaanxi and Gansu
provinces—more than 6,770 hectares of forest have been destroyed
and converted into agricultural land in recent years. This has resulted
in serious soil erosion and flooding and completely damaged more than
95 hectares of farmland, destroying the equivalent of 203 hectares of
crops. In Minqin county, Gansu, some 1,625 hectares of Ordos sage-
brush and sand willow trees have been chopped down, causing more
than 1,963 hectares of farmland to be wiped out by sandstorms. In the
Qilian Mountain region, owing to deforestation in recent years, as
well as the attempt to turn grassland into farm fields, the snow line has
risen, which has considerably reduced the amount of water resources.
[. . .]

· Document 45 ·

Comrade Liu Jianxun's report on the problem of waterlogged and alkalized farm fields [in Hunan province], as well as a proposal to solve the problem, December 24, 1961

In recent years, a number of Yellow River irrigation projects have been built unsuitably, causing the problems of alkalization and water-logging to become even worse. [. . .] In the twenty-eight counties in northern Henan, the amount of agricultural land being damaged by alkalization has risen from 324,960 hectares in 1958 to 744,700 hectares. There is no sign of it slowing down, either. In fact, the problem is worsening fast; the situation is rather urgent.

Alkalization is very destructive. There is a local saying: "The drought happens for just one season, but alkalization will last a lifetime." Alkalization not only prevents crops from growing but also damages houses and causes them to collapse. Last year in Qingfeng, Nanle, Neihuang, and other counties, more than 340,000 houses collapsed [due to alkalization]. This year again, more than 300,000 houses have collapsed. In areas being badly affected by alkalization, famine is widespread, and local farmers are in real anguish. There has been a mass exodus of the local population. To survive, many families were compelled to sell their children; many girls at a very young age were forced into marriage; many married women had to leave their husbands and remarry elsewhere. Edema and premature death have increased sharply. If no appropriate rescue plan is introduced to stop the problem, in a few years the vast plain along the Yellow River will turn into a total wasteland, and there will be no more people left. [. . .]

One other problem is Anhui's Linhuaigang dam project on the Huai River. The project was started a few years ago, and in 1960 it began to create a reservoir of water. But to build it, many counties along the riverbank were flooded. Last year, when this happened, many villages were completely immersed. We had to send out airplanes to drop rubber boats to rescue the villagers. [. . .]

· Document 46 ·

"My Witness: Traveling through the Countryside [of Hunan Province] in Twenty-Five Days, Covering 1,800 Kilometers," by Hu Yaobang, October 1, 1961

From September 4 to the 29th I traveled with three comrades across the Yellow River plain as well as through regions around the Huai

River. [. . .] We witnessed devastating floods in most of these areas. The majority of the counties in Shandong's Dezhou and Liaocheng regions, as well as a number of counties in Jining region, were among the worst-affected areas. Throughout our journey, we saw villages surrounded by water, just like small islands in an ocean. No crops were left. Gaotang is a county with a population of 60,000; 40,000 houses there have been destroyed. According to our information, Dezhou, Liaocheng, and Huimin were the three worst-hit regions, with more than one million local people affected. From what we saw, the people here are facing extreme hardship.

The rainfall this year has not been particularly heavy, and the affected areas stretch no more than 600 or 700 kilometers. How come the flooding was so bad? One of the causes of the problem is the irrigation work. In the Yellow River delta there is now a labyrinth of canals. Many of these are surface canals. And they are not linked up properly. Each county and each commune has its own network of canals. Once the rain gets a little heavier, water starts to accumulate in one spot. Like an evil dragon, those flooded canals turned the earth into the sea. There is much concern in Liaocheng. Because many canals were silted up by the floods, there could be terrible flooding next year with even a very small amount of rain. [. . .] Because the groundwater level is very high in this area and the soil quality is unique, irrigation canals—in particular, aboveground canals—have caused severe alkalization, affecting a huge area of cultivated land. In Heze region, the alkalization has spoiled 20.8 percent of the farmland. In Liangshan county the amount of alkalized farmland has increased to 24 percent, compared to 8.2 percent in 1957. There is a feeling of discontent among the ordinary peasants in the region; they are very unhappy about the irrigation work.

CHAPTER SIX

The Turn to Religion (1957–1962)

Religion is the heart of a heartless world.
—Karl Marx

I N December 1955, Mao read a report on the progress of collectivization in Qufu county. Qufu, in Shandong province, is the
birthplace of Confucius, China's most renowned sage. Upon reading the report, Mao remarked: "After living in poverty for more than
two thousand years, people [in Qufu] have entered collectivization.
Their life, both economically and culturally, has improved greatly since
collectivization. Their example has proven that socialism surpasses any
ancient wisdom. Compared to the Confucian classics, socialism is far
superior. I recommend that those who are fascinated by Confucian
temples and Confucian monuments visit the agricultural collective in
Qufu."[1]

In Maoist China, all aspects of popular culture, from social institutions to popular ways of life, were seen as a threat to the domina-
tion of the Chinese Communist Party and the state. In the radical
collectivization campaign launched in 1958, the "old" and "feudal"
peasant culture was to be eliminated. Chinese peasants were reorganized into militarized production brigades, which destroyed family
life. At the same time, popular religious practices were attacked as
"feudal superstitions," religious institutions were crushed as "counterrevolutionary," and temples, ancestral shrines, and graveyards
were demolished to make space for Great Leap Forward projects.
On August 20, 1958, for example, three days after the campaign to
establish people's communes was officially inaugurated at the Politburo meeting in the seaside resort of Beidaihe, a newly formed people's commune in rural Guizhou declared war on dead ancestors
and feudal superstitions. The commune Party Committee even composed a poem entitled "Ask the Dead People to Join the People's

Commune and Turn the Graveyard into a Field of Crops" (document 47).

The commune in Guizhou was not unique in its response. Just east of Guizhou, in northern Hunan, for example, temples were destroyed and gravestones were toppled. The bricks were used to construct collective irrigation projects (document 48). And in Sichuan's Guan county, the local farmers were deeply troubled when a historical Daoist monument—Erwang Temple—was almost destroyed by explosive blasts during the construction of the Yuzui hydropower station, a famous Great Leap Forward project (document 49).

Erwang Temple, erected sometime between 25 and 220 CE, was built to honor a local governor, Li Bing, and his son. Between 256 and 251 BCE, father and son had helped the local people build one of the world's earliest irrigation systems, Dujiangyan, on the Min River. For many centuries this remarkable irrigation system, still standing today, brought much prosperity to the region. Without Dujiangyan, Sichuan could not have become the "land of abundance." The local peasants remained grateful. Millions of people who lived in the west Sichuan plain traveled every summer to the temple to make offerings to Li Bing and his son and to seek their blessings for good weather and a bountiful harvest. In 1958, at the height of the Great Leap Forward, the decision was made to build a hydropower station 400 meters above this ancient irrigation system—in an active earthquake zone. Some 300 local families were forced to leave to clear space for it. But in 1960 the project was abandoned, wasting 65 million yuan and the efforts of 25,000 construction workers. Meanwhile, thirty-eight people had been killed in construction accidents, and Erwang Temple was badly damaged by the nearby detonations. The underground tunnel built to assist with the construction of the hydropower project had also compromised the temple's foundations. Few were surprised when an earthquake on May 12, 2008, finally destroyed it. Its doom had been sealed fifty years earlier.

As temples and churches were turned into commune factories, schools, nurseries, hospitals, and offices, monks were compelled to join people's communes and make their own contributions to the Great Leap Forward. Temples on Sichuan's Mount Emei—a sacred site for Chinese Buddhists and the destination of pilgrimages—suffered severely after the Great Leap Forward began. The number of monks and nuns there, as well as the number of visiting pilgrims, dropped sharply. A similar fate befell other religious institutions, causing much resentment among devout men and women (documents 50–55).

In areas with large ethnic and minority religious populations, local cadres regularly showed disrespect and prejudice toward non-Han Chinese: they were not "real" Chinese. In Henan, in central China, collectivization deprived many local Muslims of their means of livelihood (document 56). It was much the same in Gansu, in the northwest (document 57). In the southwest, in the Tibetan region in Yunnan, the local Communist authorities cut off daily supplies to the Tibetan monks, forcing many to flee. Some died. The number of monks declined significantly, and local Tibetan Buddhism was in danger of extinction (document 58). In neighboring Sichuan many religious groups were suppressed as counterrevolutionary; religious institutions were shut down, and monks and their leaders were arrested (document 59).

On October 1—National Day—1960, an editorial in the *People's Daily*, the official voice of the Chinese Communist Party, lamented that in the past two years the country had witnessed unprecedented "natural disasters." This became the official line for explaining the devastating famine and the destruction of farmland and forestland. Ordinary people did not dare to challenge the authorities, but they knew that the disasters brought by collectivization had not been "natural." Having seen that radical collectivization did not work and that the government was failing to deliver adequate famine relief, many peasants turned to the heavens and local gods for help. The Communist government's concerted effort to eliminate religion as well as popular beliefs and practices did not remove their importance in rural life. Socialism could not replace personal beliefs and family values.

Popular beliefs and practices not only provided ordinary peasants with a sense of certainty but also helped to catalyze organized opposition to the ruling powers. Although there were very few revolts in the Chinese countryside during the radical collectivization period, the ones that did take place took the form of religious insurgency. The uprisings often had a strong apocalyptic streak: the famine was a sign from heaven that the world was coming to an end. In Sichuan, Hunan, Guizhou, and Jiangxi provinces and Guangxi autonomous region, a number of secret religious societies, banned by the Communist authorities, became active again (document 60). A number of them organized several uprisings that had as their goal the overthrow of the Communist government in Beijing (documents 61–62).

The more the government tried to destroy religion and popular beliefs, the more vital they became. In different parts of the country, Christians continued to sing hymns and to worship in secret (documents 63–64). When the government failed to deliver the free health care it had promised, many peasants turned to religious healers for help and protection. Radical collectivization was creating a Communist hell, not a Communist paradise, and many villagers switched back to "feudal" religious institutions and beliefs. Millions of Chinese peasants caught in the life-and-death crisis and even some Communist Party members bowed their heads to local gods. In the aftermath of the famine, religion and popular beliefs continued to provide hope and consolation for the survivors (documents 65–68).

· Document 47 ·

"Ask the Dead People to Join the People's Commune and Turn the Graveyard into a Field of Crops," by the Party Committee of Zhengchang township, Suiyang county, [Guizhou province,] August 20, 1958

"The ancient hero did not lead the way; the real hero is born today. Thousands of years of tradition and superstition must be wiped out completely; turn the dead people's graveyard into a mountain full of potatoes." This slogan was introduced by Zhengchang township's Bayi and Wangli communes. To achieve the food production quota, both communes needed to use every centimeter of land. They therefore waged a war on the dead; they asked dead people to join the people's commune and turned all burial grounds into sweet potato fields. [...] In Bayi commune there are more than 9,000 graves, taking up 19 hectares of land. Once the graveyard was turned into a sweet potato field, the total food production figure could rise by more than 250,000 kg. Even now, many peasants still hold the belief that they must show respect to ghosts and spirits. They think that finding a good piece of land on which to bury their dead ancestors will bring them good fortune. They put their future happiness in such superstitions. Such beliefs are like a yoke that has prevented them from moving forward. By occupying a large amount of fertile land, these graveyards have reduced productivity. In the past, many villagers regarded the demolition of graves as an act of betrayal to their ancestors; it would bring the extinction of the entire family. [...] To have one's ancestors' graves damaged was considered the biggest humiliation. It often caused irreconcilable hatred between villagers, which could last for many generations. [...] After Liberation, although the Party tried to enlighten people through education, such beliefs were still strongly held.[2] [...]

Under the leadership of the township Party Committee, many peasants and local cadres have received a socialist education. They have been completely reformed. Quite a number have decided to break away from feudal superstitions. They have started the revolutionary activity of waging war on the dead and using the land to grow sweet potatoes. After three nights of hard work, they have achieved a great deal. More than 2,000 people in both communes have taken part in this war, and they have demolished 8,790 graves—equal to 17 hectares of land. [...] A total of 1,296 families have pulled down their ancestral shrines and portraits of gods and have put up Chairman Mao's portrait on their wall. [...]

There was resistance, too. For example, the night before the demolition, the father of Xue Haishan, a peasant, brought a bamboo plank to his father's grave. Holding an axe in his right hand, he told the demolition team: "I have put down a plank on this grave, so don't touch it. Otherwise, I will risk my and your lives to save it. I am old, and I no longer fear death." After the first night, the peasant Wang Ganming went home complaining of stomach pains. He pretended that he had met a ghost and refused to continue the demolition work. Some peasants agreed to join in, but deep down they were unsure. After the demolition started, they hesitated; their hands started to shake and their legs started to turn sore. They could not dig into the graves. [...]

· Document 48 ·

Report by the Party Committee of the Hunan Province Justice Department on a number of disputes over the demolition of temples and graveyards in winter construction work, February 14, 1958

This winter a number of collectives organized various irrigation projects and persuaded peasants to demolish temples and graveyards to support dam construction work. This caused a number of disputes between individual peasants and different collectives. Several fights broke out among individuals over large areas. They were extremely damaging. On December 10, for example, the Youai and Shibu collectives in Yueyang county's Dasong township gathered more than 100 peasants to demolish the Dongyue temple in order to collect bricks to build the local dam. After discovering what was happening, peasants in Dongyue collective rang the alarm and tried to stop the demolition work. A serious fight broke out. The heads of Shibu collective and Youai collective were badly injured and were detained by [Dongyue collective]. As a result, construction work on the dam was stopped.

Because of shortages of building material, cadres from Jinqiao collective tried to persuade peasants to demolish their own family graveyards and to sell the bricks and stones to the collective. Many peasants refused. So the collective decided to start with a number of Party activists, persuading them to set a good example by demolishing their ancestral graveyards and selling the tombstones and bricks to the collective. Once people realized that tombstones could be exchanged for money, robbery started. [...] After Liu Nainan discovered that the Liu family ancestral tombstone had been stolen, he gathered together a group of people from the Liu family and went over to beat up the Party activist Jiang Zhisheng. Jiang was badly injured as a result. The demolition of graveyards to gather bricks has become prevalent in the area. [...] Between December last year and the present, more than 100 graveyards have been destroyed. Dead bodies and bones have been dumped outside. There is no one to take care of them. The scene is extremely disturbing.

· Document 49 ·

Report on the incident in which Erwang Temple was damaged by a blast during construction of the Yuzui hydropower station by the United Front Work Department in Guan county, [Sichuan province,] August 23, 1960

To the Provincial Party Committee and the Provincial United Front Work Department:

Erwang Temple is a famous scenic site in Dujiangyan, and it is a protected religious site. It attracts a large number of domestic and overseas visitors every year. Recently, owing to the construction of the Yuzui hydropower station, it was badly damaged by several explosions. Damaged areas include the left section of the side entrance, walls, and the inscription plaque. The inscription plaque fell off and broke during a blast. A large number of roof tiles also tumbled down during the terrible shocks caused by the blast. At the same time, workers from various teams employed at the construction site have been using the temple as their sleeping quarters without permission. Some workers have dismantled doors and timber walls to make beds. Others have been using the timber from doors and walls to build wardrobes. They have also been picking fruit from trees in the temple's vicinity, leaving the temple in a terrible mess. [...]

· Document 50 ·

Report on the wanton occupancy of temples and churches, the destruction of trees at religious sites, and the random removal of property from religious institutions, by the Department of Religious Affairs of the Sichuan Provincial People's Committee, May 16–November 23, 1961

In September we inspected a number of protected religious sites and found that many of these places have been wantonly occupied by government work units and offices. Trees were chopped down, and furniture and tools were taken away. Such acts clearly violate Party policy.

1. The situation regarding the occupancy of temples and churches

In [Chengdu,] religious sites have been occupied by various people's communes for their schools, nurseries, factories, offices, and hospitals. The sites include two Catholic churches, four Protestant churches, four Buddhist temples and monasteries, and one mosque. Of these, Shijing Temple and the Jinsha monastery are both protected religious sites. But now Shijing Temple has been divided up and turned into Longquan district's granary, supply department, commune hospital, and brigade offices. More than thirty peasants and workers also currently live in the place. A large number of trees in the temple have been felled. Take the commune hospital, for example. In 1960 it chopped down more than 150 trees. [. . .] A number of houses belonging to various churches have been occupied, too. In most cases the occupiers did not ask for permission and refused to pay rent. Some government work units did not even bother to inform the church when they moved in. This has caused great resentment. Take, for example, the Catholic church in the city's northern suburb. In 1958, the Boji street committee took over the majority of its rooms and turned them into offices. Meanwhile, a commune nursery has built a canteen in the front churchyard. Besides the canteen, there is a stove for boiling water for tea put up by the Number 3 wooden tool factory. The rear of the church has been turned into a pigsty for the collective canteen. The factory also uses it to store material. It looks very messy. The church complained to us, saying: "They just moved in without informing us. They messed up the whole place and did not keep it clean. We could not say anything to them, since it was the decision of the street committee." There are many similar problems. For instance, after occupying the Stone Buddha Temple near Banxian Bridge in the east of the city, the district hospital refused to pay rent as stated in the contract. [. . .]

2. The situation regarding unrestricted tree felling

In a number of big temples, felling trees has become a serious problem. Shijing Temple was one of the worst-affected temples, and another is Wenshu Temple. In October 1960, the management personnel of Dufu's Thatched Cottage[3] went to Wenshu Temple and chopped down much bamboo, weighing about 1,500 kilograms. They did not have any official permission. Some monks in the temple told us that the city planning office has also been to the temple to fell trees.

3. The situation regarding temple property being pocketed

Shiyang people's commune has pocketed more than ten items from Jinci Temple, including carts, night-soil buckets, and tables. It has also taken more than 100 buckets of fertilizer from the temple. [. . .] Furthermore, a number of historical monuments have also been damaged.

· Document 51 ·

Report on the development of urban people's communes, by the Zhengzhou City Party Committee [of Henan province], April 1960

Since the city has been reorganized into various people's communes, the number of Catholic and Protestant worshippers has been reduced from 3,800 to 300. The number of observing Muslims has declined from 1,700 to 77. [. . .] A number of churches have been turned into factories, schools, or collective canteens. [. . .]

Prior to the introduction of the urban commune, there were eight different Christian sects in the city, including nine institutions located in thirteen different venues. There were also two Catholic churches, three Buddhist institutions, and nine mosques. Since the establishment of the commune, many religious institutions have been merged. For instance, various Christian groups have been merged into one church, and they have been given two venues. The two Catholic churches have been merged into one. The three Buddhist institutions have also become one monastery and one temple. The nine mosques have been reduced to five. The number of places for religious activities has decreased considerably. [. . .] The mosques used to rent out 324 rooms and more than 5,200 square meters of land. Their annual income from the rent was 2,225 yuan. Their land and properties have now been taken by the government. [. . .] Similarly the Catholic and Protestant churches, as well as the Buddhist institutions, used to rent out 356 rooms; their monthly income from the rent was 868 yuan. All their properties have been taken by the government, too. Before the establishment of the commune, only five out of eighteen top religious leaders in the city did physical work. Afterward, apart from three suffering from ill health and disability, the rest have all been asked to take part in physical labor. [...]

· Document 52 ·

Report on ideological and physical reform among Buddhist monks and nuns on Mount Emei, by the Department of Religious Affairs of the Sichuan Province People's Committee, 1959

Currently there are sixty-one temples on Mount Emei. The total number of monks and nuns is 208. Among them, 35 still have not joined the people's commune. The total number of monks and nuns who have joined the commune is 173. Of those, 46 are full-time laborers, 45 are half-time laborers, and 58 can do only some occasional work. The rest, about 24 in all, have completely lost their ability to work because of old age, physical disabilities, or mental illness. Since 1958, the financial affairs of Mount Emei have been controlled by the Buddhist Association. The monks and nuns receive free food, shoes, and medicines. It was agreed that apart from those living in Jinding Temple, who would receive a 3 yuan living allowance each month, and those living in Fuhu Temple, who would receive a 2 yuan living allowance each month, the other monks and nuns would each receive a 5 to 10 yuan living allowance each year. However, after March 1959, the association stopped giving out allowances. The monks and nuns constantly complain. They told us: "We work all day long, but we could not get money even to buy tobacco. How could we have enough strength to carry on working?" Some also said: "Whether we work hard or not, it's all the same. There is no incentive [to work]." [...] Some of the religious leaders complained that "[the commune] does not discuss anything with us, making it hard for us to try to push forward any policies." Abbot Puchao is not happy at all. He said: "Last year, during the Great Leap Forward, we were given different tasks each day. We had no clue what was going on."

Some monks and nuns have never done any physical labor before. Last year during the Great Leap iron- and steelwork, they had to carry goods weighing 20 kilograms or more. Some complained: "The work was so demanding that we could hardly breathe." Last year six different Great Leap projects were assigned to Mount Emei: making konjac jelly,[4] planting herbal medicine, doing agriculture work, constructing a copper factory, transporting iron and steel, and doing road construction work. The copper factory workers were responsible for digging copper and coal, making charcoal and coke, transporting cement, smelting copper, and searching for copper mines. Since there are only forty-six full-time laborers, many felt so exhausted that they could not take it anymore. They complained: "We worked hard every day till dark, but nothing was accomplished in the end."

Also the jobs were very irregular. The monks and nuns were moved around all over the mountain. [. . .] Furthermore, a number of small temples at the summit were demolished during the Great Leap Forward in 1958, and many Buddhist statues were damaged. A number of them have been left without heads or limbs. [. . .]

· Document 53 ·

Report on the reform of Buddhist monks on Mount Emei,
[Sichuan province,] March 13–November 10, 1959

A number of monks openly resisted the reform. Some complained that the authorities forced Buddhist monks to do physical labor. Lirong, a monk of Taiziping Temple, even wept in grief, saying: "[The authorities] do not treat us like human beings. I am extremely upset." Some complained that they were treated the same as the "rightists." Tongyong, a monk of Daping Temple, says: "We are treated no better than the rightists. Like them, we have to work all day and all night." [. . .] Chanyu, a monk of Guangfu Temple, refused to do any physical work; he says: "Socialism is hard work." Last December, Changyi, a monk of Daping Temple, tried to carry more than 15 kilograms of mined stones on his back one day, but someone told him that he should carry 30 kilograms instead. He became extremely unhappy about this. He complained that socialism made life more and more difficult. After he returned to his room, he overdosed himself with sleeping pills and committed suicide.

· Document 54 ·

Regarding the current political standing of monks and nuns on Mount Emei,
[Sichuan province,] February 28–September 18, 1960

Owing to the progress of the socialist revolution and the improvement of people's living standards, the monks' and nuns' socialist consciousness has grown deeper, and the influence of religion has diminished considerably. In the past two years, twenty-seven monks and nuns have left the Buddhist order and resumed secular life; thirty-seven monks and nuns have died. Compared to the number in May 1958, the number of monks and nuns has dropped by 26.5 percent. Apart from the three big temples in Jinding, Jiulaodong, and Hong Chunping, where one or two old monks still carry out such religious activities as reciting sutras, making offerings, and ringing the bell, the temples have all been closed down. Only on major Buddhist holidays, such as the Buddha's birthday, do some of these closed temples resume religious ceremonies. The number of pilgrims to the mountain [Emei] has also dropped considerably. According to statistics, between January and September this year, only 3,000 pilgrims visited the mountain. Compared to 57,000 in 1957, that is a 94.8 percent drop. The income of these religious institutions has also decreased sharply. In 1957 the temple in Jinding received 15,000 yuan, but this year its annual income is only 1,800 yuan—that is an 88 percent drop. Similar decreases have also occurred at other temples. This shows that the decline of religion is inevitable as society progresses. No power can stop it.

· Document 55 ·

Religious personnel's reaction to the policy to increase productivity and to be economical in order to fulfill the country's export quota, by the Department of Religious Affairs of Chengdu city, [Sichuan province,] September 29, 1960

During the movement to increase productivity and to practice economy, [Chengdu's] religious personnel were organized into groups to study government policy. Many followed the Party's appeal and started to open up wasteland and to grow vegetables. Monks and nuns in Wenshu Temple cultivated 2,708 square meters of vegetable fields. In Daci Temple, the monks and nuns cultivated 677 square meters, and in Zhaojue Temple the monks and nuns cultivated more than 8 square meters. All of the [cultivated land] has been planted with vegetables. These temples have also fulfilled the government quota for raising pigs. Zhaojue Temple has already contributed two pigs and is raising another twenty-five for the state. Daci Temple has also contributed two and is continuing to raise three more for the state. Wenshu Temple currently has raised five pigs for the government. [. . .] Although some of them were motivated by the thought that they could get some pork to eat by raising pigs for the government, they still make a significant contribution to the government export quota.

However, there are a few who have tried to resist and attack the Party's policy. For example, the Catholic priest Yang Guozhen has been saying: "I have started slow suicide. I am not well and I don't want to take any medicine. There is no food available in any stores, and we could not even buy alcohol. [...] That's the way to be economical. Everyone will die. Let God take my soul." The Catholic bishop Tang Jun has been spreading rumors like "We cannot even buy cigarettes anywhere." He has also tried to attack Party policy: "The government policy changes all the time. Take food rationing, for example. The amount of the ration has changed three times within one year. It was reduced in June this year; by September we were told to economize again. [...] My brain cannot cope any more. The meat coupons were cut down two or three times, too, and in the end they have cut down meat supply completely. [...] In my opinion, the food we saved was not used for famine relief but for export. [...] It's a political game." [...]

After hearing that food coupons will become invalid, a number of monks and nuns rushed to restaurants. [...] A monk from Wenshu Temple attacked the Party, saying: "All coupons will become invalid once the newspaper announces it, just the way it was before Liberation. The two systems[5] are the same. They are both extremely dark." [...] A number of monks in Zhaojue Temple are also extremely unhappy about the ration policy. [...] The monk Hongkai refused to do any physical work. [...] The Daoist monk Liu Liquan also complained: "[The government] asked us to go all out. How? There is hardly anything to eat." [...]

· Document 56 ·

Report on the situation of ethnic groups in the Shifodian area, by the United Front Working Team of Gushi county, [Henan province,] January 1957

The total population of the Shifodian area is 976 people, or 234 families. More than 49.48 percent of them are Muslims; that is a total of 483 people, or 111 families. About eight businesses in the area are run by Muslims. [...]

There is one mosque in the area. Before the land reform, the annual income of the imam was 645 yuan. Shortly before collectivization, it was reduced by 41.2 percent, to 384 yuan per year. Since collectivization, it has been reduced again, by 53.1 percent. The current annual income of the imam is 180 yuan. To make a living, the imam has to do physical labor and to practice traditional Chinese medicine. The mosque has become very rundown, and there is no water supply. [...]

A number of cadres and government offices in the area have regularly violated the ethnic policy. For instance, Liu Guanming, one of the managers in the local government food company, assigned the Muslim worker Hu Anhe to sell pork in three different collectives. Hu did not dare to refuse for fear of losing his job. In December last year, Hu sold a pig weighing 50 kg to Xinsheng collective. He was deeply depressed over this. Earlier on, in May, another manager, Xu Junshan, told Hu to send some pigs to Zhangguangmiao town. Hu wept all the way and said: "Being a Muslim is so miserable."

Not only this, Muslim workers also get paid less [than Chinese workers]. For instance, in March 1956 the monthly salary of the Muslim Hu Anhe was 15 yuan. It has been increased to 21 yuan per month. The salary of the Chinese worker Gao Guoyou was originally 13 yuan per month. It has been increased to 24.5 yuan. On top of that, Gao received a 4.46 yuan heating allowance for the winter, but Hu Anhe received nothing.

The head of management in the local food company, Guo Zihou, made the decision to sell beef and pork in the same place. [...] The cutting knives and [meat] hangers were not kept separate, and a number of staff did not differentiate pork from beef. In December, there were two incidents of Muslims being sold pork instead of beef. Again on January 7, the Muslim Zhang Peiying—the wife of a soldier—was given pork when she tried to purchase beef.

On another occasion, the Muslim Hu Anhe went to the office of the Zhangyao district People's Committee for lunch. Because all the dishes were cooked with lard, Hu ordered a plain bowl of rice with soy sauce. But the canteen staff member Gao Xiangpu added some lard to his rice.

In this area, more than twenty Muslim families have become unemployed. [...] Since 1955, the government has banned all market stores, causing many Muslim store owners to lose their livelihood. They have no income, and their lives have become very difficult. For example, Bai Ruying used to own a small business, but after joint state-private ownership was established for it, replacing private ownership, he was given a monthly salary of 13 yuan. It was impossible to feed the eight mouths in his family. So Bai took back his share and rented out his shop for 18 yuan. He left 12 yuan to his family and took 6 yuan with him to Anhui, hoping to start a small business there. Since he left, the family has not heard a word from him. It was impossible for seven people to live on 12 yuan. Bai's sixty-eight-year-old father, Bai Jinyou, even fought with his little grandson for a bowl of tofu dregs. The family lived in borrowed accommodations, and there was no bedcover to keep them warm. When the weather turned cold, Bai Youjin became seriously ill because of malnutrition, lack of clothing, and lack of sleep. After twenty days, the landlord asked the family to move Bai into the mosque, since he did not want Bai to die in his house. Bai stayed in the mosque for another seven days, where the imam tried to treat him. But there was no medicine to give to him. Not long afterward, Bai died.

Since collectivization, the nine family graves of the Muslim Chang Xiabing have been demolished.

· Document 57 ·

Report on the Rectification Campaign in Qingshui, [Gansu province,] by the Qingshui branch of the Investigaton Team of the Central Committee of the Chinese Communist Party, February 14, 1961

To the Gansu Provincial Party Committee and the Tianshui Region Party Committee:

[. . .] In Qingshui, one-third of the local population is Muslim. Ethnic conflict happens here regularly. [. . .] Many Muslim cadres have suffered persecution, and some were forced to eat pork and dog meat. A number of Muslim farmers have also been ordered to raise pigs. [. . .]

· Document 58 ·

Comrade Zhou Chiping's report on the situation in Lijiang region, [Yunnan province,] July 18–October 27, 1959

Regarding the problem of religion in the Tibetan area [of Yunnan]: According to Comrade Zhang Gaolin's report, there used to be more than 1,000 Tibetan monks in the Tibetan area. At the moment there are only around 200 left. Most of them are old and weak, or sick and crippled. Previously they received a living allowance from the government, but that has been stopped. [. . .] Although the local authorities have not publicly announced the elimination of religion, they are in fact denying religion by cutting off all supplies to the monks. Some cadres have been preaching atheism in an attempt to weaken religion. [. . .] This is a serious issue, since it affects the majority of people in the Tibetan area. Moreover, this will also have an impact on Tibet. [. . .]

· Document 59 ·

The opinion of the Party Committee of the Sichuan Province Public Security Bureau on how the campaign to suppress counterrevolutionaries should be carried out in ethnic areas, December 8, 1958

In 1958 and 1959 the total number of arrests was 3,513 in Liangshan, 1,776 in Ganzi, and 1,224 in Aba. During the recent battle to suppress the revolt in Xichang, 492 rebels were captured. In 1959 we plan to arrest 10,000 counterrevolutionaries in total, and 8,000 will be from ethnic groups. The number of arrests in various lama temples should, however, be limited to 0.3 to 0.5 percent of the total number of monks: we reckon 300 to 500 monks. The other 2,000 arrests will be Han Chinese. [. . .] We also plan to execute a number of counterrevolutionaries: 220 will be from various ethnic groups, including 70 in Ganzi, 40 in Aba, 60 in Liangshan, and 50 in Xichang. As for the Han Chinese, each local authority must take their circumstances into consideration. Even if they should be executed, permission from the Party must be granted first. [. . .]

· Document 60 ·

Report on wiping out the True Jesus Church, by the Department of Religious Affairs of the Sichuan Province People's Committee, 1959

In 1952 the True Jesus Church[6] raised a clarion call: "Break tough areas, settle firmly in southern Hubei, cross many mountains, and bring the True Jesus Church to rural villages." In [Sichuan]'s Xichong, Yanting, and Wusheng counties and other mountainous regions, the True Jesus Church has been practicing supernatural healing and has recruited more than 1,000 believers. Under the leadership of He Shouwu, a deacon in the Yanting church, and Li Huijiang, an activist in the Xichong church, as well as Liu Jingshan, the local bandit chief, a counterrevolutionary revolt has been plotted. In March 1958, Xia Quanshou, another deacon in the Yanting church, asked a church member, Wang Tianyuan, to play the role of God. More than 400 people from Yanting and Jian'ge gathered together inside [the True Jesus] Church in Yanting county and prayed for the miracle of transfiguration: from a god to a water ghost.[7] They caused quite a disturbance in the area. When some local cadres tried to stop them, a number of them started to attack the cadres physically. After the incident, more than 100 of them signed a letter of complaint defying the local authorities in an attempt to overthrow the government. [. . .] Among the church members are quite a few counter-revolutionaries, rightists, and other bad elements. We proposed to strike them hard. [. . .] We have now arrested 120 church leaders, about 62.5 percent of the total number of leaders in the area; 35 of them were put in prison, and 40 were sent to do hard labor. We determined to fight them until the public starts to see their true face. Thanks to our hard work, the church's top leadership has now been successfully crushed.

· Document 61 ·

Report on the counterrevolutionary revolt in Taiping village in Wuxian township, Yingjing county, by the Party Committee of the Sichuan Province Public Security Bureau, December 16, 1958

On November 18, an armed counterrevolutionary revolt broke out in Wuxian township's Taiping village. The leaders are Huang Ziqing and Xia Wanhong. Their motto was "March to Beijing and overthrow Chairman Mao. Restore the emperor back to the throne." [. . .]

Early on in this village, in March, the counterrevolutionary shamans Peng Wanfeng and Xia Wanhong dressed up and pretended to be gods. They performed magic healing by burning candles and incense and by chanting charms. They claimed that their daughter Zhang Guanglian was "the child from heaven, the goddess destined to marry the Yellow Emperor."[8] They also claimed that "once the emperor has been restored, all old people will become high officials, and there will be food to eat and clothes to wear." [. . .] This incident had a huge impact on the local people. [. . .] After July the former landlord Ma Guangyuan and others started to organize a revolt. [. . .] They openly incited villagers with statements like "So much work day and night: what a tough life ordinary people live"; "Under the Nationalists we ate cornbread; now we have to work day and night, and we still eat cornbread"; "The heavenly army is coming soon, and Chairman Mao will not last long." [. . .] In August following their failed attempt to revolt, the leader, Ma Guangyuan, continued to spread rumors and perform magic to recruit villagers in order to expand the counterrevolutionary organization. In preparation for their rebellion, they also invited Huang Ziqing, a counterrevolutionary practitioner of feudal superstitions, to be their general. After Huang arrived in the village, he ordained himself "bishop" in charge of the altar of the gods and started to organize activities. From November 13 to November 16, he performed the ritual of "carrying gods on the back" every evening and shouted: "The dynasty is going to change soon," "The current regime will be turned upside down," and "Let's pray for the downfall and death of Chairman Mao." In the meantime, Yang Xuelun, who was actively preparing for the revolt, used hunting as an excuse and bought and collected quite a few guns and bullets. On the eve of November 17, the villagers made a number of flags with signs of the Big Dipper, the Eight Trigrams [*bagua*],⁹ and the Yin-Yang [*taiji*] diagram on them. [...] On the morning of the 18th, the revolt broke out. More than forty people joined in. [...] They first went to the local temple and tore down the portrait of Chairman Mao. They then ransacked the local supply and marketing cooperative and took away all the goods stored there. Meanwhile, some of them surrounded the county inspection team, including the deputy chief of the county court, Li Maorong, and eleven others, and snatched their guns. [...] The revolt was later suppressed by the police and the local militia.

· Document 62 ·

The minutes of a telephone conference of Hunan provincial and regional Party secretaries on rural work and security, December 30, 1958

Recently a number of counterrevolutionary revolts have broken out in Hunan, as well as in neighboring Guangxi, Guizhou, and Jiangxi. Secret societies are also extremely active. So far they have organized ninety-seven counterrevolutionary revolts. In Anxiang county's Guhuatang more than 200 people joined a local uprising, which eventually affected the nearby five counties. The organizers formed a "Heavenly Supreme National Salvation Army" and appointed "marshals," and so on. Initially they plotted to revolt on September 18, but later on they changed the date to March next year. In Nan county a secret society meeting was held at the Hall of Bright Virtue on December 17. In Lingling county the seven-member counterrevolutionary group "Central Anti-Bandits National Salvation Army" is currently quite actively trying to recruit followers. In Dongan county, there were also eight revolts involving secret societies. Furthermore, about thirty-one secret society members have now gone into hiding in the mountains.

· Document 63 ·

Regarding the collectivization situation in Yonghe [township, Cangyuan Wa autonomous region, Yunnan province], October 30–December 15, 1961

Yangpin in Yonghe is a Wa village.[10] Before 1958 the village had forty families and 209 villagers. [. . .] At the beginning of 1958, the local authorities in Yonghe started collectivization and have tried to persuade villagers to open up wasteland for farming. [. . .] A number of villagers have run away as a result of [collectivization]. By the end of this year, thirty-five families had left, amounting to 156 people—that is 87.6 percent of the local population. A majority of the people from Yangpin also left in 1958, about 104—making up twenty-three entire families altogether. [. . .] The main reason for villagers to leave is collectivization: many were afraid that collectivization might result in class tension. [. . .] The other reason for many villagers to leave is the ban on Christianity. For two days during the autumn harvest season in 1958, villagers were forbidden to go to church. Some complained: "They are trying to destroy our religion, [so] we'd better leave." [. . .]

In 1958 the local Christian religion came under severe attack. In 1959 a number of cadres again tried to undermine Christianity. On the surface, it looks as though there are no more believers in the area. However, many among the local population secretly resented the local government's decision to ban their religion. According to our investigation, 34.3 percent—that is, a total of twelve people out of thirty-five adults in Yonghe—still have some belief. There are at least eighteen committed believers in the area—that is, 51.5 percent of the total population. Among them are five very devoted Christians who still secretly sing Christian hymns. The majority of those who refused to join the collective continue to go to church on Sundays. Those who have joined the collective have also been going to the church in secret.

· Document 64 ·

Report on improving the poor standard of living of Catholic villagers in the Shanhe administrative district of the Bailu people's commune, by the United Front Department of Peng county, [Sichuan province,] May–September 1960

The local population in the Sanhe administrative district of the Bailu people's commune in Peng county is predominantly Catholic. In the early 1950s, the area had one church and more than 300 believers. Some have since died, and others have moved away. At the moment there are 196 Catholics left. The percentage of the Catholics in the area is 35 percent of the total population. [...] Recently we did a survey among 116 adult believers: 76 regard themselves as devoted Catholics, and 35 said they believed a little. [...] At the moment, religious consciousness is still strong in the majority of believers, and most of them continue to pray at home. When it is busy at work, some even recite prayers on their way to work. Because of the absence of a priest in the area, a number of devoted believers go to Chengdu or Qionglai to attend services during the major Catholic festivals. Some local devotees even have permission from priests to recruit and baptize new believers. [...] Since the Great Leap Forward, Catholicism has shown some signs of declining. This has caused resentment among a few devoted believers. They complain that "since the Great Leap Forward, there is no time to take care of our hearts and souls." Some even questioned the government's policy toward religion. [...] A number of them continue to talk about former foreign missionaries as their "patrons." Some say: "Our area used to be so poor. If it weren't for the help of foreign priests, how could we manage to find a wife?" Hitherto, eleven believers from this area have married someone from the nunnery in Chengdu. Others also say: "This area used to have many orphans, and they were all being taken care of by those foreign priests. If it weren't for those foreign priests, many of them would have died." [...] Last year, because of food shortages and slips by some cadres, the local church has been stirring up trouble, and more than 100 villagers have been involved. Seventy percent of these villagers were Catholics. They surrounded the commune's inspection team and requested the dismissal of the local Party secretary. Some have also been spreading antigovernment sentiment among ordinary people. They say: "When we used to worship God, we had food to eat. Now we can no longer worship God, and there is no food to eat"; "Life is so hard these days; let's prepare our souls and wait on God," and so on. They harshly attacked socialism and tried to damage the relationship between the Party and ordinary people. [...]

· Document 65 ·

On rural affairs, by the Hunan Provincial Party Committee, 1957

Since April this year, there have been several outbreaks of epidemics in the province. Although the situation is getting better in cities and towns, the problem is still endemic in the countryside. In addition to flu and meningitis, measles is also widespread, particularly in the Binxian and Qianyang regions. There are more than 5,000 people in Yuanling's Bairong township, and 40 percent of them have become ill. In Bingxian, at least 80 percent of the local population became ill. There are 400 families in Rucheng's Xinhu collective, and more than half of them have at least one sick family member at home. More than forty entire families have also become ill, and no one is left at home to take care of them. The majority of people are very frightened. As a result, an increasing number of people have started to pray to gods and to take part in religious activities. Of the fifty townships in the Shaodong region, superstitious activities have become widespread in at least thirty-two. Each case involves from fifty to several hundred people. In Laiyang county's Yuqing township, almost every family has been found praying to local gods, and incense burners have been lit in every village. Every month local peasants have refused to work on the first day and fifteenth day of the lunar calendar.

According to a report from Laiyang county, local monks and Daoist practitioners are much busier than doctors at the moment. The main reason is that the doctors' fees are too high. In Hengyang, Laiyang, and Lanshan counties, the local traditional Chinese medicine clinics charge 0.2 to 0.4 yuan for each consultation and 0.3 to 0.5 yuan for each visit. The payment is required in advance.

In Huarong county 6,187 local people have been reported to be suffering from bad cases of flu; 36 people have died as a result. In Taojiang and Shuangjiang townships, more than 1,000 strong laborers have been taken ill. In Shizi brigade all the strong laborers have become ill and there is no one left to do the farm work. In Huaihua county, measles has become widespread among the local children. In Changde and Fuxiang, the majority of villagers could not afford to go to the doctor or pay for medicine. While a number of them just stayed home in bed, others have started to pray to the gods to seek healing and protection. In Niutouhu township's Ma'anshan village, every month on the first day and fifteenth day of the lunar calendar, more than 100 men and women go to the local shrine to pray to the local god. A number of young people and Party secretaries have also joined in. On one occasion, more than 200 villagers from Laihuaping township's Xi'nan collective went to the local shrine to pray. A cadre from the commune reacted harshly and smashed the statue of the local god. Local peasants were very unhappy about this. Some villagers have being going around collecting donations in an attempt to rebuild the statue and the shrine.

· Document 66 ·

An investigation into health care in the eight different communes in Chuxiong county, [Yunnan province,] 1964

Since 1961 a huge number of people and animals have become ill. Owing to lack of adequate health care in the area, deaths of human beings and animals have become prevalent. In the past three years, at least 409 people have died, plus 1,111 goats. As a result, supernatural healers have become popular again, and there has been a resurgence of spirit mediums and exorcism involving a large number of the local people. According to one estimate, at least 117 villagers in the eight communes have been making a living by practicing supernatural healing.

The majority of people take these superstitions very seriously. A number of cadres and Party members have also taken part in supernatural healing activities. In Mahuangjing commune, there have been quite a few such activities since 1961, including 135 collective activities and 629 individual ones. A total of 1,762 yuan was spent on such activities. In Candoutian commune there have been 29 collective divination events and 227 individual activities involving exorcists. The total cost was 1,814 yuan. Take an example: when the wife of Zhe Zhengwang—head of Upper brigade in Mahuangjing commune—became ill, instead of trying to find a doctor, she sent for a diviner to read her fortune. [. . .] Out of eleven healers in the Bijifang and Candoutian communes, five practice supernatural healings. [. . .]

· Document 67 ·

On the famine in Xichang region, by the Bureau of Civil Affairs, Sichuan province, 1960

[Owing to a number of crises] in the countryside, feudal superstitions are on the rise again. A number of villagers have turned to local gods to pray for rain. In Huidong county's Xincun commune, a number of cadres and peasants from Haiguang big brigade's Number 4 production brigade have been praying to the dragon god for rain because of the drought. They have performed animal sacrifices and made offerings to the dragon god. Such events have affected agricultural production, since no one has turned up to work anymore. In Yanyuan county, local shamans have become very active. They encourage villagers to participate in religious ceremonies and to pray for rain. In Miyi county's Pingshan commune, the Number 2 brigade spent 50 yuan to hire a shaman to perform divination. [. . .] In Xichang's Xijiao and Chuanxing communes, many villagers asked the local authorities to grant them permission to perform the water dragon dance and other rituals in Qinglong Temple at Qionghai Lake. Some even complained about the local government, saying: "In the old days, the local governor would make offerings outside the local government office to ask for rain. Nowadays the county heads do nothing."

· Document 68 ·

Report on fighting enemies in the rural countryside [Zunyi region, Guizhou province], 1963

Recently local feudal powers have become active again. They have been engaged in a number of reactionary counterrevolutionary activities. These include remaking the book of the family tree, electing clan leaders, building ancestor halls, and making offerings at ancestral tombs. Some of them are extremely active. [. . .]

A number of secret societies have also been plotting reactionary counterrevolutionary activities. In Ceheng county's Banba commune, the former landlord Wang Mieyan and the rich peasant Lu Jiaren have been performing witchcraft. They claim they are the reincarnations of gods and spirits. They told ordinary peasants: "If you want to have food to eat, you should follow spirits, not cadres," and "To leave the collective and to work independently is the only way to have a good life." Under their influence, a number of peasants have been distancing themselves from cadres and have lost any desire to work for the collective. Last year, in Zunyi county's Sidu commune, during the busiest time of the autumn harvest season, the rich peasant Feng Guangrong and the former landlord Zhou Yunquan from Sijiaba big brigade encouraged more than 1,000 local villagers to take part in the Hungry Ghost Festival.[11] It lasted for five days. They quoted from Buddhist teachings on suffering and salvation and claimed that "the real salvation is coming soon from heaven" and "Chairman Mao's regime will last only another two and a half years." They also incited people to complain about the "bitterness" they have been suffering under the Communist Party. They even led people in reciting verses such as "Oh, the dead, what a terrible life you suffered and how miserable was your death. In 1959 there was no food and you starved to death just like that." [. . .] In Tongzi county's Songkan district, the secret religious sect Guanyin Laomu Dao, which has been suppressed several times by the authorities, has also started to become active again. Since last year, the sect's three leaders have organized a number of religious activities. They have now recruited more than 1,200 followers and have set up one central altar and seven branch altars throughout the area. They have appointed an "emperor," "representatives," an "accountant," and so on, among their leadership. They are currently extremely active.

CHAPTER SEVEN

Strategies for Survival (1959–1962)

THE Communist state built an elaborate hierarchical system to enforce its control. The system was effective: people lived in constant fear of imprisonment, punishment, or death. But it also permitted corruption at all levels. To survive, people developed a wide range of strategies to exploit the system and outwit the Party and the state. In the time of famine, the human will to live superseded stated socialist moral standards and the new order the Communist Party tried to enforce. Skill in cheating took an individual much further than readiness to obey. Cadres and those in charge of foodstuffs feasted while others starved to death (documents 69–78). Theft, robbery, speculation, profiteering, and simply defrauding the system were widespread (documents 79–84). Many people dealt in the black market (documents 85–87).

As the famine unfolded, people employed a whole range of strategies to stay alive, from stealing or hiding food to robbing state granaries. As the famine worsened, they developed or rediscovered ways to cope with hunger by eating earth, worms, decomposing animals, and human flesh (documents 88–89, 96). Some fled their village or sold everything they had, including their children, for a bowl of grain. Women left their husbands and children to cohabit elsewhere for the same reason (documents 90–92). Some went into prostitution. When the famine in Sichuan reached its height in 1961, there was a resurgence of prostitution in the provincial capital, Chengdu (document 93).

In times of extreme scarcity, money loses its value. Access to goods and services depends almost entirely on whom one knows and on one's ability to flatter or to bribe (document 94). A network of personal contacts and social connections developed. This mesh of obligations became an essential tool for survival—for families and for individuals regardless of family. For those facing calamity, selfishness became the norm. One person's gain was always another person's loss. To secure the odd mouthful of food, desperate people were ready to steal from one another or even to murder. Time and again within many families, there was violent strife over food, leading to many broken marriages and cases of brutal treatment (documents 95–98).

The devastating famine in China ceased by degrees toward the close of 1962. The catastrophe had left tens of millions dead. Now, fifty years later, with the economy booming in many cities and a staggering growth in the gross national product, Mao's vision of a China on par with industrialized nations of the world, the aim of his Great Leap Forward, seems to have finally come to pass. Yet the consequences of the famine still cast a long shadow over the country. Cases of fraud by factory managers and corruption among cadres are discussed every day. The tainted milk scares in 2008 and 2011, the school buildings "collapsing like tofu" during the Sichuan earthquake of May 2008, and the abuse of child slave laborers in factories all occurred because someone somewhere tried to cut corners, cheat the system, and increase profits. Even with China the world's second-biggest economy, most Chinese struggle to survive. After sixty years of life under Communism, they live by the hard lesson beaten into them during the famine: the only way to keep going, to have access to goods and services, is to disobey, to steal, to cheat, and to manipulate the system.

· Document 69 ·

Report on excess waste among some cadres and ordinary people in the countryside, by the Jilin Provincial Party Committee, September 21, 1959

1. In some areas cadres have been using the harvest celebration as an excuse to kill a large number of pigs and goats for lavish banquets. Take the Huancheng administrative district in Jiutai county's Jiutai commune for an example. Within half a month, it hosted three banquets and wasted the equivalent of 400 to 500 yuan in cash. In Yushu county's Shuangjingzi commune, one brigade from the Dafangzi administrative district decided to celebrate before the harvest. They hosted a banquet for the entire brigade and indulged in excessive eating and drinking. Many villagers became very drunk and two died of alcohol poisoning as a result. [. . .]

2. In recent months, large amounts of fish, meat, tobacco, alcohol, candies, and tea have been squandered to entertain government

inspection teams. The waste is so enormous that it has caused many villagers to be publicly angry. Take the Yedian county's inspection team, for example. Under the leadership of Li Jingxiang, deputy head of the county Agricultural Work Department, the team consumed three pigs, one cow, two chickens, and many bottles of alcohol within half a month. When the inspection team from Jiutai county's Jiutai commune went down to one village to inspect the local agricultural work, the local cadres put on a lavish banquet to show their generosity. They even hired a manager to take charge of catering and drinks. Grain and fruit liquors and beer flowed freely, and mountains of cigarettes, tea, and white sugar were on offer. That was still not enough. They also put on a special feast for all commune-level cadres. [. . .] Many villagers complained to us: "What kind of inspection team is this? Clearly they came for the food." Some say: "This kind of corruption should be stopped. How can we afford such terrible waste?" [. . .]

3. Some communes and brigades have also wasted a lot of cash purchasing extravagant equipment; most of it was not for agricultural production. The amount of waste was simply shocking. Jiutai county's Bonihe commune, for example, spent more than 1,000 yuan in cash to buy fifteen bicycles. Each of its administrative districts received one. The commune also bought sofas and rotating chairs for each Party secretary and one rotating chair for the head of the commune. Each office was also given a new telephone. The total waste was more than 1,800 yuan in cash. [. . .] Some districts also bought new desks for the Party secretaries and district heads. There were a few brigades that even purchased radios. Each radio costs more than 100 yuan.

Currently there is a lot of dissatisfaction among ordinary people. It is not only that a huge quantity of economic resources has been wasted; it is also extremely damaging to the Party politically.

· Document 70 ·

Report by the Hubei Provincial Party Committee on the Rectification Campaign in Mianyang county's Tonghaikou commune, January 31, 1961

In the past two years, quite a few cadres in the commune have been found taking and consuming more than they were entitled to. According to our calculations, within two years they consumed 18,094 kg of rice, 2,089 kg of pork, 3,429 kg of fish, 313 kg of oil, and 216 kg of eggs. They have also pocketed coupons worth 5,097 kg of rice, 503.7 kg of cotton, 2,973 meters of fabric, 298 kg of oil, and 484 kg of meat. [. . .] Almost all commune cadres have received more food than their allotted ration. In public many brigade cadres pretended to eat the same rations as everyone else, but secretly they consumed extra food that villagers had been told to save.

[. . .] Whenever the Department of Commerce managed to secure luxury foods, they were always offered to cadres first. Because of the scarcity of food, almost anything available was taken by cadres. In 1960 the commune bought 1,024 cartons of cigarettes, and 412 went to thirty-one different cadres in the commune. The other 314 cartons were consumed during cadre meetings, and 165 cartons were distributed among cadres in various brigades. The few that were left were also given to lower-ranking cadres. So what remained for ordinary people? Last year the commune shop manufactured 1,018 kg of sweets, but of that amount, 446 kg were divided up by cadres in the commune. Similarly, the commune bought over 60 meters of luxury fabric last year, and different cadres in the commune took over 11 meters. The commune deputy Party secretary Wang Shidong, for instance, took 4 meters himself plus nearly 2 meters of cotton fabric.

· Document 71 ·

Any bad elements must be dealt with severely, by the Central Supervision Commission, [Beijing,] April 16, 1960

Currently, corruption and waste among rural cadres are very prevalent. According to our investigation, in Hubei province's Huanggang region, 29 percent of local cadres have been involved in various types of corruption. That is almost 4,000 out of the total number of 13,000 cadres in the region. They range from brigade heads to canteen managers, granary managers, accountants, and Party secretaries. The amount of money involved ranged from over 10 yuan to more than 1,000 yuan. In Shandong province's Guan county, Peng Jianlin, the Party secretary in Qianma village, Wangfeng people's commune, managed to swindle more than 8,000 yuan in cash. Other cadres, including the deputy Party secretary, the accountant, and the brigade head, as well several Party members, have also pocketed 300 to 5,000 yuan. In the past few years, owing to corruption among cadres, ordinary people have suffered terribly. For instance, some cadres have stolen the money for famine relief or have pocketed food intended for old people's homes or nurseries, resulting in a large number of deaths.

[. . .] Last year in Guangdong province's Leibei county, the Hechun people's commune wasted more than 35,000 yuan on meetings, visits, and entertainment. During one meeting, the commune put on a lavish banquet, and each table was filled with more than thirty dishes. In Heyuan county's Yihe people's commune, Zhang Yuchun, the brigade head of Mixia big brigade, celebrated his thirty-first birthday with a huge banquet consisting of twelve tables of food. He also mobilized more than 100 people to go around collecting money and gifts for him.

[...] In Hubei province's Xiaogan county, the Party secretary of Xiaohe people's commune, Cai Fumin, kept a separate kitchen for himself. He has been eating four meals a day, and each month he has consumed nearly 25 kg of rice, 2 kg of oil, and more than 10 kg of meat. Meanwhile, more than 1,700 people have died of edema in this commune within a period of four months—from October last year to February this year.

· Document 72 ·

Minutes of the plenum of the Chishui County Party Committee, [Guizhou province,] December 16–22, 1960

In 1960 [the county Party secretary, Wang Linchi,] consumed luxury health supplements worth more than 700 yuan, including deer antler extracts and ginseng worth 400 yuan. [...] When he went into the countryside to inspect work, he never ate in the collective canteen. Instead, his private staff always took plenty of meat, sweets, and alcohol from the county's Bureau of Commerce for Wang to indulge in during his trips. [...] When he was admitted into the county hospital because of an illness, he was allocated a single room equipped with a gramophone. One doctor and one nurse were assigned to take care of him especially. On his door there was a Don't Disturb sign while he took the nurse and his private guard to the opera and the cinema. [...]

During the Chinese New Year, when many people in the countryside were starving or freezing to death, Wang took more than 300 people from the county Party Committee, county school, and opera with him to Fuxing commune to express sympathy and solicitude. To create a cheerful atmosphere, he ordered the commune to send villagers to stand by the side of road to welcome him. [...] In Fuxing commune, they feasted on pork, fish, poultry, and plenty of alcohol every day. In February this year, during a worksite meeting in Tucheng commune, Wang ordered a huge banquet for more than 180 people. Quite a few cows and pigs were slaughtered to feed them, and they drank gallons of alcohol. More than fifty waiters or waitresses were called to serve them. The county opera and [county] cinema also put on shows to entertain them. For five days of feasting and entertainment the total expenditure was 4,817 yuan. [...] Meanwhile, Wang ignored the fact that many people were dying of edema. Not only did he not carry out any action to remedy the problem, but he also tried to suppress the news and to find excuses. [...] When Comrade Ma Zhao reported that seventy-one people had died in Tucheng within one month, and nineteen had died within one day, [...] Wang called him a rightist. [...] When the county Public Security Bureau reported cannibalism in Tiantai district, Wang publicly denounced the bureau during a Party conference. He accused the Public Security Bureau of spreading rumors. He said: "Why are you so anxious about cannibalism? Why do you keep on investigating and taking photographs? Your intention is to destroy the Fuxing commune's Party Committee. Do you want to make trouble for the Communist Party?" After that incident, no cadres dared to report any problems. The number of deaths and sick people has increased. [...]

· Document 73 ·

Report on Liu Hongbin's criminal group and their activities, by the Party Committee of the southern Guizhou region, 1962

Between 1960 and 1961, while the country was suffering severe food shortages, the deputy head of the Duyun city Finance Department, Liu Hongbin, as well as the former head of the Duyun city Bureau of Commerce, Zhang Zhirong, and the deputy head of the Food Department in the same bureau, Yang Yuxia, stole a total of 122,882 kg's worth of food from the state granary and hid it in a food factory run by the Bureau of Commerce.

One method they used was to forge the figures needed for manufacturing food in the factory. [...] In the winter of 1960, when Duyun city's state granary was supplied with food for only ten to twenty days, Liu, Zhang and Yang used the New Year holiday season as an excuse to request 49,000 kg of unprocessed rice and 1,000 kg of dried soybeans from the city store, even though the factory had more than 60,000 kg of rice grain and 9,000 kg of dried soybeans still untouched. After the city government refused the request, they forged an official paper and forced the city's Bureau of Grain to release more than

15,000 kg of rice. In March the same year, when there were only 100 kg of cooking oil left in the city's state granary, whereas there were still 1,400 kg untouched in the factory storage room, they asked Yang Yuxia to use the manufacture of luxury sweets as an excuse and sent the Bureau of Grain an urgent request stating: "There are only 7.5 kg of oil left. If you don't send more, the factory will have to stop production." Under their pressure, the Bureau of Grain dispatched 100 kg of rapeseed oil to the factory and cut off the entire supply to the city's ordinary residents.

[...] They also used the government policy to "economize the use of food" as an excuse and reduced the food ration for factory and mine workers as well as for edema patients. [...] In 1961 they closed down seventeen restaurants in Duyun. The other six were also forced to reduce their size and to cut back on the quality of food. Meanwhile, they informed the city's vegetable company to stop selling tofu and good vegetables, causing serious shortages in the marketplace. In September 1960 they tried to stop the provision of cakes for workers in special units and replaced the cakes with 150 g of white sugar per month. They even cut back the special provision of cakes for edema patients. They also delayed supplying the dried porridge meal required for treating edema patients. They claimed that "the porridge is no good. To cure the disease patients need to eat fat and meat." As a result, many patients were left with nothing to eat. [...]

[...] The three of them regarded the food factory and four major restaurants in the city as their "five paradises," where they could indulge in eating and drinking to excess. According to our incomplete estimate, Liu Hongbin has consumed more than 650 yuan's worth of food by himself. More than 1,500 kg of pork, 500 kg of lard, 450 kg of sausages, and 3,000 duck eggs went missing at Yang Yuxia's hands. [...]

· Document 74 ·

Report on the condition of collective canteens in the Wuai administrative district, Sanxing commune, Jintang county, by the Wenjiang branch of the Agricultural and Grain Production Investigation Team of the General Office of the Sichuan Provincial Party Committee, April 1960

There are forty-two collective canteens in this district, and the majority of them have no order or proper system. [...] One brigade head, Xie Xianfu, has been regularly pocketing the cash from the canteen. As far as we know, he has stolen at least 60 yuan in cash. He also took oil, salt, vegetables, and rice from the canteen. Together with another cadre from the district, he ate all the dried peas reserved for planting. The store manager, Zeng Shao'an, hardly ate at the canteen. He has been stealing rice from the store on a regular basis so he could feast at home. [. . .] Xu Chaopin, the canteen manager in Number 11 brigade has stolen more than 110 kg of rice, as well as the eggs collected for the state. Even worse, Grandma Chen's eight-year-old granddaughter once ate some rice before it had been weighed by the canteen, and Xie and one cadre from the district, Liao Xianzhen, punished the whole family and deprived them of food, leaving all seven of them starving for the entire day. [. . .] Last year, 930 people from this district became ill, and there were more than 500 edema sufferers. [. . .] The number of deaths last year was 373. Between January and April this year 91 people have already died.

· Document 75 ·

Report by Comrade Hou Shunde on the condition of collective canteens in Peipozhuang big brigade [in Hebei province], October 20, 1960

There are altogether eight collective canteens in the brigade [. . .] and the problem of canteen staff eating more than what they are entitled to is quite common at all of them. In some canteens there have also been quite a few cases of corruption and incidents of stealing among the staff. For instance, Guo Congyou, the canteen manager in Number 5 small brigade, used to refuse to let his married daughter stay at his home, afraid that she would eat his food ration. After he became the manager, his daughter has been coming home every month, and she never brings along her own food ration from her husband's village. Many villagers complain that "being the canteen manager is like holding onto an iron rice bowl: not only does he get fat himself, but even his family and relatives have become fat."[1] The canteen in Number 1 small brigade once treated villagers to fried cakes. Afterward there were still 20 kg of flour left. It was sent back to the village storeroom, and the door was locked by a villager, Bai Xinyue. [. . .] While villagers were working in the field, the former canteen manager and some cadres used all the flour to make cakes and ate them all. When Bai and other villagers asked after the leftover flour, some cadres from the big brigade blamed Bai for attempting to damage the canteen and to spoil the relationship between cadres and ordinary people. They denounced Bai in public meetings. After that, no one dared to make any complaints. During the Moon Festival, the big brigade made more than 10 kg of moon cakes, but they all went astray. [...] Nor was that all. Canteen managers also treated different people differently. If they disliked someone, they would give that person less food. For instance, the canteen manager in Number 3 small brigade has been regularly encouraging the wife of the Party secretary, Bai Shenming, to go to the canteen to take wheat flour or sweet potatoes for free. However, during meal times he has been deliberately serving smaller amounts to ordinary villagers. The old villager Bai Yuxiang complains that the canteen manager has "a different heart for different people" and that the scales in the canteen are never the same. [...]

· Document 76 ·

The instruction on rectification in people's communes from the Central Committee of the Chinese Communist Party and Chairman Mao, 1959

In [Jiangsu province's] Jiangning county, a village cadre killed a peasant's chicken and ate it himself. Not only did he refuse to pay for the chicken, but he also demanded that the peasant supply oil and salt with which to cook the chicken. [...]

In Guizhou province's Taijiang county, the deputy Party secretary took some fish from villagers without paying. At the same time, a cadre from Rongjiang county took more than 10 kg of cabbage from peasants and did not leave any money [to pay for it].

Last year, in [Shaanxi province's] Xianyang city, Ma Qingshan, a cadre from Number 3 brigade in Diaotai commune, was sent by the brigade to buy food for the villagers. He stole more than 60 yuan in cash from the food money and used it to buy cigarettes and alcohol for himself.

· Document 77 ·

Some cadres in southern Guizhou have been pocketing factory workers' oil and meat rations, June 8–December 1, 1960

Recently in southern Guizhou, a number of cadres in some factories and mines have been found pocketing workers' rations for non-staple food. [...] Jiang Yelin, the head of the Duyun city agricultural tool factory, and ten members of his family have never bought any fuel, coal, or salt. They have been eating factory workers' rations. Nor is that all: they have also taken more than 25 kg of oil and coupons worth 75 kg of rice from the factory. They have been regularly taking the factory's and factory clinic's quotas of ration [coupons] to purchase alcohol, sugar, cakes, noodles, and so on, for their own consumption. Even worse, recently they sold 550 kg of coal oil, 80 kg of steel, and two engines to the Xinhua restaurant in exchange for food. Those items are in very high demand. In Duyun's electric company, a number of workers complained that the cadres ate white bread while ordinary workers ate dark bread. Some cadres have also been eating in excess, far beyond their alloted rations. Many workers are extremely unhappy about this. In Weng'angao city, some cadres from one coal mine have pocketed more than 10 kg of sugar reserved for sick workers. Not only that, many cadres have eaten more than their alloted rations; many of their family members have also been consuming the rations of ordinary workers.

· Document 78 ·

An investigation into why Mianyang county's Songya commune is so poor, by the Mianyang branch of the Rectification Campaign Investigation Working Team of the Sichuan Provincial Party Committee, January 13–September 28, 1961

The family of Shi Kaiyun, head of the Number 3 administrative district, kept three plots of land in different locations. This year they harvested more than 500 kg of pumpkins. They have also kept more than seventy chickens. Every day they feasted at home. The child of Chen Wenli, a poor peasant, once saw him frying bread, so the child quietly went to watch. Shi discovered him. It was a winter's day, and the weather was freezing outside. Shi took off the child's clothes and slapped him. The child died the next day.

· Document 79 ·

The Supervision Administration of Gushi county, [Henan province,] regarding some cadres from the County Transport Department who used the opportunity to transport coal to illegally extort nonessential food items from four production brigades in Qiyi commune, March 23, 1961

Owing to the high demand for transport and the severe shortage of fuel in the countryside, some cadres from the County Transport Department have been using the opportunity to transport coal in order to illegally extort nonessential food items from four production brigades in Qiyi commune. The state transport [system] has simply become their tool for obtaining goods. They agree to take on a transportation assignment only if the customer offers them bribes or sells goods to them cheaply. Otherwise, they use "too busy" or "vehicle is broken" as excuses and refuse to take on any work. For instance, the head of the Scheduling Department, Liu Hongqi, and other members in the department have managed to extort, in total, 692 kg of pork, beef, poultry meat, fish, and animal fat, plus 65 kg of noodles, tofu, and brown sugar. Besides what they have consumed, they have auctioned the rest to other cadres and workers at the Transport Department. Sometimes they even sold extorted food items on the black market to make a profit. [. . .] Some drivers and cadres in the department have also been using work as an excuse to force various brigades to entertain them with plenty of food and alcohol. For instance, the department took on the task of transporting coal for Hongguang big brigade. They did it three times and consumed 6 kg of rice and more than 7 kg of pork and fish. After the feast, they only paid 150 g in rice coupons to the brigade. Nor was that all. They also took all the leftovers back with them. Once, after they helped Zishu big brigade to transport some coal, they did not get a free meal. The Transport Department refused to take on any further assignments [from the brigade]. Out of fear, the brigade sent 2 kg of fish, 250 g of sesame oil, and coupons worth 1 kg of rice to the Transport Department the next day to apologize.

· Document 80 ·

Report on the current situation in the countryside, by the Department of Rural Affairs of the Sichuan Provincial Party Committee, 1961

To the Central Committee of the Chinese Communist Party and the Sichuan Provincial Party Committee:

In Qianwei county's Mamiao commune, some brigades have started to impose fines on villagers caught stealing food. If anyone fails to pay the fine, deductions are made from his or her food ration. However, it turns out that the higher the fine, the more thefts there are. Youai big brigade in Jingyan county's Wugong commune has announced that whoever is caught stealing 0.5 kg of food must pay back 5 kg, and whoever reports any stealing will be rewarded. [. . .] However, this did not stop villagers from stealing, and there has been an increase in the number of incidents. In Jiangbei county's Yuanyang commune, villagers have stolen all 4 hectares of broad beans in Paifang big brigade. [...] Some cadres even watched villagers stealing and did not do anything to prevent it. A small number of cadres also joined in the theft of food. In Jiangjin county, the Party secretary of Shimen administrative district as well as 8.8 percent of brigade heads all took the lead in pilfering. Some entire families also participated. About 22.7 percent of villagers—that is, a total of 108 people—have been involved in stealing food.

· Document 81 ·

The view of the Guangdong Provincial Party Committee on counterrevolutionary sabotage in a number of instances, including murder, arson, and granary robbery, well as on incidents in which some cadres ran away to join the enemy, December 29, 1960

On December 2, Chen Qunrong, Li En, and five other people from Baisha big brigade in Guangsi county's Didou commune stole more than 500 kg of sweet potatoes from the commune granary. On the eve of December 19, in Xinxing county's Qigong commune, Zhang Yi and another twelve villagers from Shanzhukeng village in Sanhe big brigade forced their way into Dabo big brigade's temporary granary. They threatened the two granary managers with knives and told them not to move. They took away more than 500 kg of rice.

There have also been a number of incidents of fires in various communes, involving the burning down of a number of storage rooms of the commune Supply Department. On the eve of December 20, the two storage rooms in Wengyuan county's Supply Department were burned down in a fire, and more than 10,000 items were damaged, equivalent in value to a total of 23,000 yuan. The criminal responsible also left some writing on a nearby wall, which read: "It's not possible to buy goods without coupons, but it's possible to burn the lot."

· Document 82 ·

Report on an anti-robbery campaign, by the Jiangsu Provincial Party Committee, July 30, 1960

According to an estimate by the Nanjing Railway Bureau, there have been a number of robberies at twenty stations along the Shanghai-Nanjing rail route since October 1959: 166.40 tons of steel, 148.7

tons of raw iron, 304 tons of copper, 2.7 tons of lead and aluminum, 1,025 bronze sheets of silicon, 613.8 tons of cement, 202 square meters of timber, as well as a large number of old coins, glasses, and engines and [a large quantity of] food have been stolen.

This year alone, in the fifty-five county post offices, 10,362 letters and packages have been opened, and more than 38,000 yuan in cash, coupons for nearly 5,000 kg of rice, and coupons for 2,000 meters of fabric have been stolen.

The methods employed by some are extremely wicked. One is to "borrow." The provincial Transport Department's Number 1 automotive team has been helping the Xuzhou heavy machinery factory to transport goods on a regular basis. They used collaboration as an excuse and "borrowed" 20 tons of steel from the factory. The Nanjing Hepingmen loading company has also "borrowed" eight engines, one machine, and 50,000 bricks from their customers. The other method is taking by force. [. . .] The head of the Xuzhou city Xinhua lock factory and the factory buyer have hired a vehicle and have driven around the city to steal goods. The third method is fraud. After hearing that twenty-five sheets of galvanized iron from Shanghai would arrive at Tiansheng port, [officials from] the Nantong ice factory went to the port and claimed the goods were theirs. By the time the real owner discovered what was happening, fifteen sheets had already gone. "[Taking] goods without an owner" is another method of stealing that various transport companies regularly use. The Suzhou Heavy Industry Bureau bought eight aluminum sheets, but the goods went missing after arriving at the Suzhou railway station. [People from the bureau] went to the station to inquire, but the staff there told them the goods had not yet arrived. In the end, the aluminum sheets were found in the station's "unclaimed goods" storage room. According to our initial investigation, more than 80 tons of steel and iron are being stored in this "unclaimed goods" storage room. [. . .] "Backdoor profiteering" is also common. Nanjing Central Department Store's Jinglan food shop received 45 kg of pork supply for the general market, but 20,000 kg ended up on the black market. More than 10,000 citizens with coupons in their hands could not buy any meat. They were extremely unhappy about this. In Suzhou's Pingjiang and Jinchang districts, 50 percent of soybean products, as well as the candies in Yipinxiang's and Daoxiangcun's stores, also walked out the back door and have gone missing. [. . .] Inside the dormitory of a team leader of the provincial Transport Department's automotive team there were hams hanging on all four walls. He had stolen them while on duty.

· Document 83 ·

Reports from Bureaus of Public Security in various provinces on the shocking amount of food that has gone missing from granaries or during transportation or during manufacturing, February 20, 1961

According to reports from various regional Public Security Bureaus and Departments of Political and Legislative Affairs, the amount of food that has gone missing or has been damaged since December last year is simply shocking. [. . .] In Jiangsu province's Gaoyou county, 275 boat operators have been found stealing food items during transportation. The methods involved include adding water or sand to the grain or manipulating the scales. Altogether they have stolen nearly 40,000 kg of grain. [. . .] In Guangdong province's Zhongshan county and seven other counties, 206 cases of fraud have been reported, and the amount of food lost has amounted to 22,000 kg. [. . .] In Shandong province, cadres and workers in food factories have stolen 42,000 kg of food plus coupons worth 8 kg of rice.

Group robbery is also very prevalent. According to an incomplete estimate by [the Ministry of] Public Security, from September last year to January 25 this year, there were more than 30,000 incidents of group robbery in twenty-three different provinces and regions. More than 4,000,000 kg of grain has being stolen. [. . .] In Hunan province alone, there have been 4,530 incidents of robbery; the amount of food lost has reached 920,000 kg. In Changde region, there have been 14,092 cases of stealing and pilfering; the amount of food lost has reached 906,000 kg.

· Document 84 ·

Report on food robbery and theft on trains, by the Party Committee of the Ministry of Railways, [Beijing,] January 20, 1961

To the Secretariat of the Central Committee:

Recently there has been an increasing number of cases of robbery and theft on trains. Below are some reports from the Bureaus of Railways in Beijing, Lanzhou [Gansu province], and Harbin [Heilongjiang province].

From September to December last year, there have been 1,271 incidents of food theft taking place along the railroads managed by the Beijing bureau. The amount of food lost has reached 80,415 kg. From January 1 to January 8 this year, there were 81 similar incidents within five days, and the amount of food lost has reached 7,263 kg. On November 25, after a train from Sichuan province's Youtingpu station carrying rice arrived at Beijing West railway station, it was discovered that more than seventeen sacks of grain had been cut open, and three of them were completely ripped apart: 1,340 kg of grain was stolen. On December 20, after one train carrying wheat flour arrived in Xuanhua railway station, a railway worker, He Zhenfeng, stole one sack while unloading the goods. He was caught when he was trying to smuggle the sack out of the station. On January 1 this year, after train no. 1062, carrying soybeans, arrived at Nandasi railway station, a gang of more than twenty people appeared at the station and stole the beans.

According to a report by the Lanzhou bureau, in the first half of January, there were more than 160 incidents of food robbery along the railroads managed by the bureau. The amount of food lost has amounted to 41,150 kg. For instance, at Wuwei railway station, almost every day more than 500 to 600 villagers from the nearby communes, such as Wuwei, Xinren, Jingta, Jingyang, and Jingchang, have been ganging up to rob trains. On January 5, after train no. 4278 pulled into Wuwei railway station, more than ninety villagers robbed the car carrying rice. They took more than ninety sacks of rice, and the estimated amount of rice lost was over 9,000 kg. On January 10 at the same station, a train loaded with coal was waiting to leave. Meanwhile, a gang of more than 300 villagers appeared at the station and robbed the entire train. On January 8 at Gaoyang railway station, train no. 2495, carrying cornmeal, was robbed by a gang of more than 100 people. The amount of cornmeal lost was over 300 kg. A day later at Wenzhu railway station, after train no. 2451, carrying sorghum from Shangshui to Yumen, had just pulled into the station, the head of Number 11 small brigade from Wenzhu commune's Number 5 big brigade took more than twenty villagers, as well as a number of mules and horses, with him to the station. They stole more than 2,000 kg of sorghum. On January 5, at Longxi railway station, train no. 1813, carrying rice to Lanxi, was robbed by a gang of more than ten people. They took away six sacks of rice. At the same station, almost every day there have been twenty to thirty people carrying knives, waiting to rob the next passing train. On January 16, along the Lanzhou-Urumqi railway tracks at Taipingbao railway station, a gang of more than 100 armed robbers robbed one train and took away more than 10,000 kg of corn. They were so fierce that the police could not stop them. On the evenings of January 19 and 20, more than 8,000 people from the nearby villages went into Wuwei railway station at different hours to rob trains. Altogether they stole over 1,000 kg of rice, 2,500 kg of brown sugar, an entire carriage full of liqueurs, 470 kg of salt, 1,000 tons of coal, 2,000 kg of lambs' wool, and 146 live goats. They also took away the luggage of the railway staff and more than 1,000 yuan in cash. They even tried to stop the engine. When the Party secretary of nearby Changhe commune went to deal with them, they beat him up.

Outside Harbin, at Sankeshu, Taipingqiao, and Xiangfang railway stations, food robbery has been happening on a regular basis. On the eve of January 8 and 9, two gangs of 200 to 300 people robbed the station. They carried with them big cloth bags and tools. Even the railway security guards and police could not stop them. On January 8 at 4:30 p.m., after train no. 3217, traveling from Harbin to Sankeshu, pulled into Taipingqiao station, a gang of more than 200 people appeared and robbed the carriage carrying soybeans. They even told the railway security guards: "You are carrying guns, but you don't dare shoot us. You might just as well throw your guns into the fire." When the security guards asked them where they were from, they replied: "We are passersby." On January 9 at 5:30 p.m., another gang of more than 200 people appeared at the station. They went onto one railroad car that was carrying food and unloaded a huge bag of food. They then divided the food up into small sacks. After the same train arrived at Sankeshu railway station, another gang of more than 200 people appeared. They boarded the train and took away a huge amount of grain and sugar beets. When ten railway security guards and twenty railway freight loaders, as well as ten students training to be railway electricians, tried to stop them, they threw the beets at the students. [. . .]

Similar incidents of robbery have occurred in other places. The problem is very prevalent and serious. If it continues, it will not only cause severe damage to the railway transport system but also affect the security and stability of the entire country.

· Document 85 ·

Report on conditions in Jintang and Qionglai, by the Wenjiang branch of the Agricultural Production Investigation Team of the Sichuan Provincial Party Committee, April 4–November 20, 1960

There is a black market currently active in Jintang county. Recently someone sold a goose to the county chemical factory for the price of 45 yuan. A villager from Number 2 brigade in Zhaodu commune's Number 6 administrative district also went to the chemical factory with two buckets of pumpkins. He sold them for over 30 yuan, and with the cash he bought one mosquito net, one padded jacket, and more than 10 kg of salt. Other villagers commented that he had made a fortune.

· Document 86 ·

Report on villagers from Xinfan, Zizhong, and Pi counties going to the black market elsewhere to make exchanges for food, and so on, by Comrade Ming Lang from the General Office of the Sichuan Provincial Party Committee, by the Party Committee of the Sichuan Province Public Security Bureau and by the Party Committee of the Neijiang and Yibin regions, February 2–September 14, 1962

Beginning in early March, a huge number of villagers from various famine regions have been traveling across the country attempting to secure food. Currently, the number is on the increase, and the area affected has widened. The matter is extremely urgent and serious. The villagers responsible are from more than seventy different communes in Yongchuan, Lu, Rongchang, Longchang, Dazu, Tongliang, and Bishan counties. They have been going to eighteen different communes in Neijing, Zizhong, and Ziyang to try to barter for food. Each day at least 2,000 people were found traveling on the road. That is a huge increase from the 800 in February. According to one estimate, on March 11 at least 806 people were at Yongchuan and Longchang railway stations waiting to go north to look for food. There were also countless villagers who went on foot. There are more than twenty railway stations between Yongchuan and Ziyang; they are always crowded with peasants, and there is no order whatsoever. We have been notified of a number of problems.

1. Besides begging in the countryside, many peasants have started going to cities to barter their possessions in exchange for coal, tobacco, paper made from straw, straw mats, and hemp fabric. Since they could not sell some old items, they would buy other things to barter for what they needed. The number of items that can be bartered has increased. This has helped the black market to constantly expand.

2. [. . .] In Neijiang each day one could see more than 100 peasants wandering around the city. Many villagers from rural Neijiang and Anyue have been coming into the city to sell dried and fresh sweet potato on the streets or in crowded places. They have helped to build the black market in Neijiang city. In Neijiang county there are at least five spontaneous illegal black markets. The one in Hongpaifang some-

times stretches out over 2 or 3 km, and every day more than 500 people turn up. A number of them have been involved in trafficking or peddling. According to an investigation by Lu county's Jiaming commune, at least fifty-five villagers have been involved in food trafficking; that is 27.8 percent of the total local population. A number of them have been exploiting the current difficulties and profiting from the famine.

· Document 87 ·

Report on edema treatment, by the Disease Control Team of the Sichuan Provincial Party Committee and the Sichuan Province Bureau of Health and Hygiene, October–December 8, 1961

On September 14 the director of the Liangshui commune hospital, Chen Yuan, took 290 yuan to Chongqing to buy some medicine for the hospital. He smuggled 20 kg of radish seeds back and sold them for 60 yuan. With that money he bought 6 kg of dried konjac and reconstituted it with water to make jelly. He then sold the konjac jelly at 1 yuan per 0.5 kg on the black market. In total, he made a profit of 1,200 yuan. On top of that, he bought five cloth sacks, 2.5 kg of candy, and a pair of rubber shoes from the government store [in Chongqing] and sold them at a very high price on the black market. He made a 2,000 yuan profit in the end.

The doctor at Tongliang county's Dongjiao commune hospital, Wu Dezhou, sold his ration coupons and made a profit of 176 yuan. With that money he bought some 225 kg of sweet potato at 0.4 yuan per 0.5 kg. He then went to the state granary and, invoking his profession as a doctor, managed to exchange the sweet potatoes for 65 kg of rice. Afterward, he went back to the countryside and bought more than 450 kg of sweet potatoes with the rice. He sold the sweet potatoes again, and this time he bought more than 3 meters' worth of fabric coupons. He sold the coupons at 2 yuan per 0.3 meter, and with the money he bought 0.5 kg of Chinese angelica. He then claimed that his wife was ill and got some *baizhu*[2] from various hospitals. He made up fifty sachets for prescriptions and sold each of them for 5 yuan. Altogether, he made a profit of 3,000 yuan.

· Document 88 ·

Report on the famine situation in Jiangjin, Wan, and seven other counties, by
the Party Committee of the Bureau of Civil Affairs and the State Council
Investigation Team, [Sichuan province,] January 9–November 21, 1962

To the Ministry of Internal Affairs in Beijing and the Political and Legislative Affairs Committee of the Central Committee:

In 1961 a number of villages in Changshou county were out of food supplies. Villagers have resorted to living on wild herbs and tree bark. Every day in [Chonqing's] Beifu district more than 100 people have been seen going out in groups to search for food. All the banana trees in the People's Park, the old people's home in the district, and the local state farm have been ripped up and the roots consumed by hungry villagers. One day about twenty to thirty villagers from Longxihe brigade in Changshou county's Sputnik commune forced their way into the compound of the Changshou County Party Committee. They peeled the bark off all the trees and consumed it. In [Chongqing's] Jiangbei county, more than 27,000 villagers have been consuming "immortal earth" to assuage their hunger.

· Document 89 ·

Report on edema treatment, by the Disease Control Team of the Sichuan
Provincial Party Committee and the Sichuan Province Bureau of Health
and Hygiene, October–December 8, 1961

In 1961 the number of deaths in Bishan county's Chengdong commune reached 887; that is 11.29 percent of the total local population. An increasing number of villagers have fled the famine or have sold their children in order to survive. There are twelve young girls, between thirteen and seventeen, who have married elsewhere either by their parents' arrangement or by their own will. After the death of his wife, Feng Cunqing, a poor peasant from Biquan brigade, was ill. To survive, he sold all the family possessions, but life was still very hard for the family. In desperation he sold his fourteen-year-old daughter to a peasant family in Shizi commune to be a child bride. [. . .] There are 200 families in Dayan big brigade, and 150 of them have been selling their clothes in order to survive. [. . .] In Jiangbei county's Yuelai commune, many villagers have been surviving on dead poultry and rats. Some animals had been dead for a while, and their flesh had started to decompose.

· Document 90 ·

The famine situation is very critical in the Wangu district of Dazu county, [Sichuan province,] by Comrade Chen Zhaobing, July 1962

Comments by Comrade Du Xinyuan, head of the Propaganda Department, Sichuan Provincial Party Committee:

Comrade Chen Zhaobing from our department went back to his home region, Dazu, after his wife had run away because of the food shortage. The following report by him shows that the famine in Dazu is very severe.

I arrived at Dazu Youtingpu railway station at 3 a.m. on July 12. At the station I saw 400 to 500 famine refugees. Some were sleeping and some were standing. The station was packed with crowds and looked like a busy market. A number of villagers were carrying clothes, chickens, baskets, sacks, and food with them. On inquiry, I learned that most of them were from Dazu, and they were going to Ziyang and Bishan because of a terrible famine at home. [. . .] On my way back to my home village, I saw similar situations in Longshui, Dabao, and Wangu. There were crowds of people on the road trying to escape the famine. In Wangu district, I spoke to a few villagers and cadres and learned about the famine there.

[. . .] Among the 465 production brigades in this district, a majority of villagers each managed to receive just a ration of less than 10 kg of food [. . .] and there was even a dearth of vegetables. [. . .] Stealing among villagers is very common, and all of the pumpkins had been picked before they were ripe. Because of the food shortages, many villagers have fled and gone elsewhere to look for a livelihood. That number is still increasing. Some of them have gone to Bishan county; others have gone as far away as Guizhou or Ziyang. Every day one can see 400 to 500 people fleeing from Wangu. In Aiguo big brigade's Number 3 production brigade, there used to be 120 villagers; 35 of them have fled the famine; that is 28.1 percent of the total local population. Someone in almost every family has run away. [. . .] Those who have gone to Bishan county, where some villages still have food, beg from one village to another in order to fill their stomachs. [. . .] Some sold their clothes and poultry to barter for food. [. . .] A number of them have also started to form a new family in Bishan. For instance, Li Suzhen from Wangu commune's Xiangtan big brigade, Li Shouguo from Aiguo big brigade, Han Zhaowen from Zhongxin commune's Shiniu big brigade, and Lan Huaming and Li Zeyuan from Gaofeng commune have gotten married in Bishan to people who offered them food or have found new parents. Others have been trying to make a living by doing odd jobs in Bishan.

Quite a few died on the road, and others have become very ill or have been robbed.

· Document 91 ·

Report on a number of villagers from Huishui county,
[Guizhou province,] selling their children, houses, and furniture out
of hardship, February 1962

According to our incomplete estimate, eighteen families from nine different big brigades in Huishui county have been forced to sell their children or to give their children away to other families. [...] Because of recent hardships, these families sold their children in exchange for food or cash. Jian Guoqing from Baijin commue's Changba big brigade has three children. He sold one to Yang Guangming in Jialie commune Shuiniu big brigade and the other one to a villager at Heping commune's Doupeng big brigade. In return they gave him 10 kg of corn, 10 kg of rice, 6 kg of millet, and 4 kg of dried soybeans. Several poor families also sold their daughters to other families as child brides. For instance, the daughter of Wang Xingzhi from Gangdu commune is only sixteen, and she was engaged to Chen Yongshan from the same village. They were not formally married because she has not reached marriageable age. But because of the recent hardships, her family sold her to the Chen family as a child bride in order to reduce their burden.

A number of villagers have sold houses and plots of land in exchange for food. According to an estimate, nearly thirty houses in the area have been sold, plus two plots of cultivated land and two construction sites. Tang Zonghe from Jialie commune, for instance, bartered 3,000 bricks for 30 kg of grain.

In Meitang commune's Lianhe production brigade, some villagers have also sold their agricultural tools for food. Because of hardship, some families were forced to sell their clothes and other possessions. According to our incomplete estimate, ninety-eight pieces of clothing, eighty-two cotton quilts, and seven mosquito nets have been sold in exchange for food. In Baijin district, some villagers from ethnic groups were forced to sell their silver jewelry. In total, eighty-eight pieces of jewelry were exchanged for food.

· Document 92 ·

Report on villagers from Lu, Longchang, Rongchang, and other counties who
went to Neijiang and Zizhong to make exchanges for food, and so on,
by Comrade Ming Lang from the General Office of the Sichuan Provincial
Party Committee, the Party Committee of the Sichuan Province Public
Security Bureau, and the Party Committee of Neijiang and Yibin regions,
February 14, 1962

Because of the famine, an increasing number of people have been
seen wandering around in various places. Their presence has become a
threat to the security of these places. There have been a number of murders on the road. Quite a few villagers were also injured while trying to
climb aboard a train. Cases of people selling their own children or
making unusual marriages have been happening regularly. There have
been at least sixty-three cases of marriage fraud in Neijiang's three
communes. Twenty-five women from Lu county and Rongchang went
to Number 2 big brigade in Longchang county's Qiguang commune
and got married to local villagers. All these women still have husbands
back at home. [...]

· Document 93 ·

Report on the problem of an increasing number of prostitutes and disorderly
girls in the city, by the Party Committee of the Sichuan Province Bureau
of Civil Affairs, August 1962

In July 1962, the Tianyashi Xijie homeless center in Chengdu has
turned into a special center for homeless females. So far, it has gathered together a total of 116 women and girls. The majority of them are
illegal prostitutes. According to our investigation, more than fourteen
of them are longtime prostitutes, and sixty-six of them entered prostitution in the past few years.[3] The center has also gathered in thirty-six
disorderly girls. [...]

Among the sixty-six new prostitutes, the oldest is twenty-five and
the youngest is only sixteen; fifty-five of them have also been involved
in stealing and shoplifting. In fact, many of them have close relation-
ships with a number of thieves in the city. They rely heavily on one another: many of the thieves supply these girls with money and food they
have stolen from elsewhere. In return, these girls provide them with sex
or become a "temporary wife." The nineteen-year-old Zeng Qingxiu
was a former high school student. In July 1961 she left school and

joined another three prostitutes wandering around all over the country. Since then, she has had sexual relations with six different thieves. She also followed a thief, Li Zhijun, to Xi'an, Zhengzhou, Beijing, and Tianjin, where they engaged in various criminal activities. On their journey, Li managed to steal nearly 1,000 yuan in cash and coupons for more than 20 kg of rice. [. . .] The sixteen-year-old Wang Fengzhen became a streetwalker in September 1961. She has had sexual relations with a number of thieves and sharpies. Xiang Deyuan was one of them, and together they went to Xi'an, where they committed a number of crimes. Once they stole 360 yuan in cash. [. . .] The seventeen-year-old Dou Xiurong has been stealing since 1958. Although she was caught and sent to factories and the countryside to do hard labor, in 1961 she managed to escape, and since then, she has been a streetwalker. On a number of occasions, she joined some thieves and other female prostitutes on trips to Xi'an to steal things. After she was caught and sent back to Chengdu, she continued stealing. She has also been selling sex on the street. [. . .]

Most of these newly engaged prostitutes are still fairly young, and some of them were still Young Pioneers a couple of years ago. But now their mouths are full of foul words. [. . .] They have committed a number of crimes and have become a serious threat to society. Quite a few also suffer from poor health, and some of them have been infected with syphilis.

The so-called disorderly girls have been leading lives similar to the prostitutes'. The only difference is their age. There are thirty-six of them. [. . .] The oldest is fifteen, and the youngest is only eleven. Four of them are former apprentices, and eighteen are former school students. [. . .] Six have been involved in robbery and theft, and thirty of them have sold sex.

While these young girls have been leading lives similar to those of the prostitutes mentioned before, the range of their criminal activities is wider and more complex. The fourteen-year-old Wang Ruifang [. . .] started stealing in 1959. Between July and August 1960 she boarded running trains several times and traveled to Beijing. There she committed a number of crimes and was caught. She was sent to Beijing Municipal Juvenile Correction Center for a year. In September, after she was released and sent back to Chengdu, she started picking pockets again. [. . .] Meanwhile, she had sex with three different men. Since she was sent to the homeless center, she has been found stealing coupons and fountain pens from the center staff. The thirteen-year-old Zhu Jiuju has been stealing since she was eight. Initially she stole things at home, and this led to pilfering from her neighbors. Later she went on the street. She would go to the city center every day to pick pockets. According to her, on some good days she has managed to steal more than 500 yuan in cash and coupons for more than 10 kg of rice. In 1959 she joined the thief Gao Xinlin and went to Xi'an to steal. Meanwhile she has also had sexual relations with six different thieves, and each time she charged them 4 to 6 yuan. [...]

Most of these girls claim that the cause for their ruin is their desire for food. Take Duan Yongxiu, for example. She was a former hairdresser. Her monthly salary was just over 30 yuan. But according to her, that was not enough to feed herself. She had to borrow money to buy sweet potatoes and eggs. After a while she could not repay the money she had borrowed, so she started to sell her clothes and clothes from other family members. In the end she became a streetwalker, and started to sell sex. [...] Zhou Huoyun was a former apprentice at the Chengdu steel factory. In 1960, she lost her job. There were six of them at home, and they relied entirely on her father's earnings. He is a barber, and his monthly salary is just over 30 yuan. Zhou's mother was pregnant at the time, and the three sisters were still very young. Since Zhou's father's salary could not support the whole family, Zhou was forced to sell blood on twelve different occasions. After she met Yue Junhui, Yue persuaded her to go to Xi'an with him, where she met a number of thieves. Eventually she started to sell sex. [...]

Currently there are still quite a few disorderly girls, prostitutes, and pickpockets out there threatening the security of the city. On the eve of the 14th [August 14, 1962], we took one prostitute to the railway station to see whether she could spot any other prostitutes. Near the platform she saw at least forty or fifty of them. [...]

· Document 94 ·

Report on the reduction in the labor force in Nanbu county's Jianxing commune and the plan to send people back in order to support agricultural production, by the Nanchong Region Party Committee, Sichuan province, April 2–October 8, 1960

There have been several instances in which instructions came from above requesting each town and county in the Nanchong region to count the number of laborers from the countryside and to send them back to their villages to help with the agricultural work. However, the problem persists in Nanbu county's Jianxing township. Why? According to a number of reports we received, the main problem is the local cadres. A majority of the laborers working in towns are in fact some local cadres' parents, wives or husbands, brothers or sisters, relatives or friends. A number of cadres have been using their power to bring their families and relatives from the countryside into the towns, so they can enjoy a more comfortable and privileged life. These people were given jobs at government offices, factories, companies, and schools. They no longer have to do any agricultural work. Take the deputy head of Sanguan commune, Huang Dabing, for example. Last June, after selling his house in the countryside, Huang moved his entire family to the town of Jianxing. The seven of them have been living on other people's property without paying any rent. He also managed to find a job for his wife, his sister, and his niece at the weaving factory and the embroidery factory, where they are paid on a monthly basis and have a stable income. As for his fifty-year-old mother, his two younger brothers, and his child, they were sent to the commune nursery and school, where they can eat for free.

The cook at the Jianxing administrative district office has been especially attentive to the deputy Party secretary of the district, Sun Shouxian. As a favor, last year Sun arranged for the cook's brother-in-law to be transferred from the countryside to work at a canteen in town. This year, after the government announced that all the rural laborers who had left the countryside previously should be sent back to support local agricultural production, the district Party Committee made an attempt to send a number of cooks who had originally come from the countryside back to their home villages. But Sun Shouxian used his position to secure the cook another position so he could continue to stay in town.[...]

The mother-in-law of the deputy head of Jianxing district, Yang Haimin, wanted to move to the northeast of China to join one of her daughters, but she could not get a permit for migration from the Public Security Bureau of Dingshui district. Yang not only bribed Xu Tianchen, a cadre at the bureau, with meat and alcohol; he also promised Pu Guangzhi, another cadre from the same Public Security Bureau, to relocate Pu's family to Jianxing. Since Yang managed to get Pu's family settled in Jianxing, Pu helped Yang's mother-in-law to obtain her permit to migrate.

· Document 95 ·

Investigative report on the case of Xiao Liangfu, who was beaten to death after being caught stealing peas, by Longxing commune, Chishui county, Guizhou province, March 13, 1961

Forty-three-year-old Xiao Liangfu is an illiterate poor peasant. [...] Beginning in January 1961, Xiao suffered edema. He became very thin and was too weak to work. On April 15 he stole rice from his pregnant wife—she had saved it for the time of her delivery. They fought fiercely. As a result, Xiao left home. [...] He continued to steal, and on four occasions he has stolen peas from the Xinlian production brigade. [...] This has caused conflict among the villagers in the Xinlian brigade. Zhong Shengping and Lei Qijia, as well as other villagers, suspected each other, and they blamed one another for stealing the peas. In the end they decided to form a night-watch group. After midnight on May 5, [...] Lei saw someone in the field stealing peas. So he quietly walked toward the person and beat that person's head with the stick in his hand. Xiao Liangfu fought back with the sickle in his hand. It hit Lei's forehead. Lei was badly injured, and the blood started to stream down his face. The two got into a bad fight. Lei pushed Xiao down a slope of 2 meters. Hearing Lei scream, Zhong and three other villagers ran to see what was going on. [...] When Lei saw the blood running down his face and all over his clothes, he became very angry, so he beat Xiao's lower back really hard with the stick. Zhong also joined in, and [they] beat Xiao up. [....] Because of his poor health and his heavy injuries, plus starvation and being cold, Xiao died around 5 a.m. the same day.

· Document 96 ·

Investigative report on cannibalism in Xinhua brigade, by the Chishui County Supervision Commission, [Guizhou province,] May 31, 1961

To the County Party Committee and the Zunyi Region Supervision Commission:

Recently we received a report suggesting that on May 11 the poor peasant woman Wang Zhizhen from Xinhua big brigade's Number 3 production brigade consumed the heart and liver of her six-year-old daughter, Luo Sanniü, after her daughter had died. After the incident, Longxing commune sent some public security personnel to the brigade to investigate the matter. [...] Since last year, more and more people have become ill in Xinhua brigade. [. . .] The collective canteen had no food left, and it was forced to close down in April. [. . .]

Wang Zhizhen has also been known for her ill treatment of her two daughters. She regularly beat them up and deprived them of food. Often she cooked for herself at night after her daughters had gone to sleep. [. . .] On May 11 [. . .] around lunchtime, Wang's mother, Zhang Yingzhi, heard the sound of Wang chopping. The door to Wang's house was locked. Zhang peeped through the door and saw Wang chopping a human body. Zhang informed Luo Jixun and Luo Anrong. Hearing what had happened, Luo Anrong, together with Lu Mingde, broke down the door and went in. They caught Wang eating her daughter's liver and heart. [. . .]

Wang married Luo Ancai in 1953, and in 1955 she gave birth to their daughter Luo Sanniü. According to Wang's own confession, she has been stealing food regularly ever since she was marrried. In 1960 she stole corn from the brigade four times. Once she also stole 1.5 kg of rice from her own mother, as well as one chicken and four rabbits from her neighbor. She is also known to like to consume dead animals, such as cows, horses, snakes, and frogs. [. . .] This year in January, she was asked by the brigade to feed the ox. She did not take care of the animal, and it fell down a slope. While the ox was still alive, Wang cut off two pieces of flesh from the badly injured animal and consumed it. Wang also regularly fought with her husband and beat up her children. After Luo was admitted into the edema clinic, Wang ate up all his rations. [. . .] She never ate from the same pot as her daughters. For two days before Luo Sanniü's death, the girl did not have anything to eat at all. [. . .]

On May 11, Wang opened up the dead body of her own daughter. [. . .] Why did she do that? This has something to do with her cruel character and her habit of consuming dead animals. She would eat anything she could get hold of. [. . .] However, the local cadres are also implicated in Wang's daughter's death. Before the death of Luo Sanniü, Wang went to the brigade cadre, Luo Yonglian, to ask for food. Luo [Yonglian] refused. Luo's refusal undoubtedly contributed to Luo Sanniü's death.

· Document 97 ·

The famine situation in Qihe county's two production brigades,
[Shandong province,] 1962

Qihe county was badly hit by the famine. [...] Dongyan production brigade has 165 families, and 98.8 percent of them have suffered badly because of the famine—that is, 163 families. Since 1960 villagers have sold 68 quilts, 608 pieces of clothing, 845 pieces of furniture, 110 agricultural tools, 37 pigs, 142 goats, 1,604 pieces of timber, 107 windows and doors, 15 vehicles, and 32,000 bricks in order to survive the famine.

Besides selling goods, some strange things have occurred. [...] Many family members fought fiercely with each other for food. For instance, there were quite a few fistfights at the homes of Yan Jingchang and Fang Xicai. In the end, both families were forced to split up. Quite a few previously very loving and harmonious families have also been fighting for food. Divorce has become common here.

· Document 98 ·

Working report by the Neijiang branch of the Agricultural and Grain
Production Investigation Team of the General Office of the Sichuan
Provincial Party Committee, March 15–December 16, 1960

In [Jianyang county's] Xingfu administrative district, the child of Zeng Wenbing, head of Number 3 brigade, stole and ate a few broad beans from the big brigade. He was caught by some cadres at the big brigade. They fined Zeng 8 yuan. Zeng did not have the money to pay. In outrage, he chopped off his child's thumb.

CHAPTER EIGHT

Letters of Complaint (1957–1962)

A S people in China struggled to survive catastrophic shortages, more and more became disillusioned and disgruntled by collectivization and the corruption that had infected the cadres. Since authorities consistently obstructed access to the truth about the famine, rumors spread. Many were about death and starvation, and quite a few were apocalyptic in scope. Rumor had become a tool for many peasants to voice their anger, to denounce cadres, and to seek redress. Others took up the tradition of complaint by writing letters and petitions to the Party.

In a one-party authoritarian state where public debate or protest is not permitted, speaking out can lead to serious trouble, however. Under Mao, the Communist Party tried to silence voices of opposition by launching endless political campaigns. Among them were the Anti-Rightist Campaign and the rural Socialist Education Campaign, both of 1957.

The last quarter of 1956 and the first half of 1957 were rather troublesome months for the ruling powers in China. After the short-lived Hungarian Revolution in the autumn of 1956, Mao had decided to promote the Hundred Flowers Campaign in China. He wanted to encourage the public to criticize the bureaucracy in order to push the government to do better: "Correct things develop from struggle with incorrect things," he said, and "every new thing [. . .] develops from struggle with old objects, old things."[1] This sentiment was expressed in the increasing number of public protests taking place in various parts of the country. Around the end of 1956 more than 10,000 factory workers and 10,000 students went on strike. A huge number of people throughout China were showing their dissatisfaction with the low wages and poor working conditions in state factories and work units, as well as with many undelivered promises (document 99). Public petitions and letters of complaint reached an unprecedented number (document 100). According to an estimate by the Central Committee of the Chinese Communist Party, between January and June 1957 more than 2,700 villagers from fourteen different provinces journeyed to the capital, Beijing, to hand in their petitions. And in the month of July, in a period of twenty days, 334 people turned up outside the Central Rural Affairs Commission to complain about falling standards of living, injustice in the countryside, and the destruction caused by the first wave of collectivization (document 101). A few even lined up outside the central headquarters of the Communist Party and the State Council in Zhongnanhai asking to see Mao (document 102). Zhongnanhai, a closed compound in central Beijing near the Forbidden City, is the location of many government offices.

It seemed that the situation might be getting out of control. Had Chairman Mao made a mistake? In July 1957, Mao and the Party launched a counterattack to "criticize rightist opportunist ideas within the Party, the departmentalism of certain cadres, and the capitalist and individualist ideas of so-called well-to-do middle peasants and to strike at the counterrevolutionary activities of landlords and rich peasants." The main target of the criticism was the "vacillating well-to-do middle peasants whose capitalist ideas should be struggled against by arguing things out."[2] There was, in fact, no "arguing things out." In the countryside, anyone opposed to collectivization or not willing to follow orders given by the cadres was publicly denounced, physically tortured, or deprived of food. In cities and towns, those who spoke out to criticize the Party were purged as "rightists" and sent to labor camps to be reeducated. According to a later government estimate, 552,877 people were labeled "rightists."[3]

Following these two campaigns Mao pushed forward the Great Leap as well as radical collectivization in the countryside. By the end of 1958, a massive 99 percent of China's peasant population had joined the people's communes.

Yet despite the efforts of local cadres and the Bureau of Public Security to silence the public, ordinary people continued to send letters of complaint to the authorities (documents 103–110). Since speaking out in public was not advisable, rumors circulated, as did mockery full of black humor. Posters devised by the government as propaganda tools became weapons against collectivization and local cadres (documents 111–119). Although very few revolts broke out in the countryside, a number of individuals used words as their weapons. They voiced their discontent, questioned the socialist system, and exposed corruption at the local level.

· Document 99 ·

Reports and documents relating to a number of recent strikes and public disturbances, by the Central Committee of the Chinese Communist Party and the Hunan Provincial Party Committee, January–August 1957

In April 1957 the Binxian region had to handle a case involving over 700 temporary workers from the geological prospecting team. Among these workers, 400 were ex-soldiers, urban residents, or temporary workers transferred to the team from other mines and factories. Most of them had no other means of livelihood. When they heard they were going to be made redundant, they crowded into the team office and demanded that their jobs be made permanent. They shouted slogans such as "Unite together and we will not leave." Some even struck tables and chairs and shouted abuse. They also smashed office windows. In the following two days, all the workers went on strike, and they sent representatives to appeal to the Binxian Region Party Committee. [...]

Since the end of 1956 there have been a rising number of strikes among workers and students. Over 10,000 workers and 10,000 students have taken part in various strikes throughout the country. Public protests and petitions are also on the increase. [...] According to our estimate, in 1956 there were at least twenty-nine public strikes and fifty-seven petitions. Cadres from the Xi'an Workers Union came to Beijing and reported orally that there had been more than forty strikes and petitions in Xi'an alone. In Shanghai, fifty-seven similar incidents took place in some joint state-private enterprises, and ten of them were public strikes. Some strikes involved over a thousand people, and a majority of these people were workers at various loading bays or docks, newly employed workers (quite a few were middle school students), workers being transferred from coastal regions to sustain newly constructed cities, construction workers, and forestry workers. These types of incidents have been happening throughout the country from northeast to northwest, east, central south, and southwest. [...] Some workers even claim that "we have no option but to follow the example of Hungary." While such incidents are becoming more frequent, the area affected is also expanding, and the problem is becoming more serious. We have noted some examples below. [...]

When officials from Inner Mongolia went to Shanghai to recruit workers, they promised to supply tractors, motorcycles, brand-new dormitories with double glazing, and heating. But the reality was nothing like that. Life in Inner Mongolian factories was very harsh, causing many workers from Shanghai to complain and to escape. [...] After being transferred to Yunnan, the salaries of some workers from Anhui were reduced by 17 yuan per month. A number of workers suffering health problems could not carry out the heavy duties assigned to them. When they asked to be transferred back to their original work units in Anhui, the officials ignored their requests. They were left with no choice but to make formal appeals. [...]

In the northeast, the loading co-op in Andong city, [Liaoning province,] reduced its charges, which led to a considerable reduction in workers' income. As a result, 80 percent of workers and their families have to survive on cornmeal mixed with tofu dregs and wild vegetables. Most workers were forced to borrow money from their relatives to stay alive.[...] Liu Guide, a worker, has five children; the oldest one is only eight. His monthly income varied from 32 yuan to 12 yuan. The family could not afford to buy bread for the children, so they had to sell the only quilt they had. There were also four workers who were driven to divorce because of hardship. [...]

In Jiangxi, Zhejiang, Beijing, and Sichuan, more than 10,000 students went on strike because of the poor living conditions, lack of facilities, and poor hygiene in their schools or universities. [...] In 1956, owing to a number of job cuts in the Ministry of Geology and Mine Resources, all the graduates from the Hebei Province Geological Cadres College were deprived of the prospect of a job. On January 9, 1957, they held a public protest, shouting, "Down with fascism" and "We don't want the bloodshed in Hungary recurring here." They looked very fierce and blocked the traffic in the city. They also stopped the trains and wanted to go to Beijing to petition. As a result, train service stopped for more than twelve hours. [...]

In [Hunan province's] Zixing mine, many workers could not sustain the heavy, intense workload. A number of them were exhausted; some even started to spit blood. This has caused much discontent among workers. [...] A number of them refused to go down into the mine and started a number of disturbances. [...]

· Document 100 ·

Report of the conference on how to deal with letters of complaint, by the General Office of the Sichuan Provincial Party Committee and various municipal and regional Party Committees, 1957

From the end of 1956 through the first half of 1957, Wenjiang region has received 9,186 letters of complaint from ordinary people. For the year 1956, various government offices in Wenjiang region's fourteen different counties received 10,000 letters of complaint. [. . .]

Mianyang region has also been receiving more than 10,000 letters of complaint each year. According to an incomplete estimate from seven counties, there were 6,513 letters of complaint in the first half of 1957. [. . .] For the entire region, the number of letters has reached over 15,000, which, in comparison, is two to three times greater than the number the previous year. [. . .] Of these, 24 percent were letters exposing injustice or corruption, 10 percent were letters critical of the government or letters of recommendations for change, and 13 percent were petitions. [. . .]

Since Chairman Mao Zedong's speech "On the Correct Handling of Contradictions among the People," the number of letters of complaint in the Suining region has increased significantly. [. . .] The number of letters to the local Public Security offices has increased by 51 percent in 1957 over the year before. [. . .] Fifty percent of the letters were written to expose local problems [. . .]; 6 percent were asking for a job or a place to live or education or a solution to livelihood issues. There were also four letters abusing local cadres.

· Document 101 ·

The concerns of the Central Rural Affairs Commission [in Beijing] over the number of complaints and petitions from ordinary people, as well as some suggestions on how to handle such matters in the future, 1957

Since January this year, the number of petitioners to this commission has increased significantly. In the first half of the year, we received 2,700 visits. Each month at least 400 to 500 people turn up at the commission to petition or complain. That is three to four times more than turned up last winter. [. . .] According to our estimate, 334 people turned up outside the commission between July 5 and July 20, an average of 20 petitioners per day. Some days the number even went up to as high as 40 to 50 petitioners. Although we have put in much effort to try to resolve various cases, we are, however, unable to cope with the increasing demand. We end up having to accommodate those people whose cases were not resolved. Every day at least 30 to 50 petitioners stay the night here. Sometimes the number even goes up to 70 or 80.

These people are from fourteen different provinces, including Jiangsu, Zhejiang, Shanxi, Henan, Shandong, Hebei, Shaanxi, Liaoning, Jilin, and Heilongjiang. [...] Their main complaints concern problems caused by agricultural collectivization. Since March this year, about 50 to 80 percent of appeals were to do with villagers wanting to leave the collective, their reason being that since collectivization, their income has decreased considerably and their living standard has fallen sharply. A number of them are facing serious livelihood problems. About 70 to 80 percent of the petitioners are upper-middle peasants. They are the most eager to leave the collective. There are quite a few families wanting to leave the collective because they cannot cope with the hard work. A number of small-business owners and handicraft workers are also among them. The last group consists of those who are childless and infirm. The collective is supposed to guarantee them free food, housing, clothing, medical care, and burial expenses, but this has not happened. [...]

· Document 102 ·

Documents of the General Office of the Sichuan Provincial Party Committee on letters of complaint and petitions by ordinary people, May 28–July 15, 1957

In recent months, an increasing number of petitioners have come to Beijing. Every day they gather outside the gate into Zhongnanhai asking to see government officials. Some come in quite big groups, while others act odiously. For instance, a few days ago a woman marched outside the State Council with her four children. She was wearing a sign that said "Hungry." Similar incidents also happened earlier. Once, in broad daylight, a man holding a lighted lantern marched all the way to Xinhua Gate[4] asking to see Chairman Mao. What he was trying to imply was that the entire country was covered in darkness, and he needed the lantern to be able to see. Incidents like this put a lot of pressure on us and are very upsetting. These people are being deliberately provocative. [...] There have been at least several hundred incidents like this happening in Beijing.

· Document 103 ·

Report on a number of letters from the public being unlawfully opened
and withheld, as well as cases of individuals being persecuted for
writing letters, by the Guizhou Province Bureau of Public
Security, 1961

The Provincial Party Committee:

Following the recent instruction from the Provincial Party Committee and the Ministry of Public Security [in Beijing], we have made some
preliminary investigations into the matter of letters from the public being unlawfully opened and withheld and anonymous letters being mis-
handled by some local Public Security offices.

The problem of local Public Security offices and post offices open-
ing and withholding letters from individuals has become widespread.
According to our investigation, the Zunyi city Public Security Bureau
issued an instruction that all letters addressed to the Central Committee of the Chinese Communist Party and the Provincial Party Committee must be checked by the local Public Security Bureau first
before they could be sent on. Last year, they withheld thirteen letters
addressed to Chairman Mao and the Central Committee of the Chinese Communist Party. In Sinan, under the instruction of the former
county Party secretary You Panjing, the local Public Security Bureau
opened and withheld more than 100 letters. In Meitan county, the local Public Security Bureau instructed the post office to check any letter
addressed to government offices or officials and to hand any anonymous letters over to the Public Security Bureau for investigation. [. . .]
Anyone who wrote an anonymous letter was labeled as being "anti-
Party," "anti-socialist," or "counterrevolutionary" and was purged,
arrested, or sent to do hard labor. For instance, Huang Zhi, an official
in Zunyi city Department of Propaganda, wrote an anonymous letter
to Chairman Mao in the winter of 1959 concerning the "Wind of Exaggeration" and mass starvation. The letter was withheld by the Zunyi
Public Security Bureau and handed over to the city Party Committee.
Huang was denounced as a "rightist," and publicly humiliated for
more than half a month. In the end he was sent to a brick factory to do
hard labor. In Zhijin county, Du Shida, a villager from Najia commune,
wrote to Chairman Mao reporting corruption and fraud among local
cadres, but the letter was passed on to the commune by the post office.
The commune Party secretary sent Public Security officers to arrest
Du. Du was labeled "dangerous" and was detained at the local Public
Security Bureau for more than two months. [. . .]

Between June and July 1959, Liang Huachang, a retired soldier from Suiyang county, wrote two separate letters to Chairman Mao and President Liu Shaoqi exposing the widespread corruption and bullying found among local cadres. The letter was handed to the commune by the county Party Committee, and Liang was publicly denounced. Under pressure, Liang was forced to flee. In November he was caught by the police and sent to a labor camp for seven years. [. . .]

· Document 104 ·

Report on various types of cadres in Leshan county's Jinshan commune, by the Leshan branch of the Rectification Campaign Working Group of the Sichuan Provincial Party Committee, 1961

In 1959 the Party secretary of Xingguang brigade, Song Youyu—twenty-six years old—forced villagers to hand over their grain ration so he could get a reward for surpassing the production target. He was awarded a thermos bottle by the Wutongqiao district. But Song was not satisfied. He also handed over all the grain rations from other brigades, causing the collective canteen to be completely out of food. Villagers were forced to survive on grass and bark. Quite a few died as a result. Meanwhile, Song boasted about the high standard of living in his brigade. A villager, Du Xingmin, wrote a letter to the higher authorities to expose the local reality. At the end of the letter, Du wrote "Please save our lives" three times. For fear of trouble, Du did not sign his real name. This letter was handed over to Jinshan Commune Party Committee for further investigation. After reading the letter, the Party secretary, Li Tianfu, became enraged. He passed the letter to Song and asked him to find the author. After a frantic search and careful study of the handwriting, Du was unmasked. Song then forged evidence and accused Du of deliberately trying to sabotage the people's commune. The investigation team from the local Public Security Bureau believed Song's accusations and ordered Du arrested. Prior to the arrest Song sent a group of local roughnecks to beat Du up. Du had both his eyes gouged out. Since Song's misconduct was covered up, 128 villagers had died of starvation by April 1960. Whenever villagers see Song Youyu's thermos bottle, they begin to weep.

· Document 105 ·

Report on the use of the local post office by the Shizhu County Party
Committee and Public Security Bureau to withhold letters of complaint
from ordinary people, by Wang Deming and Zhang Junying of the Working
Group of the Sichuan Provincial Party Committee, May 2, 1961

From 1959 to January 1961, thirty-three letters of complaint by local
people were withheld by Shizhu county. [...] The former county Party
secretary Xu Zhengmin and his colleagues Xi Hongyuan and Kang
Maogui made every effort to cover up their errors and crimes, including
beating a number of people to death during the Anti–Right Deviation
Campaign. [...]

Under their pressure, anyone in the commune, brigade, or post office
could open and withhold letters from individual people. [...] According to our investigation, in a number of local post offices, no letters
were allowed to be sent out without being checked. Despite their effort
to try to block any information from being released, some villagers still
walked hundreds of kilometers to neighboring Fengdu county, Zhong
county, Wan county, and Lichuan county to send off letters of complaint.

· Document 106 ·

Memorandum from Chairman Mao and the Central Committee of the Chinese
Communist Party to the Xinyang Region Party Committee, Henan province,
after reading the report on the Rectification Campaign and famine relief
work in Xinyang, December 31, 1960

In Tongxin brigade, in Luoshan county's Zhugan commune, a poor
peasant girl, Xiang Xianzhi, wrote a letter of complaint to Chairman
Mao. But instead of sending the letter out, she stitched the letter inside
her jacket, [where it stayed] for over a year. Later she handed the letter
over to the government investigation team, asking them to redress the
wrongs done to her father and sister; they had died as a result of an
injustice committed by local cadres.

· Document 107 ·

Letter to the Fuyang Region Party Committee, by Liu Yuqing of Guodamiao township, Taihe county, [Anhui province,] 1958

To those bureaucrats at the regional Party Committee:

All day long you sit high on your chairs inside your offices. Do you have any idea what has been going on in the countryside? [...] Take local water conservation work, for example. The cadres forced families from every village to leave in order to build [irrigation canals and reservoirs.] [...] Even worse, they destroyed crops in order to build ponds. Their actions have caused a lot of public anger and discontent among ordinary people. [...] We were told the government would compensate us 0.1 yuan per every cubic meter of earth to build the local dike. However, the local cadres decided to deduct one-third of the money and use it to repair the tunnel. This is purely exploitive. It is unlawful, and it is contrary to Party policy.

Oh, you bureaucrats, there are many examples like this, and I don't even know where to start. I wish you'd step down from your official chairs and come to the countryside to see [the situation] with your own eyes. Three people from our collective have recently been hounded to death. Why don't you do something about it? Come down to wipe away the scourge for us and to emancipate us from oppression.

From Liu Yuqing, a retired soldier[5]

· Document 108 ·

Regarding a number of letters of complaint in the first half of February stating that there are food shortages in the countryside, by the Shandong Provincial Party Committee, August 10, 1959

Between February 1 and February 15 we received 266 letters of complaint passed down by the Central Committee of the Chinese Communist Party or sent directly to the Provincial Party Committee. All the letters are concerned with food crises in the countryside. Most of these letters are dated January; only a few are dated February. In regard to the content, most of them complained that a number of collective canteens have run out of food completely and that there is widespread fear in the countryside. Many villagers have fled or have become ill. Agricultural production has almost come to a halt. [...]

It seems that the crisis in Jinxiang county is the most critical. Since the Chinese New Year, there have been at least nine letters of complaint describing the food crisis there. [. . .] For instance, Wang Weizhen, a student at Shandong Finance and Economics College, as well Sun Dehua and five other soldiers from the People's Liberation Army No. 0408 force in Weihai, went back to Dongfanghong people's commune during their holiday break. They wrote letters stating that each villager could get only 200 to 250 grams of food ration per day. A similar situation is depicted in a letter from Zhao Chuanran and four other people in Guting commune and in an anonymous letter. These letters reveal the lack of food or even the absence of food in the countryside and that people are constantly worried about their livelihoods. Many villagers ended up having to fill their stomachs with wheat stubble. [. . .] On the first day of the [Chinese] New Year, many villagers from Zhou Yingli village went to the fields to look for rotten sweet potatoes and carrots to fill their stomachs. In some villages around Yucheng and Guting, [. . .] a huge number of people have fled to other counties to beg for food. In Damin village, owing to a lack of money, six people died of illness within eight days without any treatment. In Xulou village, six people died of starvation within ten days. In Huazhuang and Liuzhuang quite a few villagers have also died of starvation. [. . .]

Wang Xunyi and another three Party and Youth League members from Yucheng commune's Xieji village wrote that in their village each villager could manage to eat just 100 to 150 grams of rice. Most villagers are emaciated, and their faces look pale. Quite a few have tried to commit suicide.

An anonymous letter from Guancheng commune describes the hardship that villagers are facing. Each person manages to get just 100 to 150 grams of rice or 250 grams of carrots—as the letter calls it, food for "ghosts." [. . .] It says that many villagers have been complaining and wanting to go to Beijing to inform Chairman Mao about the hardship people are facing. They want Chairman Mao and the Party to seek revenge for them. [. . .]

· Document 109 ·

Letter to Comrade Zheng Ying from Liu Zhugui at the Department of Civil Affairs, Lushan county, [Sichuan province,] July 20, 1962

Comrade Zheng Ying:[6]

I am a cadre in charge of civil affairs. In the past few years, Lushan county has been badly hit by natural disasters. In addition, with the damage caused by the "Wind of Communism," and so on, local peasants have lost their enthusiasm for agricultural production. The local population has dropped considerably, and agricultural production has plummeted. The standard of living has also fallen sharply compared to the standard in 1957. Many ordinary people ask: "Since the Chairman loves us peasants, we wonder whether he knows about the hardships we have to endure?" [...] The local population was 74,483 in the 1956 census. This year it has dropped to 57,314. The number of deaths in the past few years, excluding the deaths of a few who moved away, was over 14,000. Most people died of edema. [...] Likewise, the number of orphans has increased. There are more than 900 orphans in Lushan county. Although the county Party Committee and the People's Committee have tried to solve the current crisis, the general standard of living is still far lower than it was in 1957 because of the enormous damage. [...] We still see people fighting over bread in the marketplace.

There are also many thieves. In extremely poor communes, many villagers continue to leave. Fortunately Secretary Liao [Zhigao] visited our county a few months ago and spoke to some of the villagers. After he learned of the hardships that people in Lushan had been suffering, he gave orders to send us some food relief. His visit was a great encouragement to people here. [...] To help improve the life of the people in Lushan and to help rebuild local agriculture, I would like to ask the provincial government to send us food, cash, and nonessential food items. [...] A number of damaged houses also need urgent repair. [...] Furthermore, we also need some health workers to come here to help treat the huge number of sick people in our county.

These are just some of my personal ideas. Since you were elected by the people in Lushan county to represent us at the People's Congress, I would ask you to use your discretion to share some of my points at various Party conferences. I would be most grateful if Secretary Liao and other Party secretaries on the provincial Party Committee would study the local situation in Lushan and find a suitable strategy to help us recover.

Yours sincerely,

Liu Zhugui, Lushan County Department of Civil Affairs

· Document 110 ·

"Our View of China's Agriculture," a letter by Niu Weixin and Cai Fumin
[of Nanjing], February 1962

A note from the Fuling branch of the Working Group of the Sichuan
Provincial Party Committee, February 19, 1962

To the Provincial Party Committee:

Recently the Fuling County Party Committee received a counterrevolutionary letter from Nanjing. It is a printed letter, and it is quite clear that the authors of this letter are trying to incite trouble. The Fuling County Party Committee made two copies of the letter and sent one to us and one to the Fuling Region Party Committee. We fear that this letter might have been distributed to various other places. Please pay attention to it. The Fuling Region Party Committee has told various counties to destroy the letter if they happen to receive one. We have made a copy of it for your reference.

"The Letter"

The two of us wish to express some concerns about China's agriculture. We are both very young and naive. Our information comes from what we have witnessed in Jiangsu and Anhui since 1958 as well as what we have heard from a number of villagers in those regions. What we write may not be correct, but our desire is to help our country to eliminate poverty, since we love our country and people dearly. We kept this letter for two years, but in the end we decided to send it out to you. Our aim is for you to read this letter first and to decide whether what we wrote was correct or not. If you could also present some of our concerns about China's agriculture to the government, it would undoubtedly help the Party to make a better policy.

1. Agricultural collectivization and the people's communes are a failure. The current reality is proof.

At the moment the majority of the people in China are living in poverty. To improve the material and cultural life of the people is one of the basic policies of the Communist Party. It is also a way to determine whether the Party's work has been successful or not. Since the implementation of agricultural collectivization, the people's standard of living in the countryside, as well as in the cities, has fallen. Particularly after the people's commune became the new form of economic and political organization in rural China, China's peasant population sank into extreme poverty. In recent years, thousands and thousands of rural villagers have died of starvation. In some areas there have been horrific incidents of humans eating human flesh. Currently 600 million Chinese are suffering from starvation. In many places people are facing food shortages, fuel shortages, and clothing shortages. Malnutrition and poor health are widespread and becoming worse. The birthrate in the countryside has fallen sharply, and the death rate is on the rise.

The quality of the labor force is fundamental to agricultural development. But in our country we are currently facing a severe shortage of labor since a huge number of peasants have died during the famine, and in some areas the death rate has reached 50 percent. In the past few years, women have taken up the role of chief laborers in the countryside. While many of them lack experience in agricultural production, they are also suffering ill health, for they are extremely undernourished. Owing to the poor quality of their diet and the heavy workload, the birthrate in the rural countryside has almost hit rock bottom. Between 1958 and 1960, hardly any babies were born in the countryside, and most children have been suffering from malnutrition and are in very poor health. This will mean that in the foreseeable future our country will continue to suffer serious shortages of agricultural labor.

Furthermore, the problem of alkalization and nitrification is very prevalent, and the majority of agricultural fields have been severely damaged. [. . .] Take rural Jiangsu, for example. No matter where you turn, all you see is the surface of the earth covered in salt.

Pig excrement used to be a major source of agricultural fertilizer. As a consequence of the radical collectivization in 1958, however, there are hardly any pigs left in the country. [. . .] In most rural villages today, peasants have to use old earth and grass to make fertilizer. The quality is very poor [compared to pre-collectivization fertilizer]. Almost half of the farm animals have died or been killed deliberately. Those still alive are poorly fed and are overworked. They are all suffering from poor health. Furthermore, most agricultural tools have been severely damaged. Shortage of farming tools is a big problem in many places.

2. Agricultural output has also plummeted. [. . .] Most peasants tell us that the current average grain output each year is only half of what it was before collectivization.

So, what has triggered the failure? We consider that the major reason for the failure is human action. The aim of collectivization was to develop agricultural production, to increase agricultural output, and to improve the living standard of the people. But the result is the opposite. [. . .] The reality shows that collectivization and the people's communes are a total failure. [. . .]

We suggest the Central Committee of the Chinese Communist Party inform other Communist countries [about the results] and warn them not to make the same mistake.

"Appendix: An Appeal"

Dear comrades:

Our country is one of the biggest countries in the world. Its progress and failure will not only affect the Chinese race but will also have a huge impact on the global Communist movement. [. . .] But let's look at the current reality in our country:

All normal human beings, peasants in particular, are extremely concerned about the current crisis in our country. [. . .]

Dear comrades, we are very worried about the future of our country if this crisis continues. Out of our sacred responsibility for our country and the Chinese people and as members of the Communist Youth League, we would like to make the following appeal to veteran revolutionaries. You are all heroes of our country, since you have sweated and shed blood for the birth of the New China; you should cherish the fruits you have fought for with your life more than anyone. Also, since you have seen the current reality, you understand the problem better than anyone else. We trust you completely, and we would like to ask you:

- To go to the countryside as ordinary members of society and listen to what average peasants have to say. This will help you to profit from all the mistakes our country has made in the past twelve years and to make an economic policy that will benefit the majority of the people in the country.
- To suggest to the Central Committee of the Chinese Communist Party that land be released to individual farmers and that an agricultural output quota be fixed for each household.
- To throw away dogma and proceed according to the current reality and condition of our country.

Dear comrades, please take action now! Our country and people are waiting in great anticipation! We appeal to you once more to save our country, which is on the verge of extermination.

From Niu Weixin and Cai Fumin, February 1962

· Document 111 ·

Survey of the Socialist Education Campaign in various ethnic regions in Xichang, [Sichuan province,] by the Xichang Region Party Committee, February 4, 1959

During the [Socialist Education] campaign, a small number of landlords, rich peasants, counterrevolutionaries, and bad elements used the opportunity to spread anti-Party and anti-socialist rumors. For instance, someone in Xichang's Lianhe township defied Chairman Mao by saying: "Chairman Mao is more brutal than Deng Xiuting.[7] We are treated worse than slaves. [Mao] is the despot under heaven.[8] In the past, a number of ethnic groups had managed to unite together and to overthrow the tyranny of slave owners. Today we can also get organized to wreck this so-called people's government." Another rumor was: "[...] The Chinese cadres are much worse than cadres of ethnic origin. In our ethnic area, we don't need Chinese cadres to lead our work." In Yanbian county some bad elements have been spreading rumors such as: "Before Liberation, there was no collectivization, and we had food to eat. Since collectivization, we work day and night, but we only have rice porridge to eat"; "As slaves, we could eat two meals a day, and we did not have to do much work. With collectivization and the Great Leap Forward most of us are leaping into death"; "When it comes to grain procurement, the people's government is much more brutal than former slave owners. We cannot get away [with taking grain] even if [the total amount] is just one grain short." [...]

In some areas, a number of bad elements have been using the opportunity to sabotage and organize counterrevolutionary activities. [...] In Yanbian county's Hongbao, Yankou, Ningnan, and Liuting [villages], eight rebels have gone into hiding in the mountains to plot revolt. In Shanshu and Liuting, a number of former slave owners and bad elements have been holding secret meetings—we are currently interrogating them. Meanwhile, a number of rumors have been going around. In Xichang's Lianhe township, Shama Hanjia was found spreading rumors such as: "Chiang Kai-shek and the Nationalists are coming soon." In Sanhe township, one rumor says: "In Dechang county, quite a number of people have died of starvation in collective canteens." [Another says:] "A [Nationalist] airplane recently flew over the sky in Aqigou township." [...] In Ningnan township, there are also rumors such as: "The Nationalist army is coming!" [...] It looks as though the enemy is very active at the moment.

· Document 112 ·

Report on the Rectification Campaign, changes in agricultural production, and people's standard of living, by the Yibin branch of the Rectification Campaign Working Group of the General Office of the Sichuan Provincial Party Committee, September 12–October 12, 1961

In Jiang'an county many rumors are currently circulating. Some even say things like: "Chairman Mao has passed away, and the land will be returned to the original owners"; "The days of the Communist Party are numbered, and the ration coupons have expired," and so on.

· Document 113 ·

A survey of Huaminglou commune in Ningxiang county by the Central
Committee of the Chinese Communist Party, the Investigation Team of the
Hunan Provincial Party Committee, and Comrade Yang Shuqing, April 4, 1961[9]

From November 1960 to January 24 this year, there have been
more than 1,100 cases of theft in this commune. [...] Recently quite
a number of villagers have been spreading rumors and carrying out
sabotage. Some have been making up counterrevolutionary ballads
or writing counterrevolutionary posters. [...]

In Nantang, Tanzichong, and Heye big brigades a number of rumors have been circulating, saying: "Chairman Mao has seconded
Peng Dehuai to Changsha and asked him to be the provincial governor of Hunan. Initially Peng refused, but later he made some deals
with Mao, such as [a deal] to abolish the ration coupons and increase
the amount of the grain ration. Mao agreed to his requests, so Peng
came."

After learning the news of President Liu Shaoqi's visit to Huaminglou [...] his niece heard people saying: "President Liu is here. He is
going to open up the granary and abolish the ration coupons." [...]
On March 28, two counterrevolutionary posters appeared on an electric pole just 1 kilometer away from President Liu's former family
home. One says "Down with Mao Zedong!" and the other says "Mao
Zedong and Liu Shaoqi, step down!" [...]

· Document 114 ·

Report on protecting agricultural production and on the Rectification
Campaign [in Guizhou province], 1959

A small number of enemies have been using the Rectification Campaign as an opportunity to carry out sabotage, to seek revenge, and to
stir up trouble. For instance, [...] in Huishui county's Dangyou
[township], a counterrevolutionary poster was found on the wall of a
collective canteen. It says: "The people's commune is great, and we
have no food to eat. The collective canteen is wonderful, and we have
to beg for food at each meal. The Communist Party cares for us, and
we are forced to do hard labor. After one day of hard work, we get only
three bowls of watery rice porridge to eat. We work day and night, but
we are paid nothing. Dear friends, the days of eating rice have gone

forever." In Kaiyang county's Guancheng people's commune, an anti-revolutionary poster was found on the wall of a public toilet. It says: "What's good about the Communist Party? All we get is 2 meters of fabric and 0.2 kg of oil. If we want to eat any more oil, we squeeze hard and our tears run out." [. . .]

· Document 115 ·

A collection of anti–people's commune posters in rural Lingui, Yulin, Pingnan, and Tiandong, collected by Comrade Wu Jinnan, the Party secretary of Guangxi Zhuang autonomous region,[10] April 1, 1959

Six Transformations:

1. In the people's commune everyone shares a bowl of rice porridge.
2. In the people's commune coarse grains have replaced rice.
3. In the people's commune private housing has been replaced.
4. In the people's commune the [collective] accommodation is not rainproof.
5. In the people's commune old people and children have become soldiers.
6. In the people's commune people's clothing has become shabby.

Ten Withouts:

1. In the people's commune married couples cannot bear any children.
2. In the people's commune there is no meat to buy at the market.
3. In the people's commune villagers cannot build individual housing.
4. In the people's commune there is no tobacco to smoke.
5. In the people's commune people have no hats to wear in the rain.
6. In the people's commune people have no cash in their pockets.
7. In the people's commune no one has any relatives or family left.
8. In the people's commune there is no household furniture, and no oil or salt to cook vegetables with.
9. In the people's commune villagers cannot keep poultry; there is no alcohol to drink and no porridge for lunch.
10. In the people's commune if someone dies, there is no coffin to bury [that person] in.

· Document 116 ·

Report on a number of problems in the collective canteen, by the Rural Affairs
Working Group of the Sichuan Provincial Party Committee and the Office
of Welfare and Benefits, 1961

In Jianyang county's Dongxi commune, a number of villagers from
Number 3 administrative district are dissatisfied with the collective
canteen. They make fun of the canteen, saying: "The good thing about
the canteen is that many people got 'fat'"—by which they meant that
many people suffered from edema. [...] In this village, more than thirteen people are opposed to the collective canteen; that is 36 percent of
the local population.

· Document 117 ·

Survey of agricultural production and the Rectification Campaign in various
regions of rural Sichuan, by the General Office of the Sichuan Provincial Party
Committee, May 25, 1959

In Dazhu county's Xihe commune, [...] the deputy head of the
Fenghuang administrative district, Lu Longan, pocketed 10 yuan from
the public funds, but [during the Rectification Campaign] he would
admit only that he had embezzled 4 yuan. The villagers put up twenty
posters denouncing him. He was so badly humiliated that he refused
to take the lead in agricultural production. While villagers were busy
harvesting, he went fishing.

· Document 118 ·

A letter from Tan Qilong and Wang Ying to Chairman Mao and the Central
Committee of the Chinese Communist Party regarding the current crisis
in Jining region, [Shandong province,] April 11, 1959

In Chao county the leader of a Daoist sect has been going around
actively recruiting followers and plotting revolt. In recent days, a number of airplanes from Taiwan have been flying around in the sky trying
to cause disturbances. Meanwhile, in Jinxiang, Jueye, and Dan counties colorful light signals have been flashing. It looks as though the
enemies are very active. There have been quite a few counterrevolutionary posters around making claims: "In the Soviet Union 70 percent of the population starved to death in order to build Communism.

And Chairman Mao has given orders to let half of the population starve to death in China," and "If we want to have enough to eat, we should unite together to kill corrupt officials and rob granaries." [...]

· Document 119 ·

Speech by Comrade Qin Chuanhou[11] at the provincial and regional Party secretaries' meeting, [Sichuan province], May 1962

So far this year there have been eighty-five public disturbances and twenty-eight robberies [in Sichuan]. [...]

Meanwhile, more than 20,000 people are still wandering about looking for work. Between March 28 and April 2, more than 500 people in Qingbaijiang district, just outside Chengdu, were involved in a coal robbery, and they stole more than 50 tons. The problem of fuel shortages is still very severe. In Hanyuan county six cadres were beaten up by villagers for corruption, and two members of cadres' families were also assaulted physically. [...] There have been more than sixty-seven incidents involving counterrevolutionary posters. In Langzhong some people came up with an eight-point manifesto claiming they would invade Beijing. They printed out many copies of the manifesto and distributed it around Chengdu. They also put up more than 100 posters all over the place.

Epilogue (1961–1962)

ON April 2, 1961, the president of China, Liu Shaoqi, embarked on a journey to Huaminglou, his home village in Hunan province. While traveling from the provincial capital, Changsha, to Huaminglou, Liu was surprised by what he saw. The hills that used to be covered in fruit trees were completely barren, and nothing except wild grass was growing in the nearby fields. Villages along the road looked deserted, and the majority of the houses had been torn down, leaving only a few cracked walls standing. The huge pig farm—a Great Leap Forward project—had very few pigs in it, and those that were there looked wretchedly thin and unhealthy.

In Huaminglou itself, Liu was horrified to discover the damage that radical collectivization had caused. Deeply distressed, he decided to carry out further investigations. On April 12, Liu and his team arrived at Tianhua brigade in Guangfu people's commune in Changsha county. The brigade was hailed as one of Hunan's model organizations. It had won many "red flags" of commendation during the Great Leap Forward. Liu stayed in Tianhua for eighteen days, and on May 11 he wrote a long letter to Chairman Mao in which he described the devastation found there: one-third of the houses had been pulled down, and 60 percent of the villagers had no homes to return to. Pigs had been killed and consumed by local cadres while many villagers were dying of edema.

On May 31, after returning to Beijing, Liu made an emotional plea, at a leadership gathering, for the Central Committee of the Communist Party to take responsibility for the disasters and errors of the past three years (document 120). Several months later, in January 1962, Communist cadres gathered inside the Great Hall of the People in Beijing. Better known as the Seven Thousand Cadres Conference for the number of cadres who met there, it marked a turning point in the history of the Great Famine in China. At the conference Liu Shaoqi gave a three-hour presentation echoing his earlier speech at the Central Committee leadership gathering. He repeated a local assessment of the famine as "three-tenths natural calamity and seven-tenths man-made." And he openly addressed a number of problems of the past few years and challenged the "nine fingers to one" expression—Mao's favorite phrase to describe the achievements of the Great Leap Forward as greater than its setbacks. Encouraged by Liu's presentation, a number of regional cadres spoke out about the problems in their areas and criticized collectivization at group meetings. The conference lasted nearly thirty days. By its end, the delegates maintained that the general Party line was correct but that errors had been made in implementing it. Mao was clearly losing Party support.[1]

The famine, meanwhile, continued.

In May 1962, a Central Committee working meeting was held in Beijing. At the meeting, headed by Liu Shaoqi, it was decided to curb the damage caused by the Great Leap Forward by introducing "special economic measures for special times." Chen Yun, a vice chair of the Central Committee, was put in charge. Chen proposed introducing a free market within a centrally controlled economy. In July 1962, Chen and the minister of agriculture, Deng Zihui, together with Mao Zedong's secretary, Tian Jiaying, proposed to Mao the policy of "more farm plots for private use, more free markets, more enterprises with sole responsibility for their own profits and losses, and fixed farm output quotas for each household." Mao disapproved, but Liu Shaoqi supported the plan, and it was carried out in various parts of the country. But Minister Deng Zihui was stripped of his position and criticized at the Tenth Plenum of the Eighth Central Committee Meeting in September 1962 for taking the "capitalist path."[2]

Not until the end of 1962 did the famine finally come to an end. The birthrate began to increase, and the death rate began to fall (document 121).

· Document 120 ·

Speech by Comrade Liu Shaoqi [in Beijing], May 31, 1961

Currently the main problem is grain, and the other conflicts are directly linked to it. Everyone must eat. People in the city consume more than people in the countryside. Besides grain they also demand

nonessential food items. Over the past few years, peasants and workers in our country have been very weak physically. In cities, nonessential food items have become scarce. According to Marx, industrial
development is backed up by a supply of plenty of food commodities
and a strong labor force. In feudal society, the landlord used to squeeze
peasants out of their grain ration. Today it turns out that we, too, have
been squeezing peasants out of their grain ration. We have been fighting with peasants for food, for meat, for cotton, and so on. The alliance
of workers and peasants is under serious threat. How we solve this
problem will directly affect whether our society can survive and continue to progress.

[. . .] The problem in the past few years was caused by unrealistic
grain-collecting quotas, unrealistic estimates, unrealistic procurement
figures, and unrealistic workloads. [. . .] Was the disaster [in the past
few years] a natural calamity, or was it caused by people? In Hunan
people say that three-tenths was natural calamity and seven-tenths was
man-made. Throughout the country quite a few errors have been made
while implementing [Party policies]. Although in some places the disaster is indeed a natural calamity, I don't think we can use only one finger
to describe our setbacks. We must be honest. [. . .] The problem was,
however, not due to the shortcomings of the general Party line, the
Great Leap Forward, or the people's communes. It resulted from errors
we have made while implementing the [general Party line]. These were
serious errors. Otherwise, how is it that agricultural and industrial productivity has decreased? Every level should take responsibility. The
Central Committee should take responsibility, and the provincial Party
Committees should also take responsibility. But the Central Committee
should take the main responsibility. We should take collective responsibility, not to blame individual departments or individual people. [. . .]

· Document 121 ·

Report on population figures in 1962, by the Party Committee of the Sichuan
Province Bureau of Public Security, February 23, 1963

To the Sichuan Provincial Party Committee and the Ministry of Public Security:

According to various reports from local Public Security offices, there
has been an increase of the population in Sichuan because of economic
improvement in 1962. The birthrate is on the rise while the death rate

has dropped. The population growth rate has become more or less normal. [...]

In 1961, the total population of Sichuan was 64, 591,786. In 1962 there were 1,813,089 newborn babies; that is 2.8 percent of the total population of Sichuan. The number of deaths was 946,496; that is 1.46 percent of the total population. [...] The total population increase was 1.34 percent, which is equal to 866,630 people.

Although the general figures in 1962 show that the population is on the increase, in seventeen counties the death rate is still higher than the birthrate. In Tianquan and Lushan counties the death rate has reached 5 percent or higher. In Baoxing, Ebian, and Wenchuan counties the death rate is above 3 percent. In Hechuan, Jiangbei, Bishan, Dazhu, Ya'an, Yingjing, Jingyan, Fushun, Longchang, Yuexi, and other counties, the death rate is higher than 2 percent. In Tongliang and Jianyang counties, the death rate is still higher than the birthrate. There are several reasons for this. The main reason is the famine disaster of the past few years. On top of that, there was another famine in the spring of 1962. Many people became ill as a result, and the death rate was quite high. However, in the second half of the year, the situation has gradually improved.

Organizational Structure of the Government of the People's Republic of China

The government of the People's Republic of China comprises the Chinese Communist Party, the state, and the People's Liberation Army.

Chinese Communist Party

The Party is the supreme political authority in the People's Republic of China. It controls the state and the military, as well as the media.

Central Organizational Structure

National Congress. In theory the congress is the highest body within the Party, but in practice important decisions are often made before its meetings. It meets about every five years.

Central Committee. The Central Committee is the highest authority within the Party. Its members and alternate members are leading figures in the Party, state, and military; they are elected by national Party congresses. The Central Committee includes the General Secretary and the members of the Secretariat, the Politburo and the Politburo Standing Committee, and the Central Military Commission.

General Secretary. The General Secretary of the Central Committee of the Chinese Communist Party was the highest-ranking post in the Party until 1943, when it was replaced by the post of Chairman of the Central Committee, and Mao Zedong was appointed to the position. He served as Chairman of the Party until his death in 1976. In 1982 the post of Chairman was abolished, and the post of General Secretary was reinstated. The Chairman or the General Secretary manages the Secretariat of the Central Committee.

Secretariat. The Secretariat, headed by the General Secretary of the Central Committee, is the chief administrative organ of the Party. The Secretariat manages the work of the Politburo Standing Committee and Politburo and makes personnel decisions for the Party and the state.

Politburo. The Politburo (or Political Bureau) oversees Party activities. The Central Committee appoints Politburo members, at least nominally; Politburo members are also members of the Central Committee.

Politburo Standing Committee. The Politburo Standing Committee, a subgroup of the Politburo, meets more frequently.

Central Military Commission. This commission, which exercises command and control over the People's Liberation Army, is supervised by Central Committee. Between 1949 and 1976 it was headed by Mao Zedong. See also People's Liberation Army (PLA) below.

Central Discipline Inspection Committee. Directly under the National Congress and on the same level as the Central Committee, this committee is responsible for the moral integrity and the discipline of Party members, as well as for combating corruptions.

Other. The Party has many other offices, including the General Office, the Central Organization Department, the Propaganda Department, the United Front Work Department, and the International Liaison Department. The United Front was originally a popular front established in the 1930s during the Sino-Japanese War. It served to bring the Communist Party, the Nationalist Party, and other anti-Japanese organizations together to fight the Japanese. In 1948 the United Front Work Department was formed. After the 1950s, however, it had lost its real function. In theory it represents minorities, trade unions, and mass organizations, including women and youth; in reality it is another Party organ.

See also Communist Youth League of China below.

Local Organizational Structure

Party structures are established at three levels below the national level: provinces, autonomous regions, and municipalities; cities, regions (or prefectures), and counties; and administrative townships or districts. Many of the administrative townships and districts were replaced by people's communes between 1958 and 1982. Each level has its own set of Party structures.

Party Committee. The Party Committee secretary is head of the province or autonomous region or municipality. Under the secretary are governors and deputy governors, mayors, and deputy mayors, and heads and deputy heads of counties, districts, and towns. According to the current Party constitution, the members of local Party Committees are elected every three or five years.

Party Congress. It holds a meeting every five years. In theory it is the highest body at each local level, but in practice it has little power.

Discipline Inspection Committee. The local committee has functions similar to those of the Central Discipline Inspection Committee.

Other. Any factories, workers' units, schools, universities, and street districts with more than three Party members must have their own Party Committees and Party secretaries.

The State

Central Organizational Structure

National People's Congress. The congress is the highest state body. Its membership is largely determined by the Party.

President of the People's Republic of China. The president is the head of state. He is elected by the National People's Congress. Mao, the first president, resigned in 1959, and Liu Shaoqi was appointed to the post; he served from 1959 to 1967. The president has the power to appoint and to dismiss members of the State Council as well as ministers and heads of State Council commissions.

State Council. The State Council is the executive organ of the state. It includes the premier (who heads the State Council, dealing with everyday administration), vice premiers, state councillors (who have narrower responsibilities than vice premiers), and ministers and heads of State Council commissions. There are ministries and commissions to deal with agriculture, finance, commerce, civil affairs, foreign affairs, education, culture, health and hygiene, national defense, security, ethnic affairs, population and family planning, and other areas of responsibility.

The State Council oversees the province-level governments and is responsible for carrying out the policies of the Party as well as the regulations and laws adopted by the National People's Congress.

Local Organizational Structure

Local People's Congress. People's Congresses at the local level—city, region, county—are the highest governing bodies at that level. In theory, People's Congresses at province level, for example, are responsible for laying down provincial policies. The functions and powers of People's Congresses are exercised by standing committees at and above the city/region/

county level when the congresses are not in session. Each standing committee has a chair, vice chairs, and members. Towns and districts are governed by counties directly, not by local People's Congresses, although People's Congresses oversee the counties.

Local Government. Local governments are accountable to local People's Congresses, standing committees, and the State Council. People's Congresses at the province, region, and county levels each elect local heads of government, including governors and deputy governors, mayors and deputy mayors, and heads and deputy heads of regions, counties, towns, and districts. In practice the decisions are often made in Beijing by the Central Committee of the Party.

People's Liberation Army (PLA)

The People's Liberation Army is the major military power of the People's Republic of China. It is formally under the command of the Central Military Commission of the Chinese Communist Party. Chairman Mao was the head of the PLA until his death. Currently the General Secretary of the Party is the chair of the PLA. The primary role of the army is to uphold the rule of the Party and to protect China's national sovereignty. It is now the world's largest military force. The Ministry of National Defense, which operates under the State Council, does not exercise any authority over the PLA and is far less powerful than the Central Military Commission.

Communist Youth League of China

The league is for youths aged fourteen to twenty-eight. Though officially separate from the Party, it is run by the Party and organized along Party lines. The First Secretary of the League is also a member of the Party's Central Committee. Members of the Communist Youth League support the Party and are loyal to it. One of the league's functions is to produce a new generation of Party leaders. Two of its First Secretaries became General Secretaries of the Chinese Communist Party—Hu Yaobang in 1982 and Hu Jingtao in 2004.

Chronology

1943

On November 29, Mao Zedong, head of the Chinese Communist Party, then based in Yan'an, gave his speech "Get Organized" at a reception in honor of the labor heroes of the Shaanxi-Gansu-Ningxia Border Region. He said, "Among the peasant masses a system of individual economy has prevailed for thousands of years, with each family or household forming a productive unit. This scattered, individual form of production is the economic foundation of feudal rule and keeps the peasants in perpetual poverty. The only way to change it is gradual collectivization, and the only way to bring about collectivization, according to Lenin, is through cooperatives."[1]

1949

With the end of the civil war, the Chinese Communist Party took control of the country. On October 1, Mao formally proclaimed the establishment of the People's Republic of China.

1953

Between April 3 and April 23, at the first National Rural Affairs Conference, it was announced that agricultural collectivization was the only possible path to prosperity for a majority of the peasants.

On October 4 and October 15, Mao gave speeches on mutual aid and cooperation in agriculture, in which he anticipated that 700,000 to 1,000,000 agricultural collectives would be established by 1957.

On December 16 the Central Committee of the Chinese Communist Party passed the policy of agricultural collectivization.

1955

On July 31, at a meeting for secretaries of various provincial, municipal, and autonomous regional Party Committees, Mao gave his speech "On the Cooperative Transformation of Agriculture." In it he criticized those in the Party leadership who opposed "rash advance," calling them "utterly wrong."[2]

On December 21, in a circular drafted for the Central Committee of the Chinese Communist Party, which was passed on to the Shanghai Bureau and the provincial and autonomous regional Party Committees, Mao expressed his displeasure with the speed of agricultural collectivization. He wanted the entire countryside to be fully collectivized by the latter half of 1956.

1956

The Hungarian Revolution broke out in October.

Mao launched the Hundred Flowers Campaign, relaxing restrictions and inviting criticism of Party policies.

1957

On February 27 at the Enlarged Eleventh Session of the Supreme State Conference, Mao gave his speech "On the Correct Handling of Contradictions among the People." He apparently wanted to encourage the public to criticize the bureaucracy so the government would do better. Public demonstrations and strikes broke out across the country; the number of petitions and letters of complaint from ordinary people was unprecedented.

In July, Mao countered the open criticism by launching the Anti-Rightist Campaign and the rural Socialist Education Campaign. All voices of opposition were silenced.

On November 18, in a speech at the Moscow Meeting of Representatives of Communist and Workers' Parties, Mao declared that China would overtake Britain in steel output within fifteen years. This was a direct response to Nikita Khrushchev's announcement that the Soviet Union would overtake the United States in economic production. Meanwhile, a massive water conservation campaign was launched in China; it marked the beginning of the Great Leap Forward.

1958

On March 20, Communist Party members at a conference in Chengdu passed the policy of total collectivization in rural China.

On April 20 the first commune in China was created: the Chayashan people's commune. Famine broke out in various parts of the country.

At a Party conference in May, Mao proposed the slogan "Going all out, aiming high, and achieving more, for more and faster economic results." Liu Shaoqi—who became the president of China the following year—and a number of top leaders in the Party supported it, and it became one of the central Party lines.

At the Party's Politburo meeting in the resort of Beidaihe in August, it was announced that steel output in 1958 must be double the 1957 output. The meeting also approved people's communes as the new form of economic and political organization in rural China. By October more than 90 percent of rural Chinese were "collectivized." Approximately 26,000 communes had been set up, with an average of 5,000 households in each. Most of China's agricultural labor force was diverted to massive steel-production and water-conservation projects. By the end of the year, severe food shortages became widespread in many parts of rural China.

In October a report on mass starvation and more than 40,000 deaths in Luliang county, Yunnan province, reached Mao and the Central Committee of the Party. After reading the report Mao asked that it be circulated within the Party and commented, "This is a good report. The Yunnan Provincial Party Committee made a mistake, but they have realized that there was a problem, and they have dealt with the problem correctly. They have learned their lesson, and they will not make the same mistake again. This is a good thing: turning disaster into a blessing."[3]

1959

In February at a meeting for top Party leaders, Mao indicated his belief that the food shortages had not been caused by crop failure but rather by peasants hiding grain. He maintained that the real cause for this was corruption among the local cadres. So he gave orders for the launch of the Rectification Campaign in the countryside. Meanwhile, Tao Zhu, the provincial Party secretary in Guangdong, launched an Anti-Hiding Campaign. It soon spread to the rest of the country. Starving peasants were forced to hand over whatever they had. The famine escalated.

At a Party conference in Shanghai in March, Mao pressed for even higher procurement targets in the countryside: up to one-third of all grain must be taken away from the peasants. He concluded by saying: "It is better to let half the people die so that the other half can eat their fill" (document 5).

In July and August at a plenum in Lushan, the Eighth Plenum of the Eighth Central Committee of the Chinese Communist Party, Peng Dehuai, the defense minister, and Zhang Wengtian, the minister of foreign affairs, criticized some elements of the Great Leap Forward. Their criticism was supported by a few Party leaders. This angered Mao. He launched an attack on Peng, Zhang, and three others and insisted on pushing forward the Great Leap. The Anti–Rightist Deviation Campaign, a campaign of repression against critical voices similar to those of Peng and his allies, was subsequently launched. In the countryside, violence and terror intensified. Many peasants were deliberately starved or tortured to death.

1960

In January, at an enlarged Politburo meeting in Shanghai, it was decided to continue the Great Leap Forward in 1960.

Between the winter of 1959 and the spring of 1960 starvation spread across the countryside. The news of a huge number of deaths and cannibalism in Guizhou province's Zunyi region reached Beijing's Central Committee. This became referred to as the Zunyi incident. (Twenty-five years earlier, Mao Zedong was elected to the leadership of the Chinese Communist Party at Zunyi.) Meanwhile, the Guizhou Provincial Committee made a report to the Central Committee of the Chinese Communist Party and Chairman Mao praising the people's communes and the collective canteens.

At a Politburo meeting in Tianjin in March, it was decided to push forward with the urban commune campaign, begun in the fall of 1958 alongside the rural collectivization campaign. Mao wanted 80 percent of the urban population to join collective canteens by the end of 1960.

Between March and April, at the People's Congress in Beijing, it was announced that the Great Leap Forward must continue.

On October 1, National Day, an editorial in the *People's Daily*—the official voice of the Chinese Communist Party—lamented that in the past two years the country had witnessed unprecedented "natural disasters." This became the official line for explaining the devastating famine. News of mass starvation and over one million deaths in Xinyang, Henan province, reached Mao. Mao concluded that the "Xinyang incident" and problems in the countryside had come about because the "democratic revolution" had not been thoroughly carried out at the local level and because local power was not in the hands of the Communist Party. After five months' investigation, the team headed by Tao Zhu decided to stop counting deaths after reaching one million.[4]

On November 3 the Central Committee of the Chinese Communist Party issued an emergency directive: the three-level ownership system in communes, which was based on production brigades and which had been introduced in August 1959, would be enforced and continued over the next seven years. The function of the commune was restricted, all private possessions would be returned, and individual peasants would be allowed to keep small plots of land, to engage in sideline occupations, to rest after eight hours' work, and to restore local markets. A full-scale Rectification Campaign to fight local corruption was to be carried out in the countryside.

On November 15, in a letter to Premier Zhou Enlai, Mao emphasized carrying out the "class struggle" in the countryside. He claimed that one-third of the countryside was controlled by the "enemy."

1961

In January, Mao announced that 1961 would be a "year of investigation." On the 20th, he sent out investigation teams to Zhejiang, Guangdong, and Hunan provinces headed by his ghost writer, Chen Boda; an alternate member of the Secretariat of the Central Committee, Hu Qiaomu; and his own personal secretary, Tian Jiaying. Meanwhile, Liu Shaoqi, Zhou Enlai, Deng Xiaoping, and other Party and government leaders also went to the countryside to assess local conditions.

In April, Liu Shaoqi arrived in Hunan province and began his one-month investigation in Ningxiang and Changsha counties. On April 19 in Shaoshan, Mao's home county, with the approval of Mao, Hu Qiaomu announced at a village meeting that the collective canteen in Daping brigade's Chenjiawan village was to be shut down and villagers were to be allowed to cook at home again.

On May 11, Liu Shaoqi wrote a long letter to Mao Zedong detailing the devastation caused by the collectivization in the Hunan countryside. On May 31 at a leadership gathering in Beijing, Liu Shaoqi appealed to the Central Committee of the Chinese Communist Party to take responsibility for the disasters and errors of the past three years (document 120).

Between May 21 and June 12, a Central Committee work meeting in Beijing passed a revised version of the sixty-article Regulations for Agriculture. The regulations specified that the grain ration should be distributed to each individual villager directly and that local villagers should decide whether to continue with collective canteens. In most parts of the country, the collective canteen system ended after that, and the Great Leap gradually came to an end.

1962

In January, at an Enlarged Work Conference of 7,000 Communist cadres, Liu Shaoqi described the famine as largely man-made. Mao began to lose support within the Party. The meeting was a turning point in the history of the famine.

The famine continued in many parts of the country. In Sichuan the number of deaths was still rising, and the state granary was almost empty. In March, at a meeting in Beijing, Zhou Enlai agreed that Sichuan no longer had to send grain to the rest of the country. Between April and May, more than 100,000 people left China, crossing its southern border in Guangdong province. More than 60,000 arrived in Hong Kong, but 40,000 were sent back to China by the British colonial government. Subsequently the British colonial government expanded the Frontier Closed Area in the northern part of Hong Kong along the border with mainland China. Around the same time, more than 60,000 villagers from Yili, a Kazakh autonomous prefecture in Xinjiang, fled to Soviet republics.

Beginning in May, under the direction of Liu Shaoqi, various adjustment measures for post-famine economic recovery were carried out. Chen Yun was put in charge. He introduced the policy of a free market within a central planned economy. Mao temporarily retreated.

The famine finally came to an end by the winter of 1962–1963, but it paved the way for the Great Proletarian Cultural Revolution in 1966—one of the most violent episodes in modern Chinese history. The Cultural Revolution lasted for ten years and tore the country and the Party apart. Liu Shaoqi, Chen Yun, and others critical of the Great Leap Forward all came under attack as "bourgeois elements" in the Party who attempted to restore capitalism. Liu Shaoqi was expelled from the Party and died in 1969.

Notes

INTRODUCTION

1. For further evidence see documents 23 and 93.

2. Yu Xiguang, *Dayuejin ku rizi: Shangshuji* (The Great Leap Forward and the years of bitterness: A collection of memorials) (Hong Kong: Shidai chaoliu chubanshe, 2005).

3. Yang Jisheng, *Mubei: Zhongguo liushi niandai dajihuang jishi* (Tombstone: A true history of the Great Famine in China in the 1960s), 2 vols. (Hong Kong: Tiandi tushu youxian gongsi, 2008).

4. Lin Yunhui, *Wutuobang yundong: Cong dayuejin dao dajihuang, 1958–1961* (Utopian movement: From the Great Leap Forward to the Great Famine, 1958–1961), History of the People's Republic of China series (Hong Kong: Xianggang zhongwen daxue dangdai Zhongguo wenhuayanjiu zhongxin, 2008). In English: Roderick MacFarquhar's *The Origins of the Cultural Revolution*, vol. 3: *The Coming of the Cataclysm, 1961–1966* (New York: Columbia University Press, 1999), also deals with official politics of the period.

5. Frank Dikötter, *Mao's Great Famine: The History of China's Most Devastating Catastrophe, 1958–1962* (London: Bloomsbury; New York: Walker Books, 2010).

6. Jasper Becker, *Hungry Ghosts: Mao's Secret Famine* (New York: Henry Holt, 1996).

7. Gao Wangling, *Renmin gongshe shiqi Zhongguo nongmin "fanxingwei" diaocha* (Acts of peasant resistance in China in the people's communes) (Beijing: Zhonggong dangshi chubanshe, 2006).

8. Cao Shuji, *Da jihuang: 1959–1961 nian de Zhongguo renkou* (The Great Famine: China's population in 1959–1961) (Hong Kong: Shidai guoji chuban youxian gongsi, 2005).

9. Alfred L. Chan, *Mao's Crusade: Politics and Policy Implementation in China's Great Leap Forward* (Oxford: Oxford University Press, 2001); Ralph A. Taxton, *Catastrophe and Contention in Rural China: Mao's Great Leap Forward, Famine and the Origins of Righteous Resistance in Da Fo Village* (New York: Cambridge University Press, 2008).

10. Yeh Hung-ling, "Understanding Historical Memory," *Taipei Times,* December 14, 2010, p. 8.

CHAPTER 1. FAMINE IN THE COMMUNES
(MARCH–SEPTEMBER 1958)

1. Mao Zedong, "Chinese People Have Stood Up," in *Selected Works of Mao Zedong,* vol. 5 (Beijing: Renmin chubanshe, 1977), p. 7.

2. See Mao Tse-tung, "Get Organized," in *Selected Works of Mao Tse-tung,* 2nd ed., vol. 3 (Beijing: Foreign Languages Press, 1967), pp. 153–161.

3. For further evidence and discussion see chapter 1; document 109. Also see Yang, *Mubei,* vol. 1, pp. 97–98, 448–455; Dikötter, *Mao's Great Famine,* pp. 32–33.

4. Chen Han, *Bayue de zuji: Mao Zedong 1958 nian Henan nongcun shicha shiji* (August's footprint: Mao Zedong's visit to rural Henan in 1958) (Beijing: Zhongyang wenxian chubanshe, 2001), p. 158.

5. The time span is from roughly mid-March to mid-August in the Western calendar.

6. The yuan is the principal unit of the official Chinese currency. At the time of the famine 1 yuan was roughly equivalent to 50 US cents.

7. Edema is the massive accumulation of fluids in the body and limbs caused by starvation and ingestion of poisonous substances.

8. It seems that anyone who died of "unnatural causes" was counted as dying an "abnormal death." The numbers given in the document do not add up.

9. The Chinese New Year, calculated according to the Chinese lunar calendar, was on February 18, 1958.

10. The Great Debate Campaign was part of the rural Socialist Education Campaign.

CHAPTER 2. TERROR, REPRESSION,
AND VIOLENCE (1958–1961)

1. For further evidence of terror, repression, and violence during the radical collectivization see chapter 2. Also see Yang, *Mubei;* and Dikötter, *Mao's Great Famine.*

2. See Dikötter, *Mao's Great Famine,* p. xi.

3. For further discussion see Dikötter, *Mao's Great Famine,* pp. 34–42.

4. "An Important Document from the Central Committee [February 22, 1959]," in Zhongyang wenxian yanjiushi, ed., *Jianguo yilai Mao Zedong wengao* (A collection of Mao Zedong's works since 1949), vol. 8 (Beijing: Zhongyang wenxian chubanshe, 1993), p. 52.

5. The Lushan plenum was the Eighth Plenum of the Eighth Central Committee of the Communist Chinese Party. It took place between July 2 and August 16, 1959. At the conference, Peng Dehuai, China's defense minister, and Zhang Wengtian, minister of foreign affairs, criticized elements of the Great Leap Forward. Their criticism was supported by a few Party leaders. This angered Mao. He bitterly attacked Peng, Zhang, and three others as "having leaned toward the right by 30 kilometers" with "right deviationism." After the conference, the Party launched the nationwide Anti–Right Deviation Campaign, a successor to the

Anti-Rightist Campaign launched in 1957, and insisted on pushing forward with the Great Leap.

6. For further discussion see Dikötter, *Mao's Great Famine,* pp. 84–89.

7. Li Xiannian (1909–1992), a former coffin maker with only two years of education, joined the Communist Party in 1927. Initially gaining success as a Red Army commander, Li became one of the most prominent politicians in China. Between 1954 and 1975, Li was in charge of the Ministry of Finance.

8. Old Xu is Xu Teli (1877–1968), Mao's former teacher, an educator who was in favor of a proletarian revolution.

9. Bo Yibo (1908–2007), the first minister of finance (1949–1953) in the new People's Republic of China, became the chair of the State Planning Commission (1956–1959) and presided over the economic policies of the Great Leap Forward.

10. The king of Qin took the title First Emperor when he unified China in 221 BCE. He ruled the country through tyranny.

11. The "Five Types" of people were landlords, rich peasants, counterrevolutionaries, bad elements, and rightists. They were classified as "enemies of the people" under Mao.

12. The suppression of the counterrevolutionary movement between 1951 and 1952 was the first government campaign to clean out opposition elements. It was accompanied by bans on opium and prostitution.

13. "Frying beans" is local slang for a heavy beating. The sound of the beating is as loud as the sound of frying or roasting beans.

14. "Wheel war" is the tactic used when several people take turns fighting opponent to tire the opponent out.

15. The campaign to "pull down white flags and hoist red flags" was launched in the people's communes in August 1958. Socialist and communist thinking that followed the Party line and cadres' orders was rewarded with a "red flag," whereas individualistic thinking or "unhealthy ideas" were denounced and given a "white flag," "gray flag," or "black flag."

16. To call a person a turtle egg is a great insult. It means "son of a whore; bastard." To draw a turtle on a woman's back suggests that she is a whore or indecent woman.

17. At a Party conference on August 19, 1958, Mao formally declared the people's communes to be military organizations and called for the military tradition of the Communist Party to be restored. Under his order, communes were organized into military units such as regiments or battalions.

CHAPTER 3. SEASONS OF DEATH (1959–1962)

1. In August 1958 a Politburo conference at Beidaihe passed a "Resolution on the Establishment of People's Communes in the Rural Areas" to speed up radical collectivization in the countryside. It was accompanied by the rise and spread of radical "egalitarianism," which consisted in "leveling of incomes among constituent units of a commune and indiscriminate requisition of manpower and resources," to quote the standard definition. A majority of peasants lost their private property as a result—a phenomenon that became known as the Wind of Communism.

2. The report ignored the fact that fewer children were born in the countryside than in cities during this period.

3. *Yangdihuang* is a Chinese herbal medicine made of foxglove leaves.

4. To fry salt in oil is a local custom.

CHAPTER 4. CANNIBALISM (LATE 1959–EARLY 1961)

1. See "The Instruction and Circular of the Central Committee of the Chinese Communist Party and the Central United Front Department Regarding Minority Affairs [1949–1952]," from the Western Sichuan Party Committee Archive, file JX1-879, pp. 3–6.

2. Jing Jun, *The Temple of Memories: History, Power, and Morality in a Chinese Village* (Stanford: Stanford University Press, 1996), pp. 71–73.

3. Zhangye is known as Campichu in Marco Polo's account of his travels. Marco Polo, *The Book of Ser Marco Polo, the Venetian: Concerning the Kingdoms and Marvels of the East,* ed. and trans. Henry Yule (Cambridge: Cambridge University Press, 2010), vol. 1, pp. 197–201.

4. There is clearly just one culprit. The numbers in the documents are copied faithfully, even when the math or the context suggests that there may be inaccuracies.

CHAPTER 5. DEVASTATION IN THE COUNTRYSIDE (1958–1961)

1. "Wind of Exaggeration" refers to one result of radical collectivization in 1958: the gross inflation in the setting of production targets and the false reporting of output achieved.

2. Hu Yaobang served as the general Party secretary of the Communist Party between 1981 and 1987. Before that, in 1978, he launched a nationwide campaign rehabilitating those purged under Mao during the Anti-Rightist Campaign in the late 1950s. In 1987, Hu fell from grace by supporting democratic reform in China. On April 15, 1989, Hu died of a heart attack. His funeral sparked student demonstrations throughout China, which ended on June 4 when the People's Liberation Army openly fired on demonstrators in Tiananmen Square and elsewhere.

3. In rural China, a sedan chair normally consists of a simple cane chair attached to two stout bamboo poles. Some people like to sit and rest in the chair.

4. On the Wind of Communism see chapter 3, note 1.

5. The "uncle" referred to is Mao Zedong.

6. The "Five Winds" are the "Wind of Communism," the "Wind of Blind Guidance in Production," the "Wind of Enforcing Arbitrary Orders," the "Wind of Exaggeration," and the "Wind of Cadres Acceding to Privileges." All of these resulted from the attempt to speed up radical collectivization in the fall of 1958.

7. In March 1961, the central government promulgated a new agricultural policy to address the excesses of the people's communes and to curb the damage being caused. It called for a cessation of egalitarianism and a reorganization of the commune with the big brigade as the basic unit of organization. The published policy contained sixty articles, hence its common name.

8. In a commune, peasants earned a number of points according to the tasks they were assigned and the number of hours they worked. At the end of a month or a year, each peasant received either a sum of money or an equivalent amount of food based on the number of points earned.

CHAPTER 6. THE TURN TO RELIGION (1957–1962)

1. "Yige sanniannei zengchan baifenzhi liushiqi de nongye shengchan he-zuoshe" (An agricultural collective that has increased productivity by 67 percent within three years), in *Zhongguo nongcun de shehuizhuyi gaochao* (The high tide of socialism in the Chinese countryside), vol. 2 (Beijing: Renmin chubanshe, 1956), p. 475.

2. "Liberation" refers to the takeover of China by the Communist Party after it defeated the Nationalist Party in 1949. The Nationalist Party retreated to Taiwan as a result.

3. Dufu's Thatched Cottage was first constructed in the Ming dynasty (1368–1644) in memory of the famous Tang-period poet Du Fu (712–770).

4. Konjac jelly is made from the root of the konjac plant, which grows in India, China, Japan, and Korea. The plant is also known as elephant yam or devil's tongue.

5. The two systems are the Nationalist government of the Republic of China and the Communist government of the People's Republic.

6. The True Jesus Church is a non-denominational Pentecostal-type church that sprang up in Beijing in 1917. In 1949 it claimed more than 120,000 members. Nine years later, most churches were closed down. Not until 1985 did the church resume its activities. Today it claims to have 2.4 million members.

7. A water ghost is a supernatural being in Chinese folklore. Water ghosts are usually the spirits of those who drowned. They continue living in the water and attack people, dragging them underwater and drowning them in order to take possession of their bodies, a process known as *tishen*, "to replace the body." A victim becomes a new water ghost.

8. The Yellow Emperor is the mythical ancestor of the Chinese.

9. The Eight Trigrams a set of signs from ancient Chinese cosmology, represent heaven, earth, water, fire, thunder, mountain, wind, and marshland. The trigrams have Yin and Yang elements.

10. The Wa are an ethnic group. Some members are Buddhists, some are Christians, and some have other beliefs.

11. The Hungry Ghost Festival takes place on the fifteenth day of the seventh month in the Chinese lunar calendar. Although it is celebrated together with the Buddhist Ullambana Festival, for most Chinese it is a time to make offerings to ancestors.

CHAPTER 7. STRATEGIES FOR SURVIVAL (1959–1962)

1. "Iron rice bowl" means with a guaranteed job or food.

2. *Baizhu*, or *Atractylodes macrocephala*, is a plant used in Chinese medicine for abdominal pain and gastroenterological diseases.

3. Again, the math in the documents is not always correct. Here: fourteen, not more than fourteen.

CHAPTER 8. LETTERS OF COMPLAINT (1957–1962)

1. See "On the Correct Handling of Contradictions among the People (Speaking Note)," in Roderick MacFarquhar, Timothy Cheek, and Eugene Wu, *The Secret*

Speeches of Chairman Mao: From the Hundred Flowers to the Great Leap Forward (Cambridge: Harvard University Press, 1989), p. 173.

2. "The Situation in Summer 1957," in Zhongyang wenxian yanjiushi, ed., *Jianguo yilai Mao Zedong wengao*, vol. 6 (Beijing: Zhongyang wenxian chubanshe, 1987), p. 545.

3. This number was given by the Central Committee of the Chinese Communist Party in the late 1970s and early 1980s. See Dai Huang, *Hu Yaobang yu pingfan yuanjia cuoan* (Hu Yaobang and the rehabilitation of rightists) (Beijing: Zhongguo wenlian chubangongsi and Xinhua chuanbanshe, 1998), p. 17.

4. Xinhua Gate is the main gate into the Zhongnanhai compound in Beijing.

5. Liu Yuqing, a retired soldier and a former Party member, was expelled from the Communist Party as a result of writing this letter.

6. Zheng Ying (1917–1999) was the wife of Liao Zhigao, the former General Secretary of the Secretariat of the Sichuan Provincial Party Committee.

7. Deng Xiuting, a local warlord, died in 1944.

8. "Mandate of heaven" is a traditional Chinese concept. Having the mandate of heaven makes a ruler legitimate. But a ruler who becomes a despot and fails to be virtuous, just, and compassionate can lose the mandate of heaven and the right to rule.

9. On Huaminglou commune see chapter 5; for another excerpt from the survey report see document 36.

10. The Zhuang are an ethnic group, most of whose members live in the Guangxi Zhuang autonomous region.

11. Qin Chuanhou was the former head of the Public Security Bureau in Sichuan province.

EPILOGUE (1961–1962)

1. Clearly Liu Shaoqi and Mao Zedong had parted ways at the Seven Thousand Cadres Conference. In Liu's effort to curb the damage and waste caused by the Great Leap Forward and collectivization, he disagreed with Mao on a number of issues. This displeased Mao immensely. Although publicly Mao had to give way to Liu and allow him to carry out various economic adjustments, secretly Mao was looking for opportunities to get rid of Liu and his supporters. The Cultural Revolution was on its way. This was Mao's last major effort to destroy all his rivals. After being targeted as public enemy number one, Liu was striped of all his positions and expelled from the Party. He died not much more than a year later, on November 12, 1969.

2. Chen Yun's post-famine economic policy became a focal point of criticism against him during the Cultural Revolution (1966–1976). In 1969 he was exiled from Beijing and sent to work in a factory in Nanchang, Jiangxi province. On May 22, 1966, Tian Jiaying was accused of being a "right deviationist" for distorting Mao's work. The day after, he was found dead at his home in Zhongnanhai, Beijing.

CHRONOLOGY

1. Mao Tse-tung, "Get Organized," p. 156.

2. Mao Tse-tung, "On the Cooperative Transformation of Agriculture," in

Selected Works of Mao Tse-tung, 1st ed., vol. 5 (Beijing: Foreign Language Press, 1977), p. 195.

3. "A Lesson: Report from the Yunnan Provincial Party Committee Regarding the Edema and Death Situation," from the Documents (1–35) of the Sixth Central Committee Meeting of the Eighth Party Congress, November 1958, Hunan Provincial Party Committee Archive, file 141-2-76, p. 98.

4. Mao Zedong, *Jianguo yilai Mao Zedong wengao,* vol. 9. (Beijing: Zhongyang wenxian chubanshe, 1996), p. 349.

Index of Documents

CHAPTER 3. SEASONS OF DEATH (1959–1962)

17. Report and feedback on the settlement and education of orphans, by the Party Committee of the Sichuan Province Bureau of Civil Affairs, March 5–May 24, 1962. From the Sichuan Province Bureau of Civil Affairs Archive, file JC 44-1441, p. 27.

18. A report to the Sichuan Provincial Party Committee regarding the condition of orphans in Ya'an, Bishan, and other areas, by a joint investigation team from the Provincial Internal Affairs Bureau, the Provincial Bureau of Civil Affairs, the Women's Association, and the Jiangjin Regional Office, May 24–November 20, 1962. From the Sichuan Provincial Party Committee Archive, file JC 1-3256, pp. 1–2.

19. Report regarding villagers in parts of Qu county, [Sichuan province,] who are digging for "immortal earth" to eat owing to hardship and lack of famine relief, August 31, 1961. From the Sichuan Provincial Party Committee Archive, file JC 1-2620, pp. 177–178.

20. The State Council's emergency announcement to prevent incidents of food poisoning while the movement to collect and manufacture food substitutes continues, [Beijing,] December 25, 1960. From the Sichuan Province Welfare Committee Archive, file JC 202-8, pp. 1–2.

21. A report by the Hunan Province Bureau of Civil Affairs regarding disease prevention work, 1961. From the Hunan Province Bureau of Civil Affairs Archive, file 167-1-1016, p. 186.

22. [Sichuan Province] Bureau of Health and Hygiene's special summary report on treating edema, January 1960–October 1961. From the Sichuan Province Bureau of Health and Hygiene Archive, file JC 133-219, pp. 15, 37, 48, 106.

23. Report on rickets and malnutrition currently [afflicting] children, as well as on necessary measures to treat the problem, by the Chongqing City People's Committee, Sichuan province, January 30–September 7, 1962. From the Sichuan Province Bureau of Civil Affairs Archive, file JC 44-3320, pp. 2–4.

24. Reports on edema prevention and treatment by the Department for Disease Control, Sichuan Province Bureau of Health and Hygiene, 1961. From the Sichuan Province Bureau of Health and Hygiene, file JC 133-2793, pp. 33–37, 80, 104–106, 112–116, 204, 206, 216–221.

25. Instructions regarding the prevention and treatment of edema and other diseases, by the General Office of the Sichuan Provincial Party Committee, the Chongqing and Fuling Region Party Committees, and various local Party Committees, January 10–December 20, 1961. From the Sichuan Provincial Party Committee Archive, file JC 1-2419, p. 46.

CHAPTER 4. CANNIBALISM (LATE 1959–EARLY 1961)

26. A study of cases of cannibalism in Linxia municipality, by the Ningxia branch of the Government Solicitude Group, [Gansu province,] March 3, 1961. From the Gansu Provincial Party Committee Archive, file 91-4-898, pp. 83–87.

27. Reports on two cases of cannibalism, [Gansu province,] April 15, 1961. From the Gansu Provincial Party Committee Archive, file 91-9-215, p. 94.

28. On humans eating corpses and killing children for consumption: a report by Comrade Wang Deming from the Shizhu branch of the Investigation Team of

the [Sichuan] Provincial Party Committee, January 27, 1961. From the Si-chuan Provincial Party Committee Archive, file JC 1-2608, pp. 89–90.

29. The problem of humans eating human flesh, by the Shizhu branch of the Investigation Team of the [Sichuan] Provincial Party Committee, February 9, 1961. From the Sichuan Provincial Party Committee Archive, file JC 1-2608, pp. 93–97.

CHAPTER 5. DEVASTATION IN THE COUNTRYSIDE (1958–1961)

30. Comrade Hu Jizong's speech at the December 22 meeting, from the transcripts of the [Hunan] Provincial Party Committee plenum, December 20–24, 1958. From the Hunan Provincial Party Committee Archive, file 141-1-884, p. 53.

31. An investigative report on the compensation situation in Qu county, by the Daxian branch of the Investigation Team of the Sichuan Provincial Party Committee, June 8, 1961. From the Sichuan Provincial Party Committee Archive, file JC 1-2620, pp. 61–62.

32. A report to the Bureau of Internal Affairs and the Political and Legal Com-mittee [in Beijing] regarding the current crisis in nine regions and counties, by the Sichuan Province Bureau of Civil Affairs, January 9–November 1962. From the Sichuan Province Bureau of Civil Affairs Archive, file JC 44-1440, pp. 127–128.

33. An investigative report about problems resulting from compulsory relocation due to construction of the Yangmei reservoir [in Gaoyao county, Guangdong province], 1960. From the Kaiping County Party Committee Archive, file 3-Ao.10-81, pp. 64–68.

34. Hou Shixiang's letter to the Political Department of Shaanxi [Province] Military Region, March 1959. From the Hunan Provincial Party Committee Archive, file 141-1-1322, pp. 108–110.

35. Report from the regional conference of third-level cadres, [Guizhou prov-ince,] June 23, 1961. From the Chishui County Party Committee Archive, file 1-A12-27, p. 15.

36. A survey of Huaminglou commune in Ningxiang county by the Central Com-mittee of the Chinese Communist Party, the Investigation Team of the Hunan Provincial Party Committee, and Comrade Yang Shuqing, April 4, 1961. From the Hunan Provincial Party Committee Archive, file 141-1-1885, pp. 40–41.

37. Report on collectivization in Shaoshan, [Hunan province,] by Mao Huachu, sent on April 10, 1961. From the Hunan Provincial Party Committee Ar-chive, file 141-1-1928, pp. 117, 126, 131–136.

38. A work report by the Jiangjin branch of the Agricultural Production Inves-tigation Team of the Sichuan Provincial Party Committee, March 20–November 30, 1960. From the Sichuan Provincial Party Archive, file JC 1-2109, p. 2.

39. A report on the current situation in the countryside, by the Sichuan Province Department of Agricultural Work, 1960. From the Sichuan Province Depart-ment of Agricultural Work Archive, file JC 9-108, pp. 11, 45.

40. Comrade Luo Qinan's report on grain production in Wenshi commune, Liu-yang county, [Hunan province,] November 11, 1960. From the Hunan Pro-vincial Party Committee Archive, file 141-1-1672, pp. 66–67.

41. A collection of speeches by the Yangzhou Region Party Committee [of Jiangsu province] on corruption among cadres, as reported at the regional conference of fourth-level cadres, from the documents of the Seventh Central Committee meeting at the Eighth Party Congress, March 1959. From the Hunan Provincial Party Committee Archive, file 141-2-101, pp. 141–142.

42. "My Witness: Traveling through the Countryside [of Hunan Province] in Twenty-Five Days, Covering 1,800 Kilometers," by Hu Yaobang, October 1, 1961. From the Hunan Provincial Party Committee Archive, file 141-2-138, pp. 188–189, 196–197.

43. Report on the damage to forests in Fujian and four other provinces and eight suggestions for the region, June 1962. From the Hunan Provincial Party Committee Archive, file 141-2-163, p. 17.

44. Report on the destruction of forestland in the northwest [of China], October 31, 1962. From the Gansu Provincial Party Committee Archive, file 91-18-250, pp. 2–3.

45. Comrade Liu Jianxun's report on the problem of waterlogged and alkalized farm fields [in Hunan province], as well as a proposal to solve the problem, December 24, 1961. From the Hunan Provincial Party Committee Archive, file 141-2-142, pp. 224–227.

46. "My Witness: Traveling through the Countryside [of Hunan Province] in Twenty-Five Days, Covering 1,800 Kilometers," by Hu Yaobang, October 1, 1961. From the Hunan Provincial Party Committee Archive, file 141-2-138, pp. 185–187.

CHAPTER 6. THE TURN TO RELIGION (1957–1962)

47. "Ask the Dead People to Join the People's Commune and Turn the Graveyard into a Field of Crops," by the Party Committee of Zhengchang township, Suiyang county, [Guizhou province,] August 20, 1958. From the Chishui County Party Committee Archive, file 1-A9-30, pp. 171–173.

48. Report by the Party Committee of the Hunan Province Justice Department on a number of disputes over the demolition of temples and graveyards in winter construction work, February 14, 1958. From the Hunan Provincial Party Archive, file 141-1-969, p. 19.

49. Report on the incident in which Erwang Temple was damaged by a blast during construction of the Yuzui hydropower station by the United Front Work Department in Guan county, [Sichuan province,] August 23, 1960. From the Archive of the Department of Religious Affairs, Sichuan Province People's Committee, file JC 50-315, no page number.

50. Report on the wanton occupancy of temples and churches, the destruction of trees at religious sites, and the random removal of property from religious institutions, by the Department of Religious Affairs of the Sichuan Provincial People's Committee, May 16–November 23, 1961. From the Archive of the Department of Religious Affairs, Sichuan Province People's Committee, file JC 50-325, pp. 1–2.

51. Report on the development of urban people's communes, by the Zhengzhou City Party Committee [of Henan province], April 1960. From the Hunan Provincial Party Committee Archive, file 141-2-164, pp. 78, 82.

Front Department of Peng county, [Sichuan province,] May–September 1960. From the Archive of the Department of Religious Affairs, Sichuan Province People's Committee, file JC 50-129, pp. 1–3.

65. On rural affairs, by the Hunan Provincial Party Committee, 1957. From the Hunan Provincial Party Committee Archive, file 141-1-835, pp. 27–28, 44.

66. An investigation into health care in the eight different communes in Chuxiong county, [Yunnan province,] 1964. From the Yunnan Province Bureau of Grain Archive, file 120-1-224, pp. 61–62.

67. On the famine in Xichang region, by the Bureau of Civil Affairs, Sichuan province, 1960. From the Sichuan Province Bureau of Civil Affairs Archive, file JC 44-3926, pp. 21–22.

68. Report on fighting enemies in the rural countryside [Zunyi region, Guizhou province], 1963. From the Chishui County Party Committee Archive, file 1-A14-15, p. 38.

CHAPTER 7. STRATEGIES FOR SURVIVAL (1959–1962)

69. Report on excess waste among some cadres and ordinary people in the countryside, by the Jilin Provincial Party Committee, September 21, 1959. From the Hunan Provincial Party Committee Archive, file 1-141-1363, pp. 124–126.

70. Report by the Hubei Provincial Party Committee on the Rectification Campaign in Mianyang county's Tonghaikou commune, January 31, 1961. From the Chishui County Party Committee Archive, file 1-A12-2, p. 4.

71. Any bad elements must be dealt with severely, by the Central Supervision Commission, [Beijing,] April 16, 1960. From the Chishui County Party Committee Archive, file 1-A11-59, pp. 17–18.

72. Minutes of the plenum of the Chishui County Party Committee, [Guizhou province,] December 16–22, 1960. From the Chishui County Party Committee Archive, file 1-A11-30, pp. 88–93.

73. Report on Liu Hongbin's criminal group and their activities, by the Party Committee of the southern Guizhou region, 1962. From the Chishui County Party Committee Archive, file 1-A13-27, pp. 62–63.

74. Report on the condition of collective canteens in the Wuai administrative district, Sanxing commune, Jintang county, by the Wenjiang branch of the Agricultural and Grain Production Investigation Team of the General Office of the Sichuan Provincial Party Committee, April 1960. From the Sichuan Provincial Party Committee Archive, file JC 1-2115, pp. 1–4.

75. Report by Comrade Hou Shunde on the condition of collective canteens in Peipozhuang big brigade [in Hebei province], October 20, 1960. From the Chishui County Party Committee Archive, file 1-A11-8, p. 76.

76. The instruction on rectification in people's communes from the Central Committee of the Chinese Communist Party and Chairman Mao, 1959. From the Sichuan Provincial Party Committee Archive, file JC 1-1672, pp. 76, 115, 122.

77. Some cadres in southern Guizhou have been pocketing factory workers' oil and meat rations, June 8–December 1, 1960. From the Chishui County Party Committee Archive, file 1-A11-83, p. 11.

78. An investigation into why Mianyang county's Songya commune is so poor, by the Mianyang branch of the Rectification Campaign Investigation Working

Hygiene, October–December 8, 1961. From the Sichuan Provincial Party Committee Archive, file JC 1-2418, pp. 155, 160.

90. The famine situation is very critical in the Wangu district of Dazu county, [Sichuan province,] by Comrade Chen Zhaobing, July 1962. From the Sichuan Provincial Party Committee Archive, file JC 1-3050, pp. 1–3.

91. Report on a number of villagers from Huishui county, [Guizhou province,] selling their children, houses, and furniture out of hardship, February 1962. From the Guiyang City Party Committee Archive, file 61-8-1061, pp. 52–53.

92. Report on villagers from Lu, Longchang, Rongchang, and other counties who went to Neijiang and Zizhong to make exchanges for food, and so on, by Comrade Ming Lang from the General Office of the Sichuan Provincial Party Committee, the Party Committee of the Sichuan Province Public Security Bureau, and the Party Committee of Neijiang and Yibin regions, February 14, 1962. From the Sichuan Provincial Party Committee Archive, file JC 1-3227, p. 16.

93. Report on the problem of an increasing number of prostitutes and disorderly girls in the city, by the Party Committee of the Sichuan Province Bureau of Civil Affairs, August 1962. From the Sichuan Province Bureau of Civil Affairs Archive, file JC 44-3927, pp. 2–10.

94. Report on the reduction in the labor force in Nanbu county's Jianxing commune and the plan to send people back in order to support agricultural production, by the Nanchong Region Party Committee, Sichuan province, April 2–October 8, 1960. From the Guizhou Province Bureau of Agriculture Archive, file 90-1-2247, pp. 9–10.

95. Investigative report on the case of Xiao Liangfu, who was beaten to death after being caught stealing peas, by Longxing commune, Chishui county, Guizhou province, March 13, 1961. From the Chishui County Party Committee Archive, file 2-A8-9, pp. 98–99.

96. Investigative report on cannibalism in Xinhua brigade, by the Chishui County Supervision Commission, [Guizhou province,] May 31, 1961. From the Chishui County Party Committee Archive, file 2-A8-2, pp. 71–75.

97. The famine situation in Qihe county's two production brigades, [Shandong province,] 1962. From the Shandong Provincial Party Committee Archive, file A1-02-1127, pp. 4, 23.

98. Working report by the Neijiang branch of the Agricultural and Grain Production Investigation Team of the General Office of the Sichuan Provincial Party Committee, March 15–December 16, 1960. From the Sichuan Provincial Party Committee Archive, file JC 1-2112, p. 4.

CHAPTER 8. LETTERS OF COMPLAINT (1957–1962)

99. Reports and documents relating to a number of recent strikes and public disturbances, by the Central Committee of the Chinese Communist Party and the Hunan Provincial Party Committee, January–August 1957. From the Hunan Provincial Party Committee Archive, file 141-1-840, pp. 2, 13, 16–20, 22–28, 80, 85.

100. Report of the conference on how to deal with letters of complaint, by the General Office of the Sichuan Provincial Party Committee and various

Party Committee, September 12–October 12, 1961. From the Sichuan Provincial Party Committee Archive, file JC 1-2614, p. 14.

113. A survey of Huaminglou commune in Ningxiang county by the Central Committee of the Chinese Communist Party, the Investigation Team of the Hunan Provincial Party Committee, and Comrade Yang Shuqing, April 4, 1961. From the Hunan Provincial Party Committee Archive, file Hunan, 141-1-1885, pp. 44–46.

114. Report on protecting agricultural production and on the Rectification Campaign [in Guizhou province], 1959. From the Guiyang City Party Committee Archive, file 61-8-503, p. 10.

115. A collection of anti–people's commune posters in rural Lingui, Yulin, Pingnan, and Tiandong, collected by Comrade Wu Jinnan, the Party secretary of Guangxi Zhuang autonomous region, April 1, 1959. From the Guangxi Zhuang Autonomous Region Party Committee Archive, file 1-25-316, p. 68.

116. Report on a number of problems in the collective canteen, by the Rural Affairs Working Group of the Sichuan Provincial Party Committee and the Office of Welfare and Benefits, 1961. From the Archive of the Department of Rural Affairs, Sichuan Provincial Party Committee, JC 9-464, p. 70.

117. Survey of agricultural production and the Rectification Campaign in various regions of rural Sichuan, by the General Office of the Sichuan Provincial Party Committee, May 25, 1959. From the Sichuan Provincial Party Committee Archive, file JC 1-1721, p. 4.

118. A letter from Tan Qilong and Wang Ying to Chairman Mao and the Central Committee of the Chinese Communist Party regarding the current crisis in Jining region, [Shandong province,] April 11, 1959. From the Shandong Provincial Party Committee Archive, file A1-01-465, pp. 28–29.

119. Speech by Comrade Qin Chuanhou at the provincial and regional Party secretaries' meeting, [Sichuan province], May 1962. From the Sichuan Provincial Party Committee Archive, file JC 1-2799, pp. 28–29.

EPILOGUE (1961–1962)

120. Speech by Comrade Liu Shaoqi [in Beijing], May 31, 1961. From the Gansu Provincial Party Committee Archive, file 91-6-81, pp. 69–71.

121. Report on population figures in 1962, by the Party Committee of the Sichuan Province Bureau of Public Security, February 23, 1963. From the Sichuan Province Statistics Office Archive, file JC 67-112, pp. 9–10.

Index

Acts of Peasant Resistance in China in the People's Communes (Gao), xii

agricultural collectivization: disastrous from the outset, 3; as means of eliminating rural poverty, 1–2; policy of, approved, 172. See also collectivization

agricultural planning, mistakes in, 84–86. See also farmland, destruction of

agricultural tools, 155

agriculture: complaint letter about, 154–156. See also crop failure; deforestation; erosion; farmland, destruction of; fertilizer; grain production, decrease in; irrigation; livestock

alkalization, 89, 155

Anhui province: archives of, ix; damaged by the Five Winds, 86; food shortages in, 10–11; irrigation-related destruction in, 74; water problems in, 89

Anti-Hiding Campaign, 18–20, 26, 33, 37, 47, 173

Anti–Right Deviation Campaign, 33, 150, 174

Anti-Rightist Campaign, 2, 142, 172

Bai Daolun, 6
Bai Jinyou, 103–104
Bai Ruying, 103–104
Bai Shenming, 122
Bai Xinyue, 121
Bai Yuxiang, 122
Balance the Books Campaign, 19
Bao Yousu, 65
beating frenzy, 32
Becker, Jasper, xii
beef, sold to Muslims as pork, 103
Beijing Railway Station, 72
birth defects, 53

birthrate: drop in, 6, 155; fertility, loss of, 43; improving, 164–165

black market, 114, 129–131

Bo Yibo, 24

breastfeeding, 6, 53

cadres: extorting nonessential food items, 123–124; stealing from peasants, 122–123

Cai Fumin, 118, 154–156

Cai Yayou, 30

cannibalism, 47, 59, 60–62, 139–140; class structure and, 62; in Gansu province, 59, 61–67; in Sichuan province, 68–71; spread of, 59–60

Cao Shuji, xii

Catastrophe and Contention in Rural China (Taxton), xii

Catholicism, declining after the Great Leap Forward, 109

Catholics, in Sichuan province, 109

Central Anti-Bandits National Salvation Army, 107

Central Archive (Beijing), ix

Central Committee, 167, 168

Central Discipline Inspection Committee, 168

Central Military Commission, 168, 170

Chan, Alfred L., xii

Chang Xiabing family, 104

Changyi (monk), 100

Chanyu (monk), 100

Chayashan, people's commune of, 3

cheating, to outwit the Communist Party order, 114

Chen Boda, 175

Chen Fujing, 30

Chen Jialan, 70

197

CPSIA information can be obtained
at www.ICGtesting.com
Printed in the USA
JSHW052245301122
33863JS00002B/71